KU-201-015

In A
Man's World

WP 0466756 5

IN A
MAN'S WORLD

Essays on Women in
Male-dominated Professions

edited by

ANNE SPENCER & DAVID PODMORE

POLYTECHNIC LIBRARY
WOLVERHAMPTON

466756

331.
409
41
INA

30. JAN 1989   RS

Tavistock Publications: London & New York

First published in 1987 by
Tavistock Publications Ltd
11 New Fetter Lane, London EC4P 4EE

© 1987 Anne Spencer and David Podmore

Typeset in Monophoto Photina by
Vision Typesetting, Manchester

Printed in Great Britain by
Richard Clay Ltd,
Bungay, Suffolk

All rights reserved. No part of this book may be reprinted or reproduced
or utilized in any form or by any electronic, mechanical or other means,
now known or hereafter invented, including photocopying and recording,
or in any information storage or retrieval system without permission in
writing from the publishers.

British Library Cataloguing in Publication Data
In a man's world:
essays on women in male-dominated professions.
1. Women – Employment – Great Britain
2. Sex discrimination in employment –
Great Britain
I. Spencer, Anne   II. Podmore, David
331.4'133'0941   HD6135

ISBN 0-422-60230-2

FOR JOHN,
AND
FOR DOROTHY

Contents

Contents

List of Contributors

ANNE SPENCER is Senior Research Fellow, Resources Intelligence Unit, at the Further Education Staff College, Coombe Lodge, Bristol.

DR DAVID PODMORE is Lecturer in the Social and Technology Policy Division, Management Centre, Aston University.

PATRICIA WALTERS is Senior Lecturer in the Department of Sociology and Anthropology, University of Salford.

KAREN LEGGE is Reader in Organizational Behaviour, Department of Social and Economic Studies, Imperial College of Science and Technology, London.

JANE ROSSER is Research Officer, Housing Department Sheffield City Council.

DR CELIA DAVIES is Project Officer at the United Kingdom Central Council for Nursing, Midwifery and Health Visiting, and Honorary Research Fellow, University of Warwick.

DR HILARY HOMANS is Senior Lecturer, Department of Nursing, Health and Applied Social Studies, Bristol Polytechnic.

BARBARA LAWRENCE is Research Officer, Management Centre, Aston University.

DR M. JOHN McAULEY is Senior Lecturer in Organizational Behaviour, Department of Management Studies, Sheffield City Polytechnic.

PEGGY NEWTON is Senior Lecturer in Social Psychology, Department of Behavioural Science, Huddersfield Polytechnic.

JOANNA LIDDLE is Lecturer in the School of Industrial and Business Studies, University of Warwick.

RAMA JOSHI is Faculty Member at the Shri Ram Centre for Industrial Relations and Human Resources, New Delhi.

1

Introduction

Anne Spencer and David Podmore

This book explores, from a variety of perspectives, the experience of women working in male-dominated professions. We became interested in the careers of such women through our research on women lawyers. In the legal profession women are still very much in a minority and are channelled into certain types of work and pushed to the margins of the profession by a variety of mechanisms. The other comtributors to this volume identify similar dynamics of exclusion and marginalization of women across a number of male-dominated professions. All of the contributors, either implicitly or explicitly, identify the professions with which they are concerned as representing 'discriminatory environments' for women (Bourne and Wikler 1978), environments in which the careers of women are shaped in detrimental ways as a result of their gender. The severity of the damaging effects of this for women varies between the different professions discussed, but in each case it is clear that women encounter considerable difficulties in their careers as a result of their 'deviant' gender status.

A further theme which is considered in several of the chapters is the effect, or lack of effect, of statements or policies on equal opportunities for women. Walters, for example, in her chapter on women in the higher civil service, discusses the equivocal and ambivalent treatment of women within it, despite the adoption of a formal Equal Opportunities Programme of Action. Homans explodes the myth of equality of opportunity for National Health Service scientific staff, despite the general perception of the NHS as an equal opportunities employer.

(The same point is made by Rosser and Davies with regard to the NHS as an employer of administrative staff.) McAuley shows that the statement by an institution of higher education that it is an equal opportunities employer is at best meaningless, and at worst actually damaging to women, if there is no coherent equal opportunities policy to back it up.

In an earlier paper (Spencer and Podmore 1983) we identified ten factors which contribute to the professional marginalization of women in male-dominated professions, some of which are closely interlinked.

(a) Stereotypes about women – for example that women's innate characteristics mean that they are 'emotional', 'unstable', 'not decisive enough'.

(b) Stereotypes about the nature of professions and professionals – for example that professions are physically demanding, 'combative', and hence unsuited to women.

(c) The sponsorship system – the need for young professionals to find a senior who will 'push along' their careers (difficult for women, because of the lack of senior women professionals).

(d) The lack of role models and peers – the relatively small number of women professionals means that women are often isolated and lacking in peer support.

(e) Informal relationships – women find themselves excluded from many of the informal activities which are so important to building a successful professional career.

(f) The concept of professional commitment – the 'all or nothing' notion of the professional career which women find (or are assumed to find) difficult to adhere to.

(g) The unplanned nature of many women's careers – whereas men's professional careers are typically 'planned', those of women often suffer from breaks and hiatuses.

(h) 'Women's work' – the view (of many men superiors) that women are best suited to work involving the 'expression of feelings', 'caring', etc.

(i) Clients' expectations – the claim that women professionals are unacceptable to many clients, and so can work only in less 'visible' capacities.

(j) Fear of competition – the fear that women will work for less remuneration than men and/or lower the prestige of a profession.

Introduction

Many of these issues are raised in this volume; all operate *within* professions. The importance of socialization into gender roles and the domestic division of labour within the home cannot be overstated as factors *outside* their professional lives which also operate to marginalize women in their working lives. The 'cultural mandate' (Coser and Rokoff 1971), the assumed primacy of the commitment of women to home and family, is highly significant in terms of their marginalization.

All the chapters in the book discuss some of these factors, from the different perspectives of the particular authors. We now provide a brief overview of the different contributions.

Walters, in her chapter on women in the higher civil service, discusses the impact on women of the expectation of a pattern of total, lifelong commitment to the career. The career pattern is normatively predicated on a 'male' model of continuity and commitment. Moreover, total commitment is demanded in the fulfilment of day-to-day working obligations. The career is stereotyped as 'masculine', with little accommodation being made for the women who work in it, despite the supposed operation of an equal opportunities policy. Women are, in fact, simply expected to conform to these 'masculine' norms in the pursuit of their careers. Since many woman have 'broken' or 'bimodal' career patterns, to allow for bearing and rearing children, this is obviously disadvantageous to them. The late twenties and early thirties are identified as the crucial period of career life for the higher civil servant, the 'make it' (or not) period. These are precisely the years in which, for many women, family commitments are likely to be at their most demanding. Great difficulty is experienced in obtaining shorter working hours and part-time work, due to the inflexible expectations of the employer. Walters also argues that women and men are differentially assessed for promotions and postings by their (overwhelmingly male) seniors who tend to assume that men are competent unless they prove otherwise, whilst women need most positively to establish the fact of their competence. When being considered for promotion, women are faced with the stereotype which suggests that they become too 'emotionally involved' in their work and pay too much attention to detail, at the expense of the 'broad view' considered to be so important in the higher civil service. Interestingly, within the higher civil service it seems that distinct areas of 'women's work' do not exist as such. While this eliminates the likelihood of women being 'ghettoized' in such work, it also precludes any possibility of their progressing by means of a special role and route for women.

Legge's chapter on women in personnel management addresses itself to a central paradox: that to consider the 'problem' of women's careers is to take men as the norm against which women are to be compared. This in itself involves a further implicit subordination of women, by using men as the standard by which to judge them. Legge argues that this ensnarement in constructs reflecting male dominance is difficult, if not impossible, to avoid since our social constructs are themselves products of male dominance, which they also serve to perpetuate and reinforce. This chapter is a consideration of the development of the personnel profession from its inception in the late nineteenth century to the present day. Its thesis is that, contrary to the general view of the profession as a stronghold of female managerial employment, it can be considered as an exemplar of the proposition that women will only have power within an occupation or profession when it has not yet attained power, or when it is losing power. The profession is traced from its early years as a female-dominated, primarily welfare function – and thus gender-appropriate for women because of their assumed caring and nurturing qualities – to its position at the present day as a far more powerful and significant function with an increasing emphasis on the male-dominated area of industrial relations. The welfare function is marginalized and sometimes denied altogether and thus female participation in positions of any power is significantly reduced.

Legge addresses the complex interlinking of stereotyped views of women and thus of the kinds of work within the field of personnel management deemed gender-appropriate to them, the changes in the ways in which personnel management has been perceived, and the ways in which organizational demands upon the personnel function have altered and thus changed the shape of the profession. The overarching concern is with the power relations between women and men from a feminist perspective, and with the impact of such relations on the changes in the stereotypes discussed.

The focus of Rosser and Davies's chapter on National Health Service administrators is what they refer to as the Female Office Management Function (FOMF). FOMF women are the unacknowledged base on which the administrative career structure of the NHS rests. They are ignored in career terms and in any discussion of equal opportunities for women. The FOMF women are assumed to perform only secretarial and/or clerical roles, *not* administrative ones. They occupy essentially 'dead-end' posts, which is regarded as making such jobs suitable for female occupancy, giving a clear indication of the NHS view of women's relationship and orientation to 'career' employment. The women are typically middle-aged or older and have returned to work after a break for child-rearing. This, additionally, sets up a stereotyped view of them as wanting 'jobs' rather than 'careers', and of lacking commitment to their work. These women, however, are actually performing complex and skilled administrative and personnel functions, although they are not recognized as administrators.

The jobs seem to be designed for women. This has not been done deliberately; the jobs have evolved in this way due to the lack of planning of work at this level. FOMF jobs make use of the women's professional skills – secretarial and clerical – but also of organizational skills developed in running a home and in handling crises and emotions, etc. These latter skills are exploited without being formally recognized as part of the job; they are seen as relating to the gender of the post-holder, rather than as part of the job description. The FOMF women tend to have become indispensable over the years. What this means in practice is that it is difficult for them to pursue further training as they cannot be spared from their present posts. This indispensability is actually the result of the high level of commitment to work on the part of these women, similar to that required of career administrators – yet 'commitment' is often believed by employers to be a problematic feature of women staff!

Homans discusses the myth of equality of opportunity for National Health Service laboratory scientists. Her chapter is based on a study of women and men currently working in clinical laboratories and an additional sample who have left NHS employment. She identifies the myth that all women will leave work permanently due to pregnancy as a major factor in the discriminatory treatment of women scientists, particularly as regards promotion. This myth is widely held by male National Health Service managers. Women are therefore viewed as problematic employees, liable to have a high turnover rate. She shows how this 'problem' is also located within patriarchal ideologies of motherhood and parenting, which suggest that it is 'incorrect' for women with children to continue in paid employment. She demonstrates that this myth about female labour turnover has little grounding in reality; however, its widespread credence by the men who control access to promotion has damaging and restrictive consequences for the women scientists. She indicates that promotion for women is generally contingent on their remaining childless, while limited opportunities for flexible working hours or part-time working, together with a lack of childcare provision in the workplace, make it very difficult for a woman who has had a child actually to return to work as a laboratory scientist.

Some consideration is also given to questions of sexuality at work. The way in which (some) men perceive women colleagues as sexual objects rather than competent co-professionals is identified as another facet of the discriminatory treatment experienced by women. Homans also discusses male perceptions of innate, gender-based differences in ability at work in terms of the 'feminine' stereotype. This is, of course, a further mechanism which disadvantages women, since the types of work regarded as 'naturally' more appropriate to them are the more routine, less visible and more monotonous components of the work. This is discussed in terms of the extension of women's perceived domestic role into the workplace.

Our chapter on women in the legal profession considers the stereotypes held by male barristers and solicitors about the legal profession and about the women who work in it (and indeed women generally). We argue that from these two major forms of stereotyping flow many of the other factors which contribute to women's exclusion, marginalization and trivialization in the profession. The chapter discusses the ways in which women's perceived primary allegiance to the home and family, rather than to the profession, leads to a view of women lawyers lacking proper professional commitment. Also, where women do leave professional life for a time to undertake childcare, this sets up a stereotype that women will 'always' leave when they marry or have children. The chapter considers the way in which perceptions about the nature of women leads to their channelling into types of work deemed gender-appropriate. The use of client 'expectations' as a means of masking prejudice against women on the part of the male lawyers themselves is also discussed. We argue that these kinds of stereotyping activities play a major part in ensuring that women are pushed to the margins of the profession.

Broadly, what this chapter examines is the nature of the 'double bind' for women lawyers. The dominant male majority in the profession stereotype the profession itself as 'masculine', with the characteristics regarded as necessary for competent performance

Introduction

within it being those most readily identified as 'male' rather than 'female'. In the view of the more extreme men lawyers, women are regarded as unsuited to legal practice altogether. A more moderate view is that they are suited to some legal specialisms but not to others. For women to be seen as competent professionals it is necessary for them to adopt 'masculine' attributes and values. However, to the extent that they do so, they will also be perceived as having 'failed' as women, as having become 'unnatural' and 'unfeminine'. Whatever women do, and however women behave, we demonstrate that they are still left with the problem that some men will persist in evaluating them only as sexual objects and not as legal professionals.

Lawrence's chapter draws on a wider study of single-handed women general practitioners. She begins by discussing the traditional role of the (male) family doctor, the development of group practice, and the difficulties experienced by women in medicine. She argues that gender was a key variable in the decisions of the women in her study to practise single-handedly rather than in partnerships or groups. Gender should be regarded, she argues, as a means of interpreting four other categories of explanatory factors for the decision to practise single-handedly, viz. financial, personal relationships, continuity of care, and independence. She demonstrates how women doctors working in partnerships or group practices experienced exploitation as a consequence of their gender, over and above the four other sets of factors which she identifies. Lawrence suggests that general practice should be regarded as a 'discriminatory environment' for women. Thus, as a result of the ways such an environment shapes and channels the careers of women within it, women GPs working in partnerships and group practices are channelled into certain specialisms within general practice, i.e. gynaecology and obstetrics, family planning, psychiatric problems and paediatrics. That is to say, women GPs tend to have the kind of cases where the patients are mostly women and children. Lawrence shows how this pattern is imposed on women GPs to a large extent, because of their perceived 'feminine' qualities; male principals and partners (and, to some extent, patients as well) regard this as gender-appropriate work for women. This 'ghettoism' within general practice was a major factor in the decisions of the women GPs to turn to single-handed practice, a form of practice which enables them to treat the whole range and variety of general practice cases.

McAuley's chapter also takes as a large part of its theme a

'discriminatory environment' for women, this time as constituted by a large institution of higher education, despite the fact that it claims to be an equal opportunities employer. He discusses the ways in which the attitudes, values, assumptions, and beliefs of the dominant male majority in the institution shape the experience of women academics in various ways. In this context the failure to eliminate discrimination against women in recruitment procedures is considered. McAuley goes on to look at issues such as women's access to promotion and senior management positions, and the ways in which activities leading to such opportunities for women are controlled and regulated by male gatekeepers. The attitudes of men staff to the teaching by women of women's studies and to gender divisions is considered, as is the potential for organizational change that the raising of these issues by women can create. McAuley argues that the dynamics of gender discrimination are both more complex and more subtle than is often taken to be the case. He argues that much of the problem is located in women's and men's very different world-views, together with a mutual failure to understand these differences. To a large extent he absolves the men of malice; he believes them to be acting at an unconscious or pre-conscious level. The damaging effects for women are, however, made very clear.

Newton's chapter discusses personality traits with regard to 'femininity' and 'masculinity' among young women training as technicians in engineering. The approach adopted is psychological, and femininity and masculinity are conceptualized as independent dimensions. She concludes that although it is clear that women have the ability to work as engineers, both the institutions training and educating them and the industries employing them remain unconvinced of their value. A large part of the problem is that male engineers are typically conservative in attitudes and values and tend to have highly traditional views of women's roles. This creates problems for women organizationally, as for instance with the lack of a comprehensive policy on maternity leave and childcare. Further there is a problem of stress at work for women, caused by prejudice and discrimination.

She argues that because engineering is clearly labelled as a 'man's world', the choice of engineering as a career has very different implications for women and for men. Women are more likely initially to perceive engineering in a negative way, because of its 'masculine' image, and will have made the choice of engineering at a later point in their school careers than male engineers. For men, however, the choice of engineering represents an important aspect of their gender identity. They are likely to make the choice early and to hold to it unquestioningly. Newton's sample of female engineering trainees scored high on measures of androgyny (that is, high on both masculine and feminine characteristics) compared to other female groups. This suggests that women in engineering find it necessary to balance the masculine image of the profession by emphasizing their feminine qualities. The majority of male engineering trainees were masculine sex-typed, indicating the importance of stereotypically masculine characteristics to their own self-conceptions. Newton's chapter concludes with an important discussion of the policy implications of her research.

The final chapter provides a comparative perspective. Liddle and Joshi examine the position of professional women in India in terms of the hierarchy of class and the hierarchy of gender. They indicate the complex ways in which class and gender are linked in India, and the need to examine both systems to understand the position of professional women. The privilege of class seems to precede the subordination of gender to the extent that the women (of middle-class origin) have access to education and to professional employment opportunities. However, the subordination of gender is seen to be greater than the privilege of class in the sense that the education of women is often seen by their parents and families as a means of improving their commodity value in the marriage market, as wives for educated men. Restrictions on women's physical mobility outside the home reinforce women's domestic dependence and perpetuate their position as male sexual property. Within the professions in India it is clear that women generally need to be better qualified than men to obtain equivalent work and that their careers are hampered by the extent of gender segregation within the professions. This occurs in the West too, of course, but it is very marked in India. The considerable restrictions on their physical mobility create difficulties in the performance of professional work, tending to confine women to 'desk-bound' tasks, reinforcing gender segregation.

These accounts of women working 'in a man's world' make it apparent that many different factors militate against the full and equal participation of women in male-dominated and male-orientated professional work. As this overview indicates, the dominant male members of these various professions engage in stereotyping activities

9

about the nature of the professions and about the women who work in them, such that the well-documented 'double-bind' for professional women is created. Further, because women constitute visible and 'deviant' minority groups, they have difficulty finding sponsors and role models and often lack female peers. The assumed primacy of women's domestic commitments leads to prejudice against them, detracts from the notion that women can be committed professionals and damages their prospects of promotion. Professional work tends to be very 'greedy' (Coser 1974) and the concept of professional commitment often makes it difficult for women to cope with their childcare responsibilities by working shorter or more flexible hours, or working part-time for a period. However, when women do take breaks in their professional careers to allow for the birth and rearing of children, they find that they are at a disadvantage on re-entry. In some cases, such as the higher civil service, re-entry may not be possible. Within most of these professions there is an element of gender segregation at work, which is sometimes acute. That is, some areas of work are perceived by the dominant male members (and also sometimes by clients) to be specially appropriate for women (only Walters's chapter on the higher civil service indicates that this kind of internal labour market segmentation does not take place). Where 'women's work' specialisms or areas of work can be identified within professions these inevitably tend to be lower-status, less 'visible' and less well remunerated.

As well as the personal stress involved, this situation can hardly be satisfactory for employers. As Epstein (1970) has noted, it seems likely that very able women in the professions underperform, underachieve, and underproduce, due to the exigencies of the patriarchal structures and modes of operation which define the nature of professional work. What of the future? Women continue to enter male-dominated professions in increasing numbers and, as their consciousness is raised, they are unlikely to continue to accept the limited and marginal roles indicated in this volume. There are also some indications that the organizations and professions which employ them are increasingly aware of the waste of female potential which such modes of operation encourage. Some employers are now adopting positive action programmes in an attempt to improve the position of women. As several of the chapters in this book make clear, more is needed than empty statements of equality of opportunity. Coherent, properly implemented and thoroughly monitored policies could be regarded as a first step in redressing the balance between women and men. Considerable changes in attitudes, values, and beliefs – on the part of women as well as men – will be necessary to bring real change about.

References

Bourne, P.G. and Wikler N.J. (1978) Commitment and the Cultural Mandate: Women in Medicine. *Social Problems* 25: 430–40.

Coser, L.A. (1974) *Greedy Institutions: Patterns of Undivided Commitment.* New York: Free Press.

Coser, R.L. and Rokoff, G. (1971) Women in the Occupational World: Social Disruption and Conflict. *Social Problems* 18: 535–54.

Epstein, C.F. (1970) *Woman's Place: Options and Limits in Professional Careers.* Berkeley: University of California Press.

Spencer, A. and Podmore, D. (1983) *Life on the Periphery of a Profession: The Experience of Women Lawyers.* Paper presented to British Sociological Association Conference, University College, Cardiff.

© 1987 Anne Spencer and David Podmore

2

Servants of the Crown

Patricia A. Walters

The subject of this chapter is the experience of women in the higher civil service. The term is used to denote that elite formation or officer cadre which has traditionally been a distinctive feature of the Home Civil Service in Britain. Until the early 1970s it was clearly demarcated as the 'administrative class', recruiting its members predominantly from university graduates in their early twenties into a career structure in which they competed for promotion from Principal to Assistant Secretary, Under Secretary, Deputy Secretary and finally, in the case of the few, to Permanent Secretary at the apex. This was the directorial elite of the service, helping ministers to formulate policy, supervising the implementation of programmes, and generally managing the machinery of government. Though the administrative class was formally abolished following the Fulton Committee criticisms of the rigidities of the service's class structure in the late 1960s, it is arguable that the formation remains essentially intact. Its functions remain the preserve of the same hierarchical pyramid of grades and there is still a career structure which is based on a 'fast stream' of young graduates recruited as administration trainees (Kellner and Crowther Hunt 1980). Though having no authority in offical usage, 'higher civil service' is an appropriate and necessary term to denote this small prestigious career structure of some 6,000 civil servants, the 'mandarins' of the public service.

The higher civil service became open to women in 1920, but on terms which were, initially, explicitly discriminatory. Until 1946 married women were ineligible for entry and those who married in

12

service were required to resign. Equal pay with men was not granted until 1955. Since then, however, the higher civil service has gained a reputation as an occupation of high status and high pay in which women can work and build careers on equal terms with men. 'When I was at University (in the 1970s) the Civil Service was not even seen as a "man's world" like engineering or the City,' one woman civil servant has written (Brimelow 1981: 314). 'The Civil Service culture accepts women easily,' claimed Anne Mueller (*Observer Magazine* 1984), currently head of the civil service's Management and Personnel Office and the latest of the few women who have attained the grade of Permanent Secretary. Visible career success like this fosters the impression that the higher civil service is a sympathetic environment for women. The steady increase in the number of women entering the occupation stands as a hard indicator of the attraction of the higher civil service to women and of its receptiveness of them. Women currently comprise 30 per cent of the successful entrants to the administration trainee grade. Civil service management over the past decades has insisted on a scrupulous approach to its women employees. When the Sex Discrimination Act was passed in 1975, the attitude of the service was that it merely applied to the private sector standards of conduct that were already operating throughout the civil service. There have subsequently been several reviews of management practice in relation to female employment. In 1984, after the latest of these, the civil service adopted a formal Equal Opportunities Programme of Action (Cabinet Office 1984).

Other impressions and evidence suggest, however, a more equivocal picture of the experience of women in the higher civil service. Numerically, if not culturally, the occupation remains a 'man's world'. After three decades of full formal sex equality women remain a small minority in the occupation. Currently women constitute 10 per cent of the 5,000 or so Assistant Secretaries and Principals, whilst in the grades at the top of the higher civil service there are only twenty-one women amongst 700 men. Studies of women in the higher civil service have revealed varying and sometimes contrary perceptions of their situation on the part of the women themselves. Many clearly do not see themselves as a beleaguered minority. They insist on the ease with which they, as individuals, work with their predominantly male colleagues and they emphasize that in the promotional stakes there is fairness to individuals. There is evidence, on the other hand, even amongst the majority of a sense of frustration that the service is, in crucial respects, less sensitive an employer of women than in purports to be. The problem would appear to be that the service as an employer is reluctant to display the organizational flexibility which is necessary to relieve the tensions between work and family; it is reluctant to facilitate the dual careers which most women in the occupation are pursuing. Civil service management has a centralized, uniformly applied, and well-publicized policy of equal opportunities, but it is arguable that as a management it tends in practice to move cautiously and pragmatically. It was not innovative in the early days of the sex equality movement. Equal pay was the result largely of pressure on the service exerted from parliament. In recent years, whilst proclaiming its commitment to the spirit of anti-discrimination, it has on several notable occasions been shown to be interpreting the letter of the legislation narrowly in relation to its own practice. In two important test cases it has been judged by industrial tribunals as following indirectly discriminatory employment practices.

It is not the intention of this chapter to argue that the civil service's commitment to sex equality is hollow. Rather its theme is that a picture of women's experience in the higher civil service must essentially be equivocal and that the service is ambivalent in its handling of the issue of female employment. The occupation can be characterized at one and the same time as exhibiting an accommod-ation towards women and a resistance to facing some of the important aspects of women's social lives. It is an occupation which opens itself to women and yet squeezes them out; which integrates them and yet marginalizes them. It both facilitates and impedes its women employees' efforts to realize their full potential.

The chapter develops the argument that the equivocal experience and ambivalent treatment of women in the higher civil service derives from features of the social structure and culture of the occupation. These are features which are definitive of the higher civil service and they have significant implications for women, opening up certain forms of opportunities for them and precluding and limiting others. After surveying these key features of the social organization of the occupation, the chapter reviews available evidence of women's experience, focusing on how they are judged in the meritocratic evaluation processes characteristic of career management in the higher civil service. The chapter concludes with a discussion of the politics of equal opportunity within the higher civil service, showing how the issue is articulated by the 'factions and tendencies' (Rose 1976: 312) which it has invoked. It is argued that there is a distinctive occupational politics of sex equality in the higher civil service, a politics mediated and shaped by the occupation's social organization and culture.

The occupational world

The higher civil service is, compared with many other occupations, a highly confined and socially intense occupation. To convey its nature one reaches out beyond the terminology of the sociology of occupations and professions into the language of communality. 'Tribe', 'village', 'caste', 'elite' – all of these terms have been employed to describe the higher civil service. It is built around a lifelong career with one employer, the Crown; entry is highly restricted and controlled; its numbers are small and its practitioners interact with each other a great deal; there is within it a very clear hierarchy of posts and a great deal of shared common knowledge about the appropriate behaviour required for progressing up the career ladder; it is an occupationally homogeneous world, all of whose practitioners, whilst they come to be divided into the more and the less successful, are performing the same kind of job. It presents a unitary, highly enclosed occupation at the top of one complex organization; it is an occupation characterized by career enclosure, career homogeneity, pronounced career management, and a strong shared ethos and sense of occupational identity.

The first structural aspect of the occupation to be noted is its total encapsulation in the one bureaucratic organization of the civil service. This occupational encapsulation is not true of all civil servants. There are professional civil servants such as doctors, town planners, lawyers, architects, and economists, to whom practising in the civil service is one of a number of options in professional life. There are, similarly, civil servant typists, secretaries, messengers, catering staff, and so on to whom the civil service is one of a number of employers in a large general labour market. The 'locking up' of an occupation and its practice in a single bureaucratic milieu applies most clearly to higher civil servants. This organizational encapsulation marks out the occupation of higher civil servants from most other professional occupations. Unlike such occupations and professions as medical practice, architecture, industrial management, and scientific research, it does not have a pluralistic employment structure. Higher civil servants *can* change employers, but they must change occupations to do so. To continue practising their occupation they are dependent on the employment terms offered by one monopolistic employer. They cannot maintain their occupation and choose between a variety of milieux such as public or private practice, small or large employers. Nor do they share the experience of many professionals employed in bureaucracies of having a choice of a number of employing organizations which, in some senses, compete with each other. There are top civil servants who move to the City and to industrial corporations; but this involves a few, generally at the end of careers within the one organization.

Not only is the occupation encapsulated but individual careers in the higher civil service are highly enclosed. The occupation has one major point of entry. Higher civil servants are recruited soon after graduation from university for a lifelong career within the civil service and there is not substantial movement into and out of the career at points above the initial entry gate. In this regard the higher civil service is different from the senior civil service in other democracies (such as the USA) and it is also different from, for example, industrial management. There is a marked stability of expectations attaching to the career. It is definitely located in London; job change and advancement do not involve geographical mobility. Practitioners are there for life; they are not expected to be mobile between employers. They move through their occupational life with the same broad cohort which is not constantly re-shaped by arrivals and departures. All this helps to make the career lines and the players in the career game visible and known. One employer, lifetime employment, and strong similarities of social and educational background amongst entrants make the higher civil service unified and homogeneous. On the inside of this encapsulated, enclosed world homogeneity is intensified by the construction of work roles and the structuring of career experience and career success.

Higher civil servants are spread through the different departments of central government. Almost without exception they work in the London headquarters of these departments, though there is a sizable Scottish Office in Edinburgh. Fundamental to higher administration in Britain is the principle that throughout different departments the task and practice of administration is similar. British higher civil servants are generalist administrators. The essense of generalism is that the same set of skills is involved regardless of what the particular policy is about. The British civil service has never organized itself to produce administrative specialisms; indeed it seeks to give all its higher administrators widespread diverse experience within a ministry and, for many of them, experience between ministries. It is the usual practice for practitioners to move to a new post every two to three years. These moves, even within ministries, can involve radical changes of responsibility, for instance a Principal in the Treasury can move from responsibility for naval equipment to health, or to the balance of payments statistics, or to national savings. The point of such procedures is to develop generalism, to make the administrator aware of the many considerations that affect a policy area and to make him/her able to take the all-round view. Through the problems addressed and jobs done, the policy papers written and commented upon, the meetings chaired and parliamentary questions answered, the administrative skills of detached judgement and rational decision-making are developed. The speed with which an administrator can master the detail of a completely new posting in order to take an all-round view of it is seen to be one of the key indicators of professional development.

Generalists are produced through a high degree of centralized, corporate control of individual job and career moves. The chequerboard of postings is guided from the top of a department through a highly developed network of information and consultation. The aims are twofold, developing generalism in all practitioners and also identifying those practitioners seen to hold most potential. Those identified as high-flyers then have their postings managed with extra deliberation. Generally it is from amongst young Principals that high-flyers are spotted. In terms of moving up to the very top of the service, fairly crucial decisions about individuals are made in their late twenties and early thirties. The culmination of a high-flying career is appointment to Permanent Secretary rank at about fifty years of age after some time spent as Deputy Secretary. High-flyers can expect promotions to Assistant Secretary and Under Secretary grades earlier than those who become Principals alongside them. At present high-flyers are attaining Under Secretary rank during their early forties. The job assignments of those tipped as high-flyers are carefully managed. The posts at Principal and Assistant Secretary level through which departments develop and test high-flyers are private secretaryships serving a minister, posts that are politically sensitive and involve a constant stream of pressure issues, and posts which involve weighty managerial responsibilities in running large-scale government services. The high-flying spiral is likely to take generalists into two or three departments to gain a sense of the interdependence of government departments. The Management and Personnel Office in the Cabinet Office has responsibility for managing the civil service. Departments inform it about generalists who have potential to reach the top posts and it arranges postings for them into central government departments, particularly the Treasury and Cabinet Office. Under Secretary appointments are jointly decided by a department and the Management and Personnel Office. Ministers are involved in the most senior appointments.

Securing, appraising, recording, and deciding upon individual performance is a highly developed part of the occupational world of higher administration. It is a closely interacting world where a high proportion of practitioner performance comes under direct scrutiny from other practitioners. It is also a world where, whilst practitioners control the 'how' of their occupational performance, much of the 'what' and 'when' is decided for them corporately. It is an occupation where individuals' moves are planned for them, thus making practitioners highly dependent on the steering of their managers. Higher civil servants do not in any way apply for jobs or movements up the grade hierarchy. Indeed, to suggest themselves overtly for a job is probably a strong disqualification for it; buckling down to assignments made by others is a pronounced aspect of higher administrative life. Reputation constitutes much of the formal and informal circulating currency in this world and there is a streaming effect; those tipped early as front runners are likely to be given the postings which have in them the best chances for building good reputations.

In the higher civil service there is a close interaction between occupational practice and occupational ideology. Occupational practices implement generalism and lead to its reaffirmation. The justification of generalism is that in the British political process ministers are best served by administrators who distance themselves from specialist considerations, from special interests, and from special pleading. Higher civil servants are most definitely not expected to act as advocate – unless it is as devil's advocate. Their role is to be disinterested, not too specialized, not too committed, and not too idealistic. It is the higher civil servants' generalism that makes them both accessible to ministerial will and yet able to withstand the pressure to become creatures of that will, or indeed of other vested interests. This emphasis on accessibility to the minister runs deep in administrative life. True, it is criticized by political analysts as being highly fictional but it certainly accounts for many of the everyday normative standards of the occupation. One such is the working rule that senior administrators must not in their occupational life 'watch the clock'. They must be prepared to respond to the crisis pressures of the political process as and when they arise. Indeed, higher civil servants are likely to experience more sustained exposure to these time pressures than the politicians whom they serve, many of whom hold a particular office for a relatively short time in their careers.

Women's career experience

The features of the occupation described above shape the occupational experience of all practitioners, men and women alike. But men and women are socially different practitioners; they bring to the occupation different social histories and different involvements in the bearing and rearing of children. It is important to consider what consequences for women's occupational lives are created by organizational encapsulation, career enclosure, and the ethos and practice of generalism. First there is the dependence on a monopolistic employer. True, it is an employer with a public commitment to being a 'good' employer, so that women practitioners have the assurance that their occupational lives can be lived in an employment structure with such a commitment; but, by the same token, the employer's dominance in their occupational lives means they are highly dependent on the terms in which this employer interprets and practises its commitment. Should women not be suited by these terms or satisfied with them, they do not have the alternative of practising their occupation in other employment environments that they judge to be more accommodating.

The stabilities of the higher civil service career that result from its enclosure can again, relative to other occupational structures, create a particular set of advantages and disadvantages for women administrators. Unlike occupations involving either geographical mobility or mobility through organizations, women in the higher civil service are pursuing an occupation in which much in the environment remains stable and can be taken for granted. Clearly, this can help in the process of integrating family and work careers. But the very stability and enclosure of the occupation can result in an inflexibility which makes it a relatively inhospitable environment for women's careers. The accepted and dominant pattern is built around continuous lifetime service in one career; the occupation is not structured around the incorporation of different lines of development and different experiences at various points of the career. This inflexibility can work against the ready institutional acceptance of the kind of broken career patterns – careers marked by breaks, late starts, and periods of part-time working – which empirical evidence suggests characterizes the working lives of contemporary British women.

Generalism structures women's experience both by what it promotes and what it excludes. The practice of generalism circulates them as individuals through the occupation and aids the incorporation of individual women into it. Generalism makes women's job performance visible to many colleagues and prevents their being trapped by superiors who mask or misreport their performance. In being judged, women in the higher civil service have the assurance that scrutiny is systematic and pays attention to many aspects of performance. But in all of this there is something which results from the structure, practice, and mores of the senior administrative world which is perhaps best described as 'the problem of the lack of women's groupings'. There are several ways in which this comes about: there are no processes of sub-differentiation in the administrative world producing areas of work which become women's enclaves. Furthermore, there is not a direct body of female clients whose presence, as for instance in medicine, law, or journalism, can lead to the elaboration of the claim that women must figure significantly amongst the practitioners. The direct contacts of administrators are with the socially powerful and successful – with politicians and the organized groups on whom ministries impinge. On the whole women are not amongst these contacts. What is striking about the world of the higher civil service is that the very ethos of generalism precludes the legitimacy of a point of view which argues that women in society or in areas of policy-making have interests which can best (or only) be fully understood or communicated by women. The essence of generalist administration is that it seeks constantly to effect the translation of different considerations and group interests into a common scale or language. This ethos precludes a special role for women in the administrative process and the occupational structure prevents a grouping and coalescing of women from which a potential challenge to the ethos might arise.

The process of systematic scrutiny in the higher civil service can help to counteract unidimensional judgements, but homogeneity in the occupation acts to limit the possibilities of pluralism. One period of career life, the late twenties and early thirties, tends to be identified as the 'make or break' period. Organizationally there is little career pluralism to loosen the constriction of this one take-off point, and the very important process of career steering that takes place in the late twenties and early thirties means that there is little room organizationally for late development. Yet all the social indicators are that women *are* late developers occupationally. The reasons lie in their child-bearing and child-rearing careers, which affect women who work continuously within occupations as well as those who take career breaks. Women administrators work in a situation where crucial and selective occupational advancement tends to happen only in the years when their family careers are most demanding. Furthermore, they face this experience in an occupation which assigns a powerful role to collective judgements and which severely limits practitioner autonomy. Thus it gives practitioners little work or career space from which they can surprise the organization and challenge the judgements made of them.

The broad social map which has just been drawn shows the contours which affect women's journeys in the higher civil service. It is now time to consider how women actually experience this occupational world. It is clear from all the available evidence that women practitioners never make it to the top of the service in anything like the same proportions as the men with whom they enter the service. Proportionally more women than men leave the service and, of those who stay, less make the jump into the Under Secretary grade either at all or early enough to progress beyond it. Women stay back, drop out, and are 'cooled out' for many reasons. Some of these will now be explored.

The proposition that men and women are equally capable of practising higher administration is taken, in the civil service, to be so accepted that it goes without saying. In doing the job women are measured side by side with men for access to the whole terrain of the occupation. The measuring process is highly formally organized in the first fifteen years or so of the career; evaluations are systematically put down on record. They are largely made by men of women; with what results?

In the late 1960s the civil service compared a representative sample of reports made on men and women administrators. In the manner of civil service reporting on administrators, the immediate supervisors of Principals were asked to evaluate the performance of individuals in terms of a list of specified characteristics. What emerged on analysis was that men and women overall were judged to be closely similar for nearly all the characteristics. There was little recorded difference between men and women when judged in terms of their ability to impress on short-term contact, in their handling of relations with colleagues, in their clarity of expression on paper, their mastery of 'figurework', their handling of meetings, their vigour and drive. There were, however, two ways in which women and men were seen to be significantly different. First, women, much more than men, were judged to be 'less stable'. They were, in the words of the categories used, less likely to be 'highly dependable; adapting well to new situations; taking most difficulties in their stride; reacting quite well to normal stress' and more likely to be 'occasionally flustered and put out, easily thrown off balance'. Second, women were judged to be significantly different from men when it came to estimations of the post that they were thought to be capable of filling successfully. Fifty per cent of all the men were judged capable of functioning beyond the level of Assistant Secretary, whereas only 33 per cent of the women were so regarded. It seems that when comparing men and women in terms of specific aspects of job performance, the predominantly male evaluators recorded little difference between the sexes. But when making judgements of overall style and approach and of whether someone was potentially top material, then women were judged to be lacking when compared with men.

In the world of the higher civil service, despite the systematization of evaluation, there appears to be a large element of job performance and judgement about performance that defies precise categorization. Many men administrators appeared convinced that no matter how well women compared with men on specific attributes of perform-ance, they did not measure up so well on the central core performance – they did not have the ability to take the all-round view, to see the essentials, to operate with the necessary detachment. To quote some of their expressions of judgement:

'Women are much more predisposed than men to get excited about detail – they have less capacity than men to operate on a broader plain.'

'There are few women and so one only has limited evidence to go on, but within the small sample I have known very few show any willingness to "think big". They are tidy and efficient administrators but I do not know any personally who could initiate really major policy change.'

'Few women in my experience have the top management ability to see the essentials à la Weinstock.'

'Women get too emotionally involved in their work.'

(Fogarty et al. 1971: 276)

Women administrators also tended to identify gender-related differences of style and were likely to say things like:

'Women tend not to suffer from pomposity . . . men are preoccupied with status.

'Women tend to be less secretive than men, they put their cards on the table more quickly.'

(Observer Magazine 1984)

But much more rarely than the men did they see women's different approaches as disqualifying them from effective performance of the central role. They were much more likely to conclude, as did Anne Mueller (Observer Magazine 1984) that 'It is the male style which is dominant as in any large organization [and] this may lead to bias.' Certainly in the higher civil service, an occupational world which lives by an intense process of judging, sorting, and labelling its members, the designation of individuals as 'outstanding' is unhesitatingly made and committed to record. There is a lot of evidence from the past twenty years which shows that women practitioners are, as a group, always judged as providing a smaller proportion of 'outstanding' practitioners than men.

The evidence is that women are less likely than men to be picked for the tougher, more prestigious postings. Indeed, in addition to the phrase 'high-flyers', the term 'crown princes' is sometimes used to describe those that are! The reasons often seem to lie in doubts about women's full availability to the organization – will they stay and thus capitalize on the experience? Will they be able to combine a high time and energy commitment to the post with their family and domestic commitments? A greater measure of doubt and disqualification is applied to women than to men. Survey research (Fogarty et al. 1971: 291) shows that women higher civil servants work on average no less hours than men and, presumably, evidence of this kind is also observable day by day in the work situation. Overall judgements of individuals are, however, made in terms of much more qualitative measures, such as 'edge' and 'reserves'; having children is seen for women administrators to eat into this. Managers and decision-makers make assessments of this contingency in women's lives whereas they usually do not have evidence from which to assess possible family perturbations in men's lives. One woman high-flyer has recently observed: 'I remember going to be interviewed for a job at Number 10. They asked me if I intended to have any more children. I objected to the question of course but I didn't get the job' (Observer Magazine 1984).

The higher civil service is hardly unique in all this; where it is more distinctive is in the extent to which its postings and promotions policy does not give individuals formal opportunities to apply for and to compete for highly demanding posts. Such a system can contribute to a 'playing it safe' set of judgements by managers about individuals and by individuals about themselves. The occupational structure also makes the late twenties and early thirties the age when very consequential decisions are made about individuals. As has been suggested, these are the years when many women are having children. Managers do appear to be prepared to place 'outstanding' women in the high-risk/high-potential postings; but as between the large proportion of women not so judged early on and the smaller but quite substantial proportion of men similarly not so judged, some very significant differences of treatment appear to operate. Higher civil servants are ranked on entry to departments depending on how well they have done in entry competitions. One large department in the late 1970s looked closely at how it treated entrants in the first two training years and found that it assigned top-ranked entrants, both men and women, to 'good' training assignments. Amongst the lowest rank of entrants, where there were proportionately more women than men, the department was much more likely to give the men rather than the women 'good' training assignments. One of the senior administrators in the department commented thus: 'Women entrants may be being judged by different standards compared with men. There may be truth in the contention that women have to prove clearly that they are successful, whereas men are assumed to be successful until they conclusively demonstrate that they are failures' (Fogarty, Allen, and Walters 1981: 44).

Women administrators' careers are not only affected by how they are regarded and managed by their male occupational peers in the business of postings and promotions. What they get from and contribute to the occupation are also crucially affected by the employment terms on offer in the civil service. If they want part-time hours or if they want a career break or if they seek employer-based child-care, they are dependent on the one employing organization within which their occupation is enclosed to create these opportunities. There is no employment milieu other than the large-scale bureaucratic one, and within that milieu there are no directly competing employers who might offer different opportunities.

A substantial minority of women in the higher civil service want a period of part-time work in their working lives; many of them encounter great barriers and difficulties in obtaining it and leave the occupation altogether because of the inflexibility of the options with which they are faced. Many women share the following experience:

'I, like many others of my intake, was keen to continue working after the birth of my first child but doing less hours than I had done. The department was not interested – there is a widespread dislike of such arrangements at all levels. So, instead, I've decided to have my two children as close together as possible and hope that I can get back when the younger is nearly five.'

(Fogarty, Allen, and Walters 1981: 65)

The frustration that many women experience at not being able to obtain part-time working is compounded by the fact that, publicly, the civil service says that its policy is to encourage departments to create opportunities for part-time working at all levels, so that women civil servants can have employment terms which fit in with acknowledged domestic responsibilities. In departments the policy has to fit with a whole set of considerations – 'resources implications', the 'justifiable needs' both of the department and 'of the staff generally'. The result in higher- and middle-level administration has been a negligible development of part-time posts.

In the higher civil service part-time working has an ambiguous status which is produced by the interaction of occupational social organization with the very smallness of the numbers of women practitioners. Despite the formal civil service policy of encouraging provision of part-time work, the woman higher civil servant has no kind of guarantee that should she seek such arrangements they will be forthcoming. Formal statements and collective wisdom in the higher civil service emphasize the severe limits that the nature of the occupation places on the development of opportunities for part-time working. The argument is that 'real' administrative work is incapable of being organized on a part-time basis because it involves a continuous meshing-in with a seamless flow of information and events. Normatively, part-time working is seen to run counter to the ethic of accessibility and the convention of 'not clock-watching'. However, whilst the higher administrative world is not prepared to contemplate the systematic provision of part-time work, it is prepared to encourage individual managers to give some flexibility of working conditions to women higher civil servants who want less than full-time work and whom management does not want to lose. The ambiguous status of part-time work in the occupation creates dilemmas of action for individual women practitioners. Many of them, though working, come to acknowledge the importance of options which allow career flexibility for women (and indeed for men). As individuals they are torn. Do they seek to promote organizational action through collective change or do they pursue individually advantageous arrangements? As confronted by individual women these may seem to be mutually exclusive strategies, for both demand expenditure of what is very likely to be a limited amount of time and energy. Pursuing the collective strategy can lead to challenging the occupation's ethos. Witness the public statement made by one young woman administrator:

'It is contended that people in the upper levels of the administration group and in the open structure need to be available on demand, to deal with urgent problems and brief ministers. This sounds sensible, but the fact is that senior men are not constantly available in this way. They are extremely busy people, with full diaries. They spend a great deal of time in meetings of various kinds, quite often away from their own office building. Some spend a good deal of time in Brussels. Some of these engagements can be cancelled or re-scheduled; other cannot. What is the practical difference between a

male assistant secretary who is at a meeting in Brussels, or
Manchester, or a nationalized industry headquarters somewhere
else in London; and a female one who is at home with her children?
Both represent a potential inconvenience to their colleagues. . . .
We survive it quite nicely when the absentee is a peripatetic man.
We could manage it just as well for part-time women.'

(Brimelow 1981: 328)

Challenging the organization can create risks for the individual; it can
mark them out as antagonistic, as not 'fitting in'. It might also lead to
pyrrhic victories – part-time work opportunities provided in a general
but inflexible form which satisfy few people. But there are risks
associated with pursuing an individualist strategy. There is the
possibility of having the door firmly held shut or there is the
possibility, actually experienced by some women, of being granted less
than full-time arrangements that are practically unworkable because
they are given little by way of organizational back-up.

Full-time career breaks and the collective provision of childcare are
also ambiguously treated in the civil service. Civil servants who leave
for domestic reasons can be reinstated – there are mechanisms for re-
incorporation. But whether or not it happens in an individual
instance depends on the employer's judgement of needs at the time
and evaluation of the individual applicant. Formally the civil service
regards itself as enabling occupational childcare provision, 'organized
child minding', to take place. Practically, the slight collective support
it gives to such arrangements makes it highly unlikely that any civil
servant seeking regular childcare would place much hope on
opportunities materializing through the workplace. Women in the
higher civil service face the same dilemma over reinstatement as they
do over part-time work – do they invest efforts whilst at work in
collective action to obtain more secure rights of reinstatement, or do
they put all their energy into individual work performance that will
ensure them a strong chance of re-entry if and when they seek it? Over
employer-based childcare, women administrators are, on the whole,
in a financial position to secure individual arrangements which they
judge to be satisfactory. Their relatively advantageous position makes
it less likely that as individuals they face dilemmas as to whether or
not to invest energy seeking action from the employer as a way of
securing their own needs. This is not to say that they do not
contemplate or engage in collective action to promote childcare.

The politics of equal opportunities in the higher civil service

The possibility that women higher civil servants may seek to alter their individual experience by collective action leads directly to the issue of the politics of equal opportunities in the occupation. There is an identifiable politics, with competing ideologies and programmes of action. In part the positions taken arise from differences of view and programme that exist in British society, but they also constitute a distinctive occupational politics shaped by the defining features of the occupation.

Within the higher civil service there is a view of women's present experience in the occupation which argues that women are never treated as a group, only as individuals. Indeed it is argued that given the highly meritocratic culture of the higher civil service and its small overall size, women in particular can become very well-known as individuals and treated on their merits. Hence what happens to women in the occupation – the degree of success that they enjoy and the ease or difficulty that they may encounter in obtaining leave or part-time working – are the result of their keenly and fairly judged capacities as individuals. Such a view of the experience of women in the higher civil service is related to a set of ideas about the occupational role within the civil service and about its role in the political process and within the wider society. Furthermore it supports organizational action on equal opportunities that it describes as organic and evolutionary.

This view gives fundamental emphasis to the principle of meritocracy as the hard-won, socially vital principle which governs job assignment and career progress throughout the service. In this view the legitimacy of the authority exercised by the higher civil service in managing the rest of the civil service rests on its strict observation of this principle in its own internal life. Furthermore a close connection is perceived between the principle of meritocracy and the principle of disinterested administration which constitutes the occupation's contribution to the political process. Both involve the standard of universal rationality – of seeking to weigh and judge different interests and factors within the same scale to arrive at one outcome which commands respect because of the process by which it has emerged. Measures which positively discriminate in favour of women, or racial groups, are treated by this view as constituting a threat to the principle of meritocracy because they are seen to move the organization from universalistic principles of allocation to explicit accommodation of group interests and particularistic criteria. This point of view is prepared to admit, *ad hominem*, that there may be parts of the civil service where women *do* suffer from adverse group experiences. This is seen to spring from the phenomenon of large numbers – both of personnel overall and of women. It is argued that large numbers can coarsen the operation of meritocracy and make sex-stereotyping more likely. It is insisted that such a hypothesis requires rigorous testing. Should it be confirmed, then the form of remedial action favoured is exhortation and educative action to develop further civil servants' capacity to make judgements of each other on the basis of capacity to do the job. Thus action undertaken to promote the interests of women as a group is action which strengthens the meritocratic principle.

There is within this overall view of the management role of the higher civil service a subsidiary argument which allows that, as well as being principled, management of the service must be realistic and hard-nosed about the resources embodied within functional groups of civil servants. This line of argument permits action designed to benefit women where they possess occupational skills that the civil service wishes to retain and to develop. It was on such grounds that the only day nursery for civil servants ever subsidized by the civil service – the Inland Revenue day nursery in South Wales – was established in the 1970s and then closed in the same decade on the grounds of not justifying the expenditure of resources.

This view further argues a particular interpretation of the role of the civil service as a national institution. It sees the small number of women in the higher civil service as a product of various social forces that curtail women's occupational achievement. It argues, however, that whilst the civil service has an obligation to be a good employer of women, this should not involve the use of its special, national status to trigger off, by its occupational policies, social changes which would affect women's work experience in British society. This view further holds that the civil service's interpretation of its role as a good employer is that it should follow clear trends, not seek to shape them. In particular, where the prevailing legal framework is not clear-cut, as for instance in the area of indirect discrimination, then the civil service has a clear obligation to test its practice in industrial tribunals rather than to create out of court settlements. There is no visible group in the civil service which espouses this view: it is best described in the words of Rose, writing of British political parties, as a 'tendency' that is a 'stable set or cluster of attitudes about a broad range of problems; the attitudes are held together by a more or less coherent political philosophy . . . adherents are often not self-consciously organised in support of a single policy' (Rose 1976: 314). In the higher civil service the 'tendency' described is dominant, its prevalence springs from the closed homogeneous structure of the occupational world, and it is supported by many, indeed probably the majority, of women practitioners themselves.

There is a challenging point of view on the 'women issue' which is best described as emanating from a 'faction' which has had various organized forms in the higher civil service. In the 1970s it assumed the form of the group 'Women in the Civil Service'. According to Rose, 'factions may be distinguished from exponents of a political tendency because they are self-consciously organised' (1976: 314). The 'women's rights faction' in the higher civil service is radical and challenging to the prevailing 'tendency' because it sees the stance adopted as unjust to women. This is not to say that self-identified supporters of this factional view would necessarily challenge the dominant 'tendency's' views on many other aspects of the necessary role and organization of the higher civil service.

In contrast to the 'tendency's' view, the 'women's rights faction' sees the small number of women in the higher civil service as a central, vital problem demanding strong action. It is seen as a clear result not only of impediments which women in the higher civil service commonly experience, but also it is seen to result from similar impediments experienced by the large numbers of women elsewhere in the civil service. It is these impediments which tend to prevent women from being amongst the internal transfers made within the civil service into the higher administrative ranks. The 'faction' argues trenchantly in the words of one of its representatives that:

'It deprives many of them of the opportunity for more interesting, more affluent and more satisfying lives. It keeps women in a tiny minority among the holders of high office under the Crown, and keeps them out of many positions of influence, authority and prestige. Insofar as the civil service and its practices have influence elsewhere, it helps to maintain the subjection of women in other areas too. The root of the injustice may lie outside the civil service – in the position of women in Britain today – but that does not remove the moral obligation to try to do something about it.'

(Brimelow 1981: 326)

The programmes that are supported on the basis of such an argument are widespread provision of employer-based childcare, considerable opportunities for part-time work, and, according to another of its proponents, Elizabeth Shore, a Deputy Secretary in the Department of Health and Social Security: 'Some sort of positive affirmation programme – things could then change rapidly because there is a lot of talent not being used. I would not expect change overnight, but targets could be set and a board could be established to monitor progress towards a fairer system' (*Observer Magazine* 1984).

Conclusion

Why does a view that bases itself on a social justice argument for women have such a limited factional life in the higher civil service? It is the argument of this chapter that within occupations and professions there are features of social organization and culture which affect women's place within them. In the higher civil service there is little room for the argument to develop that the service needs women as gendered subjects. At its centre there is articulated a set of values, rationality and meritocracy, which aim to be constructed in universal terms and from which gender-based qualities or experiences are judged to be absent. This leads to an organizational tendency to suppress gender rather than to incorporate it explicitly into occupational life. Women as well as men are socialized into this pattern and features of the occupational structure reinforce it. The structure scatters and individualizes women. They do not, as in some occupations, cluster in enclaves within the occupation, creating through the communality of their experience a base from which to challenge the prevailing ethos. In fact to challenge the ethos in any full sense is likely to lead to interpretations that those doing so are failures and 'deviants' who cannot comply with the necessary and demanding exigencies of the occupation. These are the features which at a fundamental level tend to marginalize women in the occupational world of the higher civil service. This is not to say that these forces are at all times unmodified by challenge. Generally the successful challenges – as in the case of the Equal Pay Campaign – require a coalition of actors inside and outside the occupation, in particular in parliament. Within the occupation, however, the dominant tendency to marginalize social justice arguments is modified internally by particular management considerations and 'resources' arguments. It is interaction between the occupational 'core' definitions and the forces modifying them which structures women's equivocal experience and ambivalent treatment in the higher civil service.

References

Allen, I., Fogarty, M., and Walters, P. (1981) Stuck on the Way to the Top. *New Society* 57: 56–8.

Brimelow, E. (1981) Women in the Civil Service. *Public Administration* 59: 314–35.

Cabinet Office, Management and Personnel Office (1984) *Equal Opportunities for Women in the Civil Service: Programme of Action*, London: HMSO.

Fogarty, M., Allen, A.J., Allen, I., and Walters, P. (1971) *Women in Top Jobs: Four Studies in Achievement*. London: Allen and Unwin.

Fogarty, M., Allen, I., and Walters, P. (1981) *Women in Top Jobs 1968–1979*. London: Heinemann.

Kellner, P. and Lord Crowther Hunt (1980) *The Civil Servants; An Inquiry into Britain's Ruling Class*. London: MacDonald.

Observer Magazine (1984) *The Mandarines* (3 June).

Rose, R. (1976) *The Problem of Party Government*. Harmondsworth: Penguin.

© 1987 Patricia A. Walters

3

Women in Personnel Management: Uphill Climb or Downhill Slide?

Karen Legge

'Where women are, power is not.'

(Rendel 1980)

'The power relationship between men and women is at the very heart of the social fabric. Once it begins to unravel, so do all other power relationships. . . . Small changes in the gender power balance can be tolerated. Many unconsciously fear, however, that a major change, one in which women could negotiate the dominant role, would prove the undoing of all other power relationships modelled so carefully after this seemingly most stable and inevitable one.'

(Lipman-Blumen 1984: 48)

Introduction

It has frequently been noted that personnel management is a 'traditional stronghold of female [managerial] employment' (Marshall 1984: 115) and, as such, is often seen to offer an unrepresentatively optimistic picture of women's opportunities in a man's world. Women may succeed in personnel, so it is fondly thought, while they may meet insuperable barriers to advancement in other, more 'masculine', managerial and professional careers, such as line management or engineering. In this chapter, I wish to argue that, rather than being a special case, *women's careers in personnel management provide an 'ideal type' model of the taken-for-granted subordination of women in employment specifically and in society*

33

generally. For, *par excellence*, the history of women in personnel management illustrates a disheartening paradox. When an occupation is seen as peripheral to central management/organizational/societal concerns, and far removed from strategic decision-making, then women may play a central role and 'reach the top'. But if that occupation becomes recognized as no longer peripheral and as a valid contributor to strategic decision-making, then women, if not elbowed out, are politely pushed aside, often with their own unconscious collusion. When women have power within an occupation, it might be asserted that that occupation has yet to attain power (Dasey 1981) or is losing power within organizations or society (Smith 1982). When the situation is reversed, the converse holds: women's position in that occupation is threatened and their contribution is downgraded.

In this chapter I wish to illustrate this paradox with reference to the development of the personnel management profession in the United Kingdom from its origins in the late nineteenth century to the present day. However, I also wish to suggest that the very statement of the 'problem' of women's careers in these terms is a further implicit subordination of women, as it assumes an essentially male perspective on working life. Hence the paradox presented will be constructed in the body of this chapter, but 'deconstructed'[1] in its conclusion.

Early days: women at the top, personnel management at the bottom

The early history of personnel management has been excellently recounted by Niven (1967) and it is sufficient here to identify a few themes of special significance to the argument that will be developed below. First, some statistics. Not only were the pioneers of personnel management women – for example Adelaide Anderson, Mary Wood, and Eleanor Kelly – all but a handful of the estimated sixty to seventy welfare workers in factories at the outbreak of the First World War were women. When at the 1913 conference the precursor of the Institute of Personnel Management (IPM) was formed, all but five of its thirty-four founder members were women, including the first president, Mary Wood. By 1927 membership was 420, but fewer than twenty members were men. Between 1918 and 1931, of the eleven institute presidents, six were women. Although in the latter statistic a familiar trend might be observed to be emerging (men represented in higher offices disproportionate to membership) it would be fair to say that women dominated the emergent profession. However, *a closer look at the early history, it might be suggested, reveals that the roots of the dominant/powerless, powerless/dominant paradox lie deep in the past.* The origins of personnel management betray several of what Lipman-Blumen (1984: 75) has termed 'control myths'; that is, 'social stereotypes about the "true nature" of women and men [which] once internalized, serve as self-control mechanisms, used by both genders to regulate their own behaviour'. Now, according to Niven (1967), personnel management arose out of nineteenth-century factory legislation (e.g. Factory Acts concerning minimum age for the employment of children and reduction of standard hours of work) which was directed at the plight of *women and children,* not at that of men, although the latter worked in similar conditions. Note here two implicit control myths, that 'women [like children] are weak, passive, dependent and fearful' and that 'men have women's best interests at heart; women can trust men to protect their welfare' (Lipman-Blumen 1984: 76, 92). Hence women must rely on men in parliament to pass protective legislation (which, at the same time, as Lipman-Blumen (1984: 94) points out, 'guarded women from a wide range of higher paid, resource generating jobs') while men could organize and fight for better conditions and wages (Niven 1967: 17). It was in the wake of such legislation that the first factory inspectors were appointed (in 1893) and, hard on their heels and sponsored mainly by Quaker employers, there came the first 'lady social workers' or 'social secretaries' such as Mary Wood, appointed to Rowntree's in 1896 and first president of the IPM, as already mentioned, in 1913.

The activities of these pioneers may be interpreted as embodying further control myths. As early as 1864, an official document (cited by Niven 1967: 16) stated that 'a female overlooker, married and of mature age is as essential to prosperity, the good government and the *moral* character of a factory as the material with which the workers are employed' (emphasis added). Furthermore, when Mary Wood was appointed to the Rowntree's factory one of her first duties, which she herself identified, was to curb rowdy behaviour in the dining room and, through raising the moral tone of the factory, partly by placing flowers in the workrooms and organizing lunch-time concerts and lectures, to attract 'more respectable girls'. Quite apart from an implicit repetition of the control myth that equates women with children, here we see lurking just below the surface of explicit pronouncement the myth that 'women's sexuality is inexhaustible, uncontrollable, and even dangerous to men' (Lipman-Blumen 1984: 86). Furthermore this control myth may be seen as implicitly reinforcing other power relationships (as suggested by the second quotation at the beginning of the chapter). 'Rowdiness' and 'poor discipline' (read 'self-assertion' and 'independence'?) are not notably characteristics desired in a direct labour force by an economy dominated by market or hierarchy.

But the nature of the work of the pre-First World War 'social workers' – who saw their tasks mainly in terms of the 'selection and education of employees, and the provision of health and safety, recreative and social institutions' (Niven 1967: 23, citing Cadbury 1912) – can also be seen, perhaps most clearly, as reflecting stereotypically 'feminine' activities. As such these underwrite the control myth that 'women are more altruistic, more nurturant and thus more moral than men' (Lipman-Blumen 1984: 83). A corollary of this myth, that women meet their own achievement needs through the success of others (usually men, or those enacting male roles) has to the present day dogged that status of the personnel function as mere 'advisers' to line management. But, equally important, this early identification of personnel management with *female* welfare activities inevitably meant that the function would be defined as low-status and unimportant, at least in comparison to central male activities such as production, finance, and so on. For as Marshall, building on Spender's (1980) work, points out and demonstrates in relation to the very structure of language and nature of conversation, 'as norms stand, male is consistently associated with superior and positive and female with inferior and negative' (Marshall 1984: 46).

A second theme which might be identified in this early history of personnel management is that the negative stereotypes of other women were already undermining both the potential status and the authority of the women pioneers. The early welfare workers, generally speaking, were educated middle-class women, drawn from the employing rather than employed class. The women whose welfare they sought to promote, who were members of a different class, not infrequently (nor unnaturally) saw them with suspicion and some hostility as middle-class 'ladies bountiful', transferring paternalistic (note the word!) calves'-foot-jelly-dispensing activities from outside to inside the factory walls. This reaction was particularly marked in the case of those women whose roles the welfare workers might be perceived as usurping, i.e. forewomen and women trades unionists. Niven has cited two revealing quotations from these quarters. When Eleanor Kelly arrived at Hudson Scotts[2] the forewoman greeted her guardedly: 'I won't do anything against you Miss Kelly. I'll summer and winter you first' (Niven 1967: 24). Stronger reservations about the early welfare workers came from a wartime meeting of women trades unionists whom Gertrude Tuckwell, in 1921, recalls as agreeing that:

> 'with some notable exceptions, the welfare worker found no place in the girls' vision of the factors which go to make a freer, healthier and more independent life for them. *She meddled and did not understand their real needs, seeking to impose on them regulations, which she thought for their good*, instead of realizing the value of self-government.'
>
> (Niven 1967: 42, emphasis added)

Nor was this opposition confined to working-class factory employees. Middle-class women were often critical of their sisters entering rough factories. As one said disparagingly of Mary Wood: 'She was one of the best teachers I ever knew and now she wastes her time cooking dinners for girls at Rowntrees' (Niven 1967: 25).

These quotations are indicative of a more general point that helps account for why women fail to exploit their potential power in organizations (and in society generally) and why they have difficulty in retaining those positions they have achieved if male competition asserts itself. Rather than bonding (Tiger 1969), women often fail to build alliances with their 'natural' allies – other women – due to the negative stereotypes they have of other groups, including the women in these groups.[3] As Lipman-Blumen succinctly put it:

> 'Middle and upper class women (and less powerful men) are kept from alliances with their gender-mates from other *socio-economic*, racial, age, and ethnic groups by the fear of contamination and loss of whatever limited advantages they currently have. Their working class sisters, alternately disdainful and desirous of the life style of middle and upper class women, *worry about the motivations of women above them in the social hierarchy*.'
>
> (Lipman-Blumen 1984: 45–6, emphasis added)

Clearly women welfare officers' failure to form constructive alliances with other women should not be overstated,[4] at least in the case of those with similar background and experience – as their role in organizing the 1913 and subsequent professional gatherings attests. But such suspicion and equivocation from *other women*, as cited here, can be used to fuel the belief that women are unsuitable for senior positions because other people, *including* women, do not want to work for or deal with women managers or professionals (Marshall 1984: 37–40).

A third theme which points to women's later loss of power within personnel management is, paradoxically, the part played by men in allowing opportunities for the role of the welfare officer to develop and in their early support of the pioneers. For not only was it men (of course) who were instrumental in passing the nineteenth-century legislation that provided personnel management's early *raison d'être*, but it was men in their role as employers who sanctioned the development of welfare functions in their organizations, acting as sponsors for the women pioneers. Niven (1967) shows clearly the sponsorship roles played, for example, by Seebohm Rowntree, Edward Cadbury, George Hargreaves, Charles Jacob, and David Crichton, 'who was later described as the prophet of the movement' (Niven 1967: 22). Perhaps it is ironic, though, that these champions of early legislation and welfarism generally were very often non-conformists and (especially) Quakers who, excluded in earlier times from the universities, professions, and public office and diverted into lower-status occupations in trade and industry, might almost be regarded, in this one sense, as 'honorary women'.[5] Nevertheless by inviting women to develop social work inside as well as outside the factory in their role as employers, such men were in fact the final arbiters of the form the activity should take.

Finally, the early history of personnel management reveals an ideological thread that eventually served to unravel women's initial dominance in the occupation (to echo the quotations introducing this chapter). In 1912 Edward Cadbury, in his book *Experiments in Industrial Organization*, writing of Bournville, made the vital connection between welfare and efficiency: 'the supreme principle has been the belief that business efficiency and the welfare of employees are but different sides of the same problem' (cited in Niven 1967: 24). This connection, which had emerged at the turn of the century (Niven 1967: 19), became fully explicit during the First World War, particularly in relation to the munitions factories. The paradox here is that although initially this connection of *welfare* and efficiency served to promote women's position in personnel management, once it could be extended to connect *personnel management* (as a more general activity) with efficiency, the days of women's dominance in the occupation became numbered. I will now consider this in more detail.

Two wars and their aftermath

Both world wars, while on the surface appearing to *consolidate* or even enhance women's position in personnel management, in practice and in the long term may arguably be considered to have *undermined* it. What is the evidence for this assertion?

The First World War, for personnel management, was characterized by two important developments: the substitution of female for male labour in many industrial sectors and a concern for the efficient production, in particular, of munitions. This in turn enhanced awareness of the health and safety issues and the dysfunctional effects on production of long hours in potentially dangerous workplaces. It also stimulated the setting up of such bodies as the Industrial Fatigue Boards, the Medical Research Council, and, specifically, the Health of Munitions Workers' Committee. The latter, in its second report on Welfare Supervision in 1916, urged that welfare supervisors should be appointed in all munitions factories where women were employed and, as a result, it was made compulsory to employ welfare workers in every factory where explosives were used, while their appointment was actively encouraged in all munitions factories. Under the guidance of Rowntree, at the Welfare Department of the Ministry of Munitions, a search was made for women to take up appointments as welfare workers. By 1919, it is estimated, around one thousand were so employed. Few had any previous experience or training, other than emergency six-week courses which London University helped to organize (Niven 1967: 39–41).

Here are several themes repeated, if to a lesser extent, in the Second World War. First, the numbers of women in personnel increased rapidly, but at the cost of dilution in training and experience. Second, while their numbers increased because of the perceived connection between welfare and efficiency, the reason why it was *women* who undertook this function (apart from the 'female' nature of the task) was because of the absence of *men*. This worked in two ways: absence of men meant women undertaking 'men's' jobs *per se*, but also more women in the workforce meant that it was appropriate (the 'moral tone' argument) to have more women to supervise them. Hence, the increase in numbers of women in personnel in the First World War, while appearing to consolidate their dominance of the nascent occupation, in fact gave a false impression. When, in the aftermath, the women workers left the munitions factories so, too, did many of the welfare workers with them. Moreover, given the dilution already referred to, women welfare workers sometimes left behind a less than glowing reputation among workers, unions, and management alike, thus enhancing the 'women are unsuitable in superordinate positions' myth.

Furthermore, during this period the connection between welfare and efficiency was being broadened. Welfare workers' contribution to efficiency, while still associated with canteens, clinics, and sports and social clubs, was also identified officially (*Industrial Health and Efficiency*, Final Report of the Health of Munitions Workers' Committee, 1918) as involving a wider range of activities. These included recruitment and selection, training, and keeping records for the monitoring and investigation of absence and labour turnover and of dismissals. Also, significantly, while not being responsible for fixing wages, these activities included receiving particulars of earnings, since the amount earned could give indication of the progress of workers (Niven 1967: 44). This broadening of the role, away from welfare towards manpower management, became even more pronounced in the Second World War, when 'labour' officers became responsible (in *addition* to the above activities) for administering the myriad of Essential Works Orders, Control of Engagement Orders, and National Arbitration Orders, thereby undertaking negotiation.

But while the Second World War repeated themes of the First – emphasizing the link between welfare and efficiency and the substitution of women workers for men and in this sense highlighting the role played by women in personnel – subtle differences are apparent which were foreshadowed in the aftermath of the First World War. Niven (1967) records how men, returning from the camaraderie as well as the horrors of the trenches, had an awakened interest in the 'personnel' aspects of management and, particularly, good workforce relationships. In this they were supported by earlier developments, such as the development of Joint Industrial Councils (JICs) following the 1917 Whitley Report and by wartime legislation making provisions about hours and welfare for men, as well as for women and children (Police, Factories, etc. (Miscellaneous Provisions) Act 1916).

Personnel management

Although, given the recession and unemployment, personnel management in the inter-war years ceased to have the importance it attained in the First World War, in industries and areas where the economy was growing (electricals, chemicals, consumer industries in the south-east), the link between efficiency and labour management continued to be developed. A special stimulus was given by scientific management and, from a different quarter, the Hawthorne studies. In 1931 the Institute of Industrial Welfare significantly changed its name to the Institute of Labour Management, giving the following rationale:

'We claim that our work is an integral part of management. At the present time methods of management are under review as never before and management generally is undergoing painfully that re-orientation necessary to refit it to a changed industrial world. In the process functions are becoming more scientifically labelled, and the label 'welfare' has become attached to a function which no longer conveys the aims of the Institute. . . . Are we to agree to an organisation of industry which includes management of buying, production, plant, sales etc, but leaves out the management of labour?'

(cited in Niven 1967: 83)

There is some evidence that these two developments, the entry of more men into welfare/labour management and the shifting emphasis from welfare to labour management, went hand in hand. Certainly, as Niven has suggested, increasingly throughout the 1920s and 1930s it became the practice in large companies for the labour/welfare departments to be split into two divisions, one for men and one for women: 'a division which some women found hard to accept especially as they could see themselves being relegated to specifically welfare aspects, leaving male colleagues to undertake the fuller functions of labour management' (1967: 79).

It is against this background that a significant difference between the position of women in personnel work in the First and Second World Wars may be identified. By 1939, the occupation was beginning to shed its 'female' image in that, of the estimated 1800 labour managers and welfare supervisors, 40 per cent were men. Hence, when war broke out and it was declared a reserved occupation (a recognition of the link increasingly argued between labour management and efficiency), not only were existing male labour officers retained in their jobs but: 'it offered a loophole to managers who found they could ease their conscience about employees for whom they felt some obligation, but whose jobs were in jeopardy because of the war: they made them labour officers.' (Niven 1967: 95). Given the Arbitration Orders male labour officers, in particular, could be justified in terms of the negotiating role they now had to fulfil. Hence the Second World War, while again increasing the number of female personnel officers (in particular to service the now conscripted female factory workers), in practice did not see such a proportionally significant substitution of women for men. Furthermore, the trend was clearly emerging for women increasingly to remain with activities involving the selection of women employees, training, and welfare, rather than to take on negotiation and broader industrial relations concerns which were left to male labour officers.

Hence, to generalize, the effect of both world wars was to demonstrate and broaden the link between welfare, other personnel activities, and efficiency. But the more this connection could be demonstrated, the more important personnel management was seen to be and, as such, the more it became visible as a suitable career for men. In the First World War women could more easily maintain their position, partly because the substitution of female for male employees was proportionally greater and partly because the connection between welfare (a 'feminine' activity) and efficiency was emphasized, in spite of the extensions to the function mentioned earlier. In the Second World War both these 'safeguards' were undermined – by reserving the occupation and by government regulations which clearly extended the function into industrial relations management. The stage was set for a male takeover of senior positions.

This occurred with gathering momentum in the years following the Second World War. The development of full employment, combined with the establishment of the welfare state, gave further opportunities for extending the link between personnel management and efficiency, whilst undermining the importance of the 'feminine' task of welfare. Full employment, in particular, prioritized the tasks of recruitment, selection, and wage negotiation, whilst the welfare state provided as of right many of the benefits previously in the gift of the employer. By 1950, not surprisingly, slightly less than half of IPM members were women; by 1960 the figure was roughly one quarter; by 1970 it was just below 20 per cent. I will next try to account for this evident decline of women from their early position of dominance in personnel management.[6]

The 1960s and 1970s: personnel management at the top, women at the bottom

I have referred to the 'evident' decline of women, but what *is* the evidence for the 1960s and 1970s in particular? Although the proportion of women in personnel (judged by IPM membership) fell between 1945 and the mid-1970s, given the vast increase in the size of the profession (in 1945 there were 2,896 IPM members and in 1979 20,194) the absolute numbers of women actually increased. The decline in the position of women may be seen rather in their absence from senior, and their clustering in junior, personnel positions.[7] A few indicative figures must suffice. Whereas between 1918 and 1931, 55 per cent of IPM (or rather its precursor's) presidents were women, between 1931 and 1961 and between 1961 and 1981 the figures were 21 per cent and 10 per cent respectively. In June 1973, the year of IPM's Diamond Jubilee and shortly before legislation on sex discrimination banned the specification by gender of applicants in job advertisements, a count of job advertisements in the IPM's own journal *Personnel Management*[8] revealed that of seventy-eight advertisements at the level of personnel/training officer, 40 per cent did not specify gender of applicant, 37 per cent specified male applicants, 13 per cent specified female applicants, and the remaining 10 per cent explicitly specified either male or female. At the level of personnel/training manager, of thirty-seven advertisements, 38 per cent did not specify gender of applicant, 59 per cent specified male applicants, 3 per cent explicitly specified either male or female, whilst *none* specified female applicants. Of the three advertisements for personnel directors, one was for a woman – to be female director of the YWCA's work with the armed forces (welfare and moral tone raise their heads again!). Similarly, a 1970 IPM survey of its members revealed that 50 per cent of the male respondents came in the top two categories of senior personnel manager or personnel manager, while 80 per cent of the female respondents came in the lower two categories, senior personnel officer and personnel officer (Roff 1973). Finally, a perusal of *Personnel Management*'s monthly feature 'Man of the Moment' (note the title), from the Jubilee year (1973) to the end of the 1970s, showed that of the seventy people featured (personnel directors, union leaders, personnel management academics, and so forth) only six (9 per cent) were women. Only one of these six women was a personnel director (three of the others were academics and two were members of quangos and the EOC and EEC Economic and Social

Affairs Committee). Of the men so featured twenty-five (39 per cent) were personnel directors or involved in senior personnel management jobs.

Why did this decline, arguably inevitable from the earliest days, accelerate from the late 1950s until the mid to late 1970s? As suggested in the introduction to this chapter the answer, paradoxically, lies in the increasing power gained by the personnel function in this period – a culmination of the long struggle to demonstrate the evolving links between personnel management and organizational effectiveness, as the link between welfare and efficiency was now reinterpreted.

Briefly, in the 1960s and 1970s five factors, born of the full employment of the 1950s and 1960s, served to identify problems of industrial performance with industrial relations and employment issues (Guest 1982). These were the increased militancy on the part of the blue-collar unions, the organization of white-collar, technical, and management staff, the implementation of and adaptation to organizational change, the higher expectations of employees about employment relationships, and, perhaps most importantly and reflecting the other four factors, the spate of employment legislation from the mid-1960s onwards (Legge 1978). To achieve organizational effectiveness it was increasingly seen that whether the strategy was to be investment, product innovation, or control of costs, this was permeated by manpower and industrial relations concerns. Further, increasing organizational complexity (in terms of concentration of ownership, the nature of control, and size) combined with a growing body of knowledge and skills associated with personnel management, encouraged specialization and stimulated a concern for professionalization (Guest 1982; Purcell and Sisson 1983). By 1975 IPM membership could no longer be acquired by experience alone, but required success in a qualifying examination.

In spite of commentators' continuing concern with the personnel function's power and status via-à-vis other management functions (see, for example, Jenkins 1973), three significant statistics indicate the enhanced centrality and status achieved by personnel management in the 1960s and 1970s. First, whilst in 1963 membership of IPM stood at 5,730, by 1979 it had soared to 20,194 and, even with the onset of recession, membership was still climbing. Second, whereas a 1971 British Institute of Management survey of the private sector found that 28 per cent of organizations had someone at board level with personnel responsibilities, by 1978 this figure had reached 74 per cent. Third, by the late 1970s personnel managers had caught up with and, in some cases, even surpassed the median salaries of other management groups (Inbucon/AIC Management Consultants 1975–80).

As poor industrial relations (the 'British disease') was seen to be at the heart of our dismal economic performance, significantly the power of the personnel function increased proportionately to the extent to which it was able to define itself, *par excellence*, as an industrial relations function. This emphasis on the 'male' activities of negotiation, wage determination, and the handling of industrial disputes, not surprisingly, went hand in hand with a distancing from and at times denial of the 'feminine' welfare function (Watson 1977: 189–90). The views of Watson's interview sample of personnel managers are probably typical of this period, where (presumably?) male respondents expressed the following views:

'We've got to stop them treating us as inefficient bumbling do-gooders.'

(p. 60)

'It's [the problem] getting rid of the image of the guy who keeps the sanitary towel machine stocked up.'

(p. 60)

'[A major dislike is] the attachment of women to it – the welfare image.'

(Watson 1977: 93)

The distancing from the welfare image and the highlighting of the industrial relations aspects of the personnel function may account, in part, for some of the proportional decline in the number of women in personnel management in this period, reaching a low ebb of 19 per cent of IPM membership in the early 1970s. For, as Watson has shrewdly commented, to avoid the feminine overtones of welfare and:

'to achieve credibility, senior personnel executives may find themselves discriminating against women in recruiting to the function. . . . There was a clear tendency amongst those men interviewees responsible for recruitment to personnel departments to lump together women with "social work types" and "churchy people". Such recruits were to be avoided.'

(Watson 1977: 190)

The same discrimination, if in a somewhat paradoxical fashion, also appeared to be affecting women's promotion chances:

> 'One respondent was clearly doing a job which would normally have been given the title personnel *manager*. However she was only called personnel *officer*, partly on the grounds that as a woman she would need to be called *manageress* which would carry unfortunate connotations connected with canteens and the like!'

(Watson 1977: 189)

The argument of this section has been that, as the personnel function achieved some measure of power, so women's influence in that function declined. What of their situation today – and tomorrow – when the effects of recession, industrial restructuring, and new technologies are once more stimulating a redefinition of personnel management (Guest 1982; Handy 1984; Hunt 1984)? Is the paradox of power still holding – and likely to hold?

Time present – and time future

If the argument developed in this chapter is valid, then it might be hypothesized that any present or future loss of organizational power on the part of the personnel function might revive opportunities for women to resume at least part of their early dominance of the activity. What evidence is there of either process occurring?

It should be said at the outset that, as far as the present and future power of the function is concerned, two contrasting arguments might be presented which point in different directions as far as the opportunities for women in personnel management go. But before I embark on these arguments, what appears to be the position of women in personnel management today? I am fortunate in having a recent IPM survey conducted by Phil Long, *The Personnel Specialists: A Comparative Study of Male and Female Careers*, to draw upon (Long 1984a). This survey was based on a 10 per cent sample of IPM members (achieving a 45 per cent response rate to a postal questionnaire) and on interviews with fifty matched pairs of men and women, which were conducted in 1982. Not only were men and women equally represented among the respondents to the postal survey (440 men and 450 women) but they were similar in terms of level of general education and grade of IPM membership attained (although differing somewhat in age and marital and parental status).

Personnel management

There were five findings which were of particular relevance to my argument. These may be summarized as follows:

(a) Pre-entry images of personnel management differed between women and men. Rather more women than men saw the function as administrative and welfare-orientated, while twice as many men as women were aware of the industrial relations aspects. For nearly two-thirds of the sample, personnel management was the most favoured career choice. However, amongst those with alternative primary career choices men favoured first management-orientated work and second engineering and technology, whilst women favoured service-orientated work, in education, health, and welfare.

(b) In early career, men were significantly more likely than women to acquire some type of industrial relations experience, although maturity on career entry enhanced the chances of such involvement for both sexes. In mid-career this trend was maintained. Men achieved far more experience in industrial relations, while women were more likely to be steered towards the routine activities of recruitment, employee conditions and services, wages and salary administration, and training. Long, interestingly, attributed this to paternalistic and protective attitudes, particularly among older male personnel managers, who attempted to avoid exposing their 'lady assistants' to the stressful conflict situations involved in industrial relations, steering them, in particular, towards welfare: 'my lady assistant is just right, very approachable, takes things in her stride, deals with all the lady staff problems, all the sickness, all the allowances, special leave and things like that' (personnel manager – male) (Long 1984a: 133). (Here, it may be noted, we have a clear statement of a number of the 'control myths' cited earlier in the chapter!)

Generally speaking, Long found that women were perceived by their bosses as holding little credibility in a negotiation situation, particularly with manual unions. This was in spite of the fact that this did not appear to be a problem for those women interviewed whose jobs *did* include major responsibility for industrial relations. Indeed, excluding the 27 per cent of women who had no contact with manual workers, the women in the sample had a higher satisfaction score with regard to their credibility with manual workers than did the men (Long 1984b)!

The other area of work experience in which the career development of men and women differed significantly was in general management activities. More men than women had some general management experience before entering personnel, and they were also more likely to acquire it during their personnel careers (for example by participating in cross-functional and divisional management meetings, by becoming involved in organizational policy-forming and corporate planning). Significantly, although only 26 per cent of the men were involved in corporate planning, this proportion was twice that of the women, who were more likely to be engaged in implementing and administering action plans drawn up by others (Long 1984a: iii; Long 1984b: 17–18). Similarly women were far less likely to receive the senior management education essential for preparation for wider responsibilities (Long 1984a: 52–7).

(c) Long found much evidence that men moved faster than women through the lower grades of personnel management and were over-represented at senior management level, the division appearing to occur at personnel manager level. Thus, 58 per cent of men were employed at personnel manager level and above, compared with 30 per cent of women. Excluding consultants, advisers, and lecturers, 51 per cent of women were employed below personnel manager level, compared with only 30 per cent of men. These results cannot be put down to the women (being younger) having less years of personnel experience. Long (1984b: 18) showed that over half of both men and women in senior personnel jobs had no more than fifteen years experience while, at the lower-middle personnel management levels, 42 per cent of women had more than ten years experience compared with just 28 per cent of men. Women's poorer promotion chances, it was suggested, may be attributed in part to career breaks, a third having experienced a break compared with only 13 per cent of men. But the majority of women had experienced only one break – mostly for less than a year – and the most common cause was redundancy, which affected 10 per cent of the sample, men and women. Furthermore only 16 per cent of the women in the sample had taken a break for reason of marriage or maternity.

Interestingly, of those women who had achieved senior personnel management positions, two-thirds were employed in small or medium-sized organizations, the industry employing most senior personnel women being public administration. As a group women were less likely to have responsibility for subordinates and were more likely to occupy the staff support roles of the personnel function (Long 1984b: 18–19).

(d) Analysis revealed that the strongest positive influence on salary level was (large) size of organization and, to a lesser extent, age. As the women tended to be younger, and more frequently employed in smaller organizations, it was not unexpected that this would have a depressing effect on their median salaries. However, even allowing for this, the extent of the 'salary gap' was significant. Women earned less than men overall regardless of the variable with which this was analysed, including education and years of service. At each management level (and including those employed in education, consultancy, and advisory work) women consistently received lower salaries than men, the median being 77 per cent of the male median salary (Long 1984a: 88–99; Long 1984b: 19).

(e) Although women were dissatisfied with their concentration in routine administrative work, their lack of development opportunities and career counselling, and by the discrimination against them in promotion opportunities, except for a minority of cases they took a less positive, structured approach towards career planning and development activities than their male colleagues. As Long put it: 'Women were thought to be more inclined to allow their careers to evolve, the expectations of their social role exerting a subtle demotivating influence' (1984a: v). Interestingly, this view was held by many of the women themselves (Long 1984a: 127), along with the almost taken-for-granted understanding that women have to be twice as good to get half as far (Long 1984a: 128).[9]

To sum up, one can only echo Long's conclusion, that the research findings show that, in 1982, 'in the personnel management profession women are still, on the average, employed in lower level jobs, less well counselled and developed, given less satisfying work and less well paid than are men' (1984a: 148).

Personnel Management's 'Man of the Moment' feature serves to confirm the picture painted by Long. Between 1980 and June 1985, of the fifty people featured, only four (8 per cent) were women, of whom two were personnel directors (the other two were a civil servant and a politician). Of the men featured, thirty-four (79 per cent) were personnel directors. Furthermore, while the journal's new series, started in 1981 and entitled 'I'm in Personnel . . .', has featured a higher proportion of women (28 per cent), it has been noticeable that the women consistently have held more junior posts than their male colleagues. Thus, for example (leaving out 'odd' jobs such as manager of a job centre, or a BP resettlement officer),whereas 40 per cent of the women featured were personnel/training officers, only 12 per cent of the men were of this grade. Whilst 50 per cent of both men and women were personnel managers, no women personnel directors were featured, compared with 12 per cent of the men. Finally, in *Personnel Management*'s series 'How I See the Personnel Function', all eight contributions came from men. Perhaps it is unnecessary to add that since 1981 no woman has held the office of president (or director) of the IPM.

Is women's position in personnel management likely to improve or decline further? Prediction is always a dangerous business as it involves both extrapolating from and questioning existing trends, the continuity of which will crucially depend on the validity of the assumptions upon which their interpretation rests. However I would reiterate that short of the radical structuring necessary to alter women's general subordination in society, it could confidently be predicted that women's position in personnel management will inversely reflect the power the function is seen to exercise in organizations. As to the latter, two contrasting views – the pessimistic and optimistic – may be presented.

The pessimistic view suggests that, with continuing recession, the decline of traditional manufacturing industry and the introduction of new technologies, the personnel function will inevitably lose a large part of the power it gained in the 1970s. The argument runs roughly as follows. With the advent of recession and of the Conservative government in 1979, problems of industrial performance have tended to be defined in financial/money supply terms, and less in terms of the industrial relations system (Guest 1982; Littler and Salaman 1984). Moreover:

'Such a view relegates industrial relations and personnel issues to a
    subsidiary role on the periphery of the economic system, whereas
    previously it had been seen as a, if not the, major influence on

industrial performance. A corollary of this is that employment concerns are subordinated to financial concerns. Personnel management therefore has to face both a recession and a redefinition of national problems which may negatively affect perceptions of the importance given to personnel and industrial relations compared with other issues.'

(Guest 1982: 37)

In support of this view Guest cites a survey of 68 engineering companies. Whereas in 1980 employee relations ranked third of eleven items in terms of its increasing importance over the previous year as an issue confronting the board, in 1981 it ranked seventh out of eleven, below 'more pressing preoccupations', such as cash flow, financial results, the order book, day-to-day operations, managerial success, and multinational operations (Korn/Ferry International 1981 cited in Guest 1982: 38). Since Guest's paper was written, little has changed to alter such perceptions – indeed the sight in 1984 of the humbling of powerful unions (as in the defeat of the NUM and the massive decline in membership of the TGWU) is likely, it might be argued, to further minimize the preoccupation with industrial relations that characterized the 1970s.

Undoubtedly a major factor in altering perceptions about the importance of employee relations issues is the fact that the pressures resulting from full employment have been ameliorated in the face of recession, unemployment, and job loss. Expectations and union demands have developed a 'new realism', as both Conservative politicians and right-wing union leaders term it. Even if economic recovery does get under way, the impact of new technologies on job loss both in manufacturing and service sectors has still to be reckoned with, if the logic of exploiting their potential for cost reduction in conditions of weakened labour resistance is adhered to (see Child 1985; Gowler and Legge 1986; Littler and Salaman 1984; Warner 1984; Wilkinson 1983). In these circumstances, it is argued, personnel management will lose the position of power it achieved in the 1970s and lapse into a largely administrative and welfare service. Indeed it has even been suggested that with continuing unemployment and the decline of the welfare state, the latter function might regain some of its old importance (Stewart 1983).

The optimistic view draws a different message from the effects of recession, future economic uncertainty, and technological change. It admits that these factors are encouraging organizations to seek manning strategies which allow a flexible response to unanticipated changes while minimizing unit labour costs (Atkinson 1984; Handy 1984; Hunt 1984). Such strategies, it is argued, involve developing three kinds of flexibility: functional flexibility (polyvalence), numerical flexibility (in terms of labour resources), and financial flexibility (in the design of reward systems and levels) (Atkinson 1984). This can be achieved by dividing the labour force into increasingly peripheral and therefore numerically flexible groups (e.g. part-timers, contract employees) clustered around a small stable core which conducts the organization's key, firm-specific continuous activities (for further details see Gowler and Legge 1986). From this perspective, organizational success will crucially depend on the quality and commitment of the small, highly skilled, 'stable core' of employees. Personnel's power essentially will rest on its role in developing such skills and commitment. In more generalized terms, its power will depend on the extent to which it can achieve responsibility for developing, sustaining, and reinforcing (by selection, induction, training, appraisal, and reward systems) key corporate values that will serve to integrate and direct organizations characterized by operational autonomy and individual contracts.

Which of these two perspectives of the power of the personnel function is likely to materialize? Possibly the most realistic view, as Guest (1982) citing Beaumont's (1982) survey, suggests, is that a polarization may occur. Small firms taking advantage of labour availability and the quiescence born of recession may choose to cut back on resources devoted to personnel management. Larger firms, particularly those undergoing restructuring, may value personnel's contribution to the management of immediate crises, such as redundancy programmes, as well as to the development of longer-term policies in areas of developing employee commitment.

Taking these pictures together, what overall conclusions may be drawn and what of women's position in personnel management? I would suggest, paradoxically, that as far as women are concerned the immediate future – say to the end of the decade – is one of 'heads I win, tails you lose'. This can be explained as follows. If one takes the optimistic picture of personnel management – as might be relevant to the high technology and service sectors of the economy – and argues that personnel will remain powerful, then men are likely to dominate the function. (Indeed, if the key task in 'search of excellence' *is* the management of the symbolic order (Peters and Waterman 1982), then the personnel management function is more likely to be challenged by other male-dominated specialist groups for control of this activity than by women within the function.) If personnel seeks to maintain its position through the management of crises (e.g. redundancy) or long-term change (e.g. new technology), while other management functions may not compete for such tasks, the very nature of such changes may undermine women's position in personnel management. For if 'managing redundancy' is defined as an industrial relations issue (as is likely, given legislative constraints and potential union involvement) then, judging by Long's research referred to above, women will tend to be 'protectively' excluded. But if 'managing change' involves technical change, a more insidious threat may be involved.

It has been suggested that the predictable uses of microelectronics will hit women's levels of employment particularly hard, whether directly (e.g. via Electronic Point of Sale technology (EPOS), word processing, reduction in assembly work via component reduction, automation in food processing) or indirectly (e.g. almost empty factories, offices requiring fewer cleaning and catering staff) (Swords-Isherwood, Zmroczek, and Henwood 1984). The replacement 'technical' jobs are likely to be those demanding skills not necessarily held by women (given their early socialization and education) and defined by management and unions alike as essentially skilled 'male' jobs. If this occurs, women may increasingly find it difficult to enter personnel management, even at the lowest levels, as their traditional role of 'dealing with all the lady staff's problems' will quantitatively be much reduced. There will not be the same numbers of women in employment, congregated in large factory or office units justifying the employment of such an 'overhead'. And if it is argued that, with better qualified more aspirant women entering the profession and more liberated attitudes generally, women are as likely as men to achieve employment and promotion in the role of personnel specialists dealing chiefly with the small core of highly skilled (male?) employees, then the following comparable observation might stand as a word of warning: 'Comments such as "we would not recruit a female technologist because her job would require her to supervise males" were typical of *personnel officers'* attitudes to women in one survey of recruitment methods' (Swords-Isherwood, Zmroczek, and Henwood 1984, citing Science Policy Research Unit 1982, emphasis added).

But what if we take the pessimistic view of the future of personnel management, and assume that if the activity diminishes in importance, women may regain their lost ground? Certainly if the function is reduced to a welfare-orientated one, this may be so (and in which case, what ground would women really have won?). However, the pessimistic view equally suggests threats to women's position. Bearing in mind both Beaumont's (1982) and Long's (1984a) findings, it might be suggested that while small firms are most likely to take advantage of present labour availability and the relative quiescence of labour to cut back on resources devoted to personnel management, it is precisely in such small/medium-sized firms that women are disproportionately employed. Furthermore, if the activity is reduced (but not to the extent of comprising welfare alone) it may still be over-optimistic to assume a female takeover – at least while the recession lasts and while men are still prepared to define personnel management as a legitimate male career, dazzled by the images of the 1970s. For as Guest, discussing the declining number of advertised vacancies in personnel management in the early 1980s,[10] has stated:

> 'When vacancies arise within an organisation, it may well be that personnel jobs are viewed as substitutable, in the sense that managers displaced from elsewhere are considered competent to fill them in preference to recruiting from outside. Where recruitment does occur, criteria are being tightened. For example, most low level jobs now ask for previous personnel experience. Other informal criteria may also be used; sadly, recent experience in helping students find jobs indicates that it is much more difficult for a woman or black student to get into personnel in a tight labour market than it is for a white man.'
>
> (Guest 1982: 37)

Sadly indeed, for this quotation returns us to those at the head of this chapter – the power structures in our society, particularly when the chips are down (in more senses than one!) serve to exclude stigmatized groups. 'Heads I win, tails you lose' is an inevitable outcome when a game is played with loaded dice.

Conclusion

Many insightful analyses have been offered as to why women 'travellers' have difficulty in succeeding 'in a male world' (Marshall 1984). One can point, for example, to early socialization and the undermining effect of sex-role stereotypes, to career timetabling based on male models, to women's exclusion from organizations' informal networks, to the problems of visibility, polarization, and assimilation associated with the 'relative number' of women and men in organizations. The list of factors has been well rehearsed and is seemingly endless (see, for example, Epstein and Coser 1982; Fogarty *et al.* 1971; Hennig and Jardim 1978; Kanter 1977; Marshall 1984; Novarra 1980). All these factors are relevant in considering women's position in personnel management today. All are difficult for women to overcome as essentially they place women in a series of 'double-binds' (Marshall 1984). For example, women are less worthy of management roles because they are seen as less committed, *but* working is socially acceptable only if it serves to support another of their life roles (providing for the family's 'luxuries');[11] women cannot be held properly accountable as they are not 'serious' managers (and hence cannot be said to be 'real' managers at all) *but* they are held more accountable as, due to relative numbers, they are more visible; women are excluded from informal male networks *but* to gain access they must be prepared to condone conversation derogatory of their gender (which, in turn, classifies them as 'one of the chaps', not a 'real' women at all, in fact); and so on (Marshall 1984, *passim*).

Furthermore the strategies often advocated for women managers to survive in a man's world, at various levels, may be seen as self-defeating. As Marshall (1984: 105) has pointed out, taking advantage of stereotypes of feminine characteristics[12] by following career paths which demand and reward such characteristics is the path to a staff position peripheral to the organization's main chain of command. Alternatively, copying male patterns of behaviour, 'gaining the skills and knowledge to pass as honorary men' (Davies 1985) enmeshes women more firmly in the double-bind, so that 'unless women behave very similarly to men they will not be considered suitable as managers . . . if they stray too far from stereotypes of femininity they will be sanctioned for deviance' (Marshall 1984: 37). Moreover copying male patterns of behaviour simply serves to reinforce prevailing culture and patterns of dominance.[13] Even when women *do* succeed, by whichever strategy, their very success similarly serves to maintain the *status quo*. If some women succeed, the illusion of equal opportunities is maintained as the unsuccessful may be portrayed as inadequate, rather than discriminated against (Davies 1985). Furthermore, it is likely that the women who do succeed will be those whose participation is not immediately threatening to those in power and who are prepared to embrace the values of the group they have joined rather than those of the excluded (Davies 1985; Epstein 1982b). Not surprisingly, then, in her interview as 'Woman of the Moment' in *Personnel Management* (December 1975), Pat Downs (then personnel director of Woolworth's) is attributed by the male interviewer with the view that:

> 'she sees herself not as a "women's libber" nor even a feminist, but rather a realist who is prepared to take on men in their own terms. Feeling as she does that men can't stand aggressive or bitter women, she argues that they must quietly involve themselves at work and be more prepared to take on responsibility when the chance is offered.'

> (Prentice 1975: 13)

So where does this leave us? As a final word I will attempt to 'deconstruct' the argument presented in this chapter. On the surface my presentation may appear critical: 'where women are, power is not' is a feminist questioning of the established order. But reflecting on this argument, what have I, in fact, really achieved? For I have unconsciously fallen prey to the very values that I have been questioning. Implicitly (note, for example, my disparaging comments about the welfare aspects of personnel management – 'what ground would women have really won?', etc.), I have presented the male as the norm and the positive value and been as guilty as any man of devaluing female values. Marshall's insightful analysis alerted me to this contradiction:

> 'Each study is bounded by the assumptions the originators bring to their work. *If they assume success in management for women is reaching the top as often as men do, they will count the number of women at senior organisational levels and report this as a percentage in relation to men.*'

> (Marshall 1984: 30, emphasis added)

Mea culpa! I have been guilty, as Marshall has pointed out, of using men as the standard by which to judge what women do. Sadly, however, I suppose that this entrapment in social norms reflecting male dominance is difficult if not impossible to break, even with the best efforts at consciousness-raising. For our social structures are not only sustained by these male values, but serve to perpetuate and reinforce them. As do these final defeated words?

Acknowledgement

My warm thanks go to Helen Brazier, of the Institute of Personnel Management library, for kindly tracking down for me many of the IPM statistics cited in this chapter.

Notes

1 'Deconstruction', a mode of analysis deriving from post-structuralist philosophy and literary criticism, may best be viewed as simply an analytical approach that uses reversals, inversions, and paradoxes to call into question the certainties of more traditional modes of analysis. For a general discussion see Culler (1983), and for an example of its application in organizational analysis see Gowler and Legge (1984).

2 Where, significantly, her only guidance from the directors as to what her job should entail was the instruction that 'there should be white tablecloths in the canteen' (Niven 1967: 25).

3 See, for example, the opposition to 'women's lib' that comes from other women (Novarra 1980) and the 'Queen Bee' syndrome whereby successful women refuse to stress the rights of other women, but identify instead with the male elites they have joined (Staines, Tavris, and Jayaratne 1974, cited in Marshall 1984: 102).

4 In some societies there is evidence of women bonding. See, for example, Murphy and Murphy (1974).

5 It is interesting in this context that Hofstede (1980) considers that Quakers represent a feminine subculture in the United States, promoting values of 'service', pacifism, and so forth.

6 This decline in women's position in personnel management throughout the century finds parallels in other professions. See, for example, Hakim (1979) cited in Davies (1985)

7 This is frequently observed about women in management and in the professions generally. See, for example, Epstein (1982a) and Whitley, Thomas, and Marceau (1981).

8 I excluded from this count jobs difficult to classify such as Industry Training Board (ITB) training advisers.

9 This latter view finds echoes in so many commentators that it has the status of a cliché. For other references to this phenomenon, see, for example, Alban-Metcalfe and Nicholson (1984); Hennig and Jardim (1978); Hunt (1975).

10 Guest draws his evidence from the *IPM Digest* of April 1982. While there is some evidence that managerial labour markets in the mid-1980s are somewhat more active, there is also evidence that the overall position vis-à-vis personnel jobs lags behind that of other management specialities.

11 In fact, of course, women often work for the family 'necessities' as well (Land 1976), particularly given the number of single-parent families and the present level of male unemployment – but to recognize this would threaten men's roles as 'breadwinners' and hence it is conventionally ignored.

12 Or to quote one male commentator (admittedly writing in 1972):

'Why shouldn't women be feminine and even seductive if that permits them to achieve success in a managerial career? This is not to advocate immorality of any sort but rather to encourage women to use all their female charms and powers and be women while being managers.'

(Basil 1972: 111)

Interestingly, Douglas Basil's female collaborator in this book, *Women in Management*, is not accorded full joint authorship, but receives that classic acknowledgement of the supportive role: 'in collaboration with' Edna Traver!

13 This, of course, is the criticism of the spate of publications – such as those by the Manpower Services Commission (1981), Cooper and Davidson (1984), and Smith *et al.* (1984) – designed to help women managers succeed in organizations. This criticism has been put forward trenchantly by Dorothy Griffiths (1985) in a review in *Journal of Management Studies* 22 (6): 573–77.

References

Alban-Metcalfe, B.M. and Nicholson, N. (1984) *The Career Development of British Male and Female Managers*. London: British Institute of Management.

Atkinson, J. (1984) Manpower Strategies for Flexible Organisations. *Personnel Management* 16 (8): 28–31.

Basil, D.C. (1972) *Women in Management*. New York: Dunellen.

Beaumont, R. (1982) *Employment Relations during the Recession*. Cambridge: Industrial Relations Resource Centre.

Cadbury, E. (1912) *Experiments in Industrial Organization*. London: Longman.

Child, J. (1985) Managerial Strategies, New Technology and the Labour Process. In D. Knights *et al.* (eds) *Job Redesign: Critical Perspectives on the Labour Process*. Aldershot: Gower, pp. 107–41.

Cooper, C.L. and Davidson, M. (1984) *Women in Management*. London: Heinemann.

Culler, J. (1983) *On Deconstruction, Theory and Criticism after Structuralism*. London: Routledge and Kegan Paul.

Dasey, R. (1981) Women in Computing. *Women and Training News* 3 (Summer).

Davies, J. (1985) Why Are Women Not Where Power Is? An Examination of the Maintenance of Power Elites. *Mead* 16 (3): 278–88.

Epstein, C.F. (1982a) Ambiguity as Social Control: Women in Professional Elites. In P.L. Stewart and M.G. Cantor (eds) *Varieties of Work*. Beverly Hills, CA: Sage, pp. 61–72.

— (1982b) Women and Elites – a Cross National Perspective. In C.F. Epstein and R.L. Coser (eds) *Access to Power: Cross National Studies of Women and Elites*. London: Allen and Unwin, pp. 3–15.

Epstein, C.F. and Coser, R. (eds) (1982) *Access to Power: Cross National Studies of Women and Elites*. London: Allen and Unwin.

Personnel management

Fogarty, M., Allen, A.J., Allen, I., and Walters, P. (1971) *Women in Top Jobs: Four Studies in Achievement*. London: Allen and Unwin.

Gowler, D. and Legge, K. (1984) The Deconstruction of Evaluation Research: Part 1, The Way Forward?. *Personnel Review* 13 (3): 3–13.

— (1986, forthcoming) Personnel and Paradigms: Four Perspectives on the Future. *Industrial Relations Journal*.

Guest, D. (1982) Has the Recession Really Hit Personnel Management? *Personnel Management* 14 (10): 36–9.

Hakim, C. (1979) *Occupational Segregation* (research paper No. 19, Department of Employment). London: HMSO.

Handy, C. (1984) The Organisation Revolution and How to Harness It. *Personnel Management* 16 (7): 20–3.

Health of Munition Workers Committee (1918) *Industrial Health and Efficiency* (Final Report) (Cmnd. 9065) London: HMSO.

Hennig, M. and Jardim, A. (1978) *The Managerial Woman*. London: Marion Boyars.

Hofstede, G. (1980) *Culture's Consequences: International Differences in Work-Related Values*. Beverly Hills, CA: Sage.

Hunt, A. (1975) *Management Attitudes and Practices towards Women at Work*. London: HMSO.

Hunt, J.W. (1984) The Shifting Focus of the Personnel Function. *Personnel Management* 16 (2): 14–18.

Inbucon/AIC Management Consultants 1975–80 (Annual) *Survey of Executive Salaries and Fringe Benefits*. London: Inbucon/AIC.

Jenkins, C. (1973) Is Personnel Still Underpowered? *Personnel Management* 6 (6): 34–5.

Kanter, R.M. (1977) *Men and Women of the Corporation*. New York: Basic Books.

Korn/Ferry International (1981) *Board of Directors' Survey: 1981 Engineering Industry*. London: Korn/Ferry.

Land, H. (1976) Women: Supporters or Supported? In D. Barker and S. Allen (eds) *Sexual Divisions and Society: Process and Change*. London: Tavistock, pp. 108–32.

Legge, K. (1978) *Power, Innovation and Problem-Solving in Personnel Management*. London: McGraw-Hill.

Lipman-Blumen, J. (1984) *Gender Roles and Power*. Englewood Cliffs, NJ: Prentice-Hall.

Littler, C. and Salaman, G. (1984) The Social Organisation of Work. In K. Thompson (ed.) *Work, Employment and Unemployment*. Milton Keynes: Open University Press.

Long, P. (1984a) *The Personnel Specialists: A Comparative Study of Male and Female Careers*. London: IPM.

— (1984b) Would You Put Your Daughter into Personnel Management? *Personnel Management* 16 (4): 16–20.

Manpower Services Commission (1981) *Practical Guide to Women's Career Development*. Sheffield: MSC, Training Services Division.

Marshall, J. (1984) *Women Managers: Travellers in a Male World*. Chichester: Wiley.

Murphy, Y. and Murphy, R.F. (1974) *Women of the Forest*. New York: Columbia University Press.

Niven, M.M. (1967) *Personnel Management 1913–63*. London: IPM.

Novarra, V. (1980) *Women's Work, Men's Work: The Ambivalence of Equality*. London: Marion Boyars.

Peters, T.J. and Waterman, R.M. (1982) *In Search of Excellence*. New York: Harper and Row.

Prentice, G. (1975) Women of the Moment: Pat Downs. *Personnel Management* 7 (6): 12–13.

Purcell, J. and Sisson, K. (1983) Strategies and Practice in the Management of Industrial Relations. In G.S. Bain (ed.) *Industrial Relations in Britain*. Oxford: Blackwell, pp. 95–120.

Rendel, M. (1980) How Many Women Academics, 1912–1976. In R. Deem (ed.) *Schooling for Women's Work*. London: Routledge and Kegan Paul, pp. 142–61.

Roff, H.E. (1973) Developments of a Decade. *Personnel Management* 5 (6): 23–5.

Science Policy Research Unit, Women and Technology Studies (1982) *Financial Times in Microelectronics and Women's Employment in Britain*. Brighton: Science Policy Research Unit, University of Sussex.

Smith, M., Wood, E., Langrish, S., Smith S.K., Davidson, L., and Mogridge, C. (1984) *A Development Programme for Women in Management*. Aldershot: Gower.

Smith, R. (1982) Women and Occupational Elites: the Case of Newspaper Journalism in England. In C.F. Epstein and R.L. Coser (eds) *Access to Power: Cross-National Studies of Women and Elites*. London: Allen and Unwin, pp. 237–48.

Spender, D. (1980) *Man Made Language*. London: Routledge and Kegan Paul.

Staines, G., Tavris, C., and Jayaratne, T.E. (1974) The Queen Bee Syndrome. *Psychology Today* 60 (January): 55–60.

Stewart, J. (1983) Whatever Happened to the Welfare Officer? *Personnel Management* 15 (6): 38–41.

Swords-Isherwood, N., Zmroczek, C., and Henwood, F. (1984) Technical change and its effect on employment opportunities for women. In P. Marstrand (ed.) *New Technology and the Future of Work and Skills*. London: Frances Pinter, pp. 192–213.

Tiger, L. (1969) *Men in Groups*. London: Nelson.

Warner, M. (1984) *Micro-processors, Manpower and Society*. Aldershot: Gower.

Watson, T.J. (1977) *The Personnel Managers: A Study in the Sociology of Work and Employment*. London: Routledge and Kegan Paul.

Whitley, R., Thomas, A., and Marceau, J. (1981) *Masters of Business? Business School and Business Graduates in Britain and France*. London: Tavistock.

Wilkinson, B. (1983) *The Shopfloor Politics of New Technology*. London: Heinemann.

© 1987 Karen Legge

4

'What Would We Do Without Her?' – Invisible Women in National Health Service Administration

Jane Rosser and Celia Davies

The position of women in health service administration has attracted some attention in recent years. In the 1970s and early 1980s a number of articles appeared in the professional journals citing discriminatory practices and attitudes towards women (Brooks 1979; Davidson 1979; Drummond 1981). Both the National Staff Committee for Administrative and Clerical Staff (NSC), the National Health Service (NHS) body responsible for setting national standards for recruitment and career development, and the Institute of Health Service Administrators (IHSA) have now considered possibilities for equalizing opportunities for female administrators (Institute of Health Service Administrators 1983; National Staff Committee 1979). In 1982, the Department of Health and Social Security (DHSS) itself became interested in the topic and commissioned research into sex discrimination.[1]

Examination of NHS statistics would suggest that this attention is justified. Staff working in administration comprise approximately 12 per cent of a total NHS workforce of over one million. In 1980, there were 115,056 administrative and clerical staff in the NHS in England alone.[2] The vast majority of these staff are on clerical and secretarial grades, and over 90 per cent of them are women. In the most junior administrative grade, men and women are found in equal proportions but, as one moves up the ladder, the proportion of women falls dramatically. Amongst the elite group of NHS administrative trainees who are expected to pursue successful careers, women do not fare well. For over a decade, women have comprised over 60 per cent of

61

trainees, yet they are still not found in senior positions in anything approximating equal proportions with men (Dixon and Shaw 1985; Stewart and Smith 1982). To date, attention has focused fairly exclusively on the elite group. Where there is any discussion of the position of women in health service administration, or any interest expressed in sex discrimination or equal opportunities, it is the administrative trainees who are cited and investigated. When we began our own investigation we, too, were encouraged, both by our reading of the available literature and by our discussions with senior managers within the health service, to see the problems of this small group of women as our legitimate concern. The vast number of staff on clerical and secretarial grades have received little attention. If their position is seen as a problem at all, it is seen as a different kind of problem because they are *not* administrators *per se*, and their work is *not* administration.

In this chapter we shall challenge this last assumption. In the course of an investigation into sex discrimination in health service administration we encountered a number of jobs, all of them occupied by women, which we called the Female Office Management Function (FOMF). In formal terms, some of these jobs were on administrative grades, some were on clerical or secretarial grades. All involved administrative work, but the women who performed them were not recognized as administrators. They were part of the vast army of staff who are assumed to be clerks and secretaries and are, therefore, of no interest to those concerned about women's careers in administration. Once we had identified these women, it became clear that understanding the position of women in administration required investigation of who was *excluded* from the definition and for what reasons, as well as examination of the position of those who are accepted as career administrators. Our aim here, therefore, is to make visible these women, their work and their position, both from their own viewpoint and from our standpoint as observers of the administrative structure in the health service. We begin with an account of the in-house view of administration and its practitioners. We follow this with a description of the Female Office Management Function, the jobs and the women who perform them, and conclude with a discussion of the implications of broadening the definition of administration to include them.

The research described in this chapter is part of a three-year investigation into sex discrimination in the NHS. The design of the project was highly action-orientated, involving detailed investigation in two district health authorities (DHAs) in England. The data came from interviews conducted as one part of this investigation, with managers and staff in both authorities explaining the nature of administrative work, job content, and career development in administration.[3]

Who is an administrator? The in-house view

Few generalizations can be made about health administration before the creation of the NHS. The role of administrators varied by region, size of hospital, type of hospital, and between the local authorities and the voluntary sector. In the voluntary hospitals the lay administrator, with the title of house governor or secretary, commanded status and respect and was directly accountable to the governing body. In the municipal hospitals the lay administrator (if there was one) was subordinate to the medical superintendent who had both clinical and administrative control of the hospital and was accountable to the medical officer of health at the town hall. In both cases much administration – the 'housekeeping function' – was the responsibility of the matron and her nurses as part of their general nursing duties. Since the advent of the NHS, however, there has been a great deal of emphasis on defining and developing lay administration. Concern has focused on the twin problems of how to administer the service most effectively and how to attract people of calibre for that task. From the beginning these two problems have been seen as interdependent. In the 1950s and early 1960s a series of review bodies produced reports on administration of the new NHS, each placing great store by the creation of a career structure which would attract professional people into the service (Ministry of Health 1954, 1956, 1957, 1963). The professionalization of health service administration was also furthered by the creation of the Institute of Hospital (later Health Service) Administrators in the 1940s and by its pattern of professional examinations and courses, as well as by the creation of the National Staff Committee for Administrative and Clerical Staff within the health service.[4] This latter body has been responsible for advising the Secretary of State on career structures, and on national standards for recruitment, selection, training, and promotion of administrative staff. It has generally endorsed the recommendations of the various review committees, complemented them, and issued guidelines accordingly.

A reading of the reports of these various bodies produces a fairly clear and uniform picture of the official view of administration and administrative careers. The most striking impression is that administration is made up of the visible few and the invisible many. There are two classes of entrants to the NHS – those with 'potential', recruited with the expectation of career prospects, and all other types of recruits (Ministry of Health 1963). For those with 'potential', whether they enter at clerical or junior administration level, there are national entry requirements – essentially educational qualifications and age. Initially, specific age barriers were recommended. Latterly, these are not evident, although discussion of the selection of career administrators clearly assumes that the careerist will be a young man or woman entering full-time and giving uninterrupted employment for a number of years.[5] For these recruits with 'potential', there are also guidelines on a period of formal training. The length and content of this period differs according to level of entry, but all incorporate courses preparing the entrant for promotion and a number of years of 'planned movement', providing experience in different departments, hospitals, and authorities. During this time, young administrators should be encouraged to sit for professional examinations and should receive management training. After this they may specialize in a particular function (personnel, for example), and are then ready either to be promoted to senior posts in that function or to senior positions in general administration.

This programme of career development was first outlined in detail by the Lycett Green Committee (Ministry of Health 1963). It was designed to ensure that, in the future, there would always be a cohort of good quality administrators to fill the most senior positions, and it was based on the principle that the interests of the health service and the interests of administrators were compatible – both requiring an attractive career structure. It operated a split focus on the top and the bottom – first to define clearly the roles and responsibilities of the most senior posts and, second, to recruit people at the bottom destined to fill those posts and provide them with a ladder to reach them. Thus an administrative elite was created, strongly supported by the existing professional associations. Since then the details have changed, with successive attempts to refine the scheme and facilitate its implementation, but the basic conceptualization of a career in administration has remained. The elite comprises only a very small proportion of all administration and clerical staff. They occupy posts on administrative grades although, occasionally, at the very beginning of their careers, they may start at the highest clerical grade (HCO). Taking the 1980 figure cited earlier, of a total of 115,056 administrative and clerical staff, less than 20 per cent would be among the elite.

The 'others', the bulk of administrative and clerical staff, have been virtually ignored in official thinking. There are no national standards for recruitment, and few guidelines for in-service training and development. These staff are not of interest to the professional associations and receive little attention from the National Staff Committee.[6]

This conceptual division of administration into career administrators and the rest is echoed in the accounts of the managers in the two health authorities where the research took place, and it is accompanied by a consensus on the types of posts occupied by each category.[7] Certain posts (in general administration in a large acute hospital, for example) are seen as 'real administration', as providing good administrative experience and as appropriate for career administrators. Others are defined as senior clerical or supervisory jobs; even if formally placed on junior administrative grades they are seen as 'dead-end' or 'ceiling' posts rather than as stepping-stones in an administrative career. The people in these posts, it is argued, are 'glorified secretaries' or senior clerks; the work does not require or give experience in administration *per se*. As a consequence, when managers are recruiting staff at the most senior clerical level (HCO) or the first grade in the administrative hierarchy (GAA), they are looking for different types of people, depending on the post. For the stepping-stone posts they seek those with initiative and ability, drive, enthusiasm, and potential – usually ex-trainees or graduate entrants. For the other posts, it is 'obvious' that you do not want a career administrator, rather 'someone who will stay and be more office-oriented . . . people coming to the pinnacle of their aspirations'. Some of these latter people are seen as vital, 'indispensable', 'salt of the earth', but not as administrators. One manager put it this way: 'The service couldn't survive without GAAs and HCOs, but because they are workhorses their outlook is narrow.'

To summarize, in the official in-house view, endorsed by managers, there is a clear conceptual division between career administrators and others, and between administrative posts (whether on clerical or administrative grades) and others. This conceptualization of administration and administrators does not slot neatly into the health service grading structure – as we have said, there are posts on clerical grades which are defined as 'real administration' and posts on administrative grades which are clearly seen as 'clerical'. In general discussion, however, managers tend to condense the two definitions, speaking as if the move into 'real administration' invariably occurred at the move from clerical to administrative grades.

How do women figure in this? There are, of course, women among the elite accepted as career administrators. They face particular problems in their pursuit of a career and, as we noted earlier, these have been investigated and documented by others (Dixon and Shaw 1985; Stewart and Smith 1982). The vast majority of women administrative and clerical staff, however, are clearly in the 'other' category. When we asked managers why women monopolized the lowest rungs of the hierarchy but were not making it to the senior positions, we were told that the explanation was simple – the majority of these staff are on clerical and secretarial grades. They are not successful in administration because they are not administrators and are not using or learning the skills required for administration in their present posts. The argument, in effect, is that they should not be included in the equation at all.

The position of women on the lowest rungs of the administrative ladder was seen as a little more ambiguous. However, if they were in dead-end posts the same kind of reasoning applied. Moreover, not only was their occupancy of the dead-end posts evidence of their lack of ability and/or aspiration, but the fact that they were *women* made them appropriate candidates for such posts:

'The chances are that the person you're appointing is going to be a female. She may be married, her husband may be working [locally]. . . . If she gets a promotion, fine, great, but she's quite happy, probably, to work there until she retires.'

'I expect they'll end up with a woman – somebody who will stay for ever . . . [it's] a little job, not too much hassle. Lots of GAA ladies are like that.'

Having described a job as fairly routine and narrow, another manager said: 'Therefore [we] tend to stick to looking for HCO secretaries who've shown initiative and a desire to better themselves – and think in terms of a woman rather than a man.'

Our interviews with *managers* provided a picture of two kinds of posts – those for the elite men and women, defined as 'real' administration and the 'others', mainly suitable for and occupied by women. The interviews with *staff*, however, suggested not two but three kinds of posts, because the 'others' group conflated two very different kinds of position. There were posts which were legitimately seen as fairly routine and clerical, occupied by both men and women, and there were those which we called Female Office Management Function (FOMF) posts.

In the accounts of the managers, these latter posts and the women who occupied them were firmly within the category 'other'. FOMF women were not administrators; their work required limited and specialized knowledge. They might be busy but the work was largely clerical and largely routine; and they themselves were not interested in pursuing a career. Obviously there *are* many such jobs in health service administration and equally obviously there *are* staff – men and women – who have no interest in future moves or development. Our interest in the FOMF women, however, is that they do not fit neatly into the slot to which they are assigned. They are administrators who are denied the status and recognition of administrators. Before considering this let us turn to an account of these jobs and the women who perform them.

FOMF – is it administration?

Jobs falling within our category of FOMF may be found in a wide range of locations within a DHA.[8] The data are drawn from interviews with administrators of small sites – a hospital, health centre, or clinic, for example; with administrators of specialist clinics/centres with authority-wide responsibility for the service, such as family planning, postgraduate psychiatry, child guidance; and with administrators servicing a department or managing an office outside administration itself, such as a works department or pharmacy.

These posts are graded at the highest rung of the clerical grades (HCO), and at the most junior rungs in administration (GAA). We suspect that there may also be some posts at the next grade up, senior administrative assistants (SAA), although none of the women we interviewed were graded at that level. We have referred to them all as administrators, although officially their titles range from 'secretary to . . .', 'office manager', 'assistant administrator', to 'administrator'.

Accounts of the work itself are complex and contradictory. On the one hand, senior administrators drew a picture of vital work, performed by worthy women; on the other hand, they saw it as largely routine with a high clerical and/or secretarial content and requiring specialized but limited knowledge. They contrasted this with the responsibilities of a real general administrator – the operational day-to-day problem-solving, the administration of buildings, the management and co-ordination of services and of staff, the management of industrial relations, and so on. The staff themselves did not concur with this view of their work. They saw their particular jobs as unique (which they frequently are, being the only such posts in the district or even the region). They tended to see the skills required and learnt in their present posts as being different from those required in mainstream administrative posts. They found it difficult, however, to be precise about the difference between their own work and mainstream administration, and usually resorted to defining the difference in terms of the kind of person who was seen as an administrator and themselves.

One way in which this emerged was when the women were asked about their chances of promotion or of their present post being upgraded. They believed that they could do the work of a higher grade, and they felt that sometimes they already were, but explained that they were not the 'right kind' of people for such posts:

'No, I haven't applied [for senior administrative assistant posts] for the simple reason that I obviously haven't got any qualifications, only very basic ones. Most of the SAA posts that I've heard have been going – generally go, I think – to national trainees . . . and basically, I suppose, because I haven't gone in for any college work, then really I'm lucky to be where I am.'

'I think I would apply for such a job recognizing that I probably wouldn't get it because of the way I've grown in this service, and because of my lack of formal training in a lot of aspects of management, which I have learned as I've gone along. And I don't think you can proceed in that way if you want to be recognized.'

Another woman felt that her job should be upgraded, but to what? The next grade was SAA, but that would not be quite right, she felt, because: 'the sort of people that are on senior administrative grading are the people in the top-line management grade for the health service, whereas my job is very different.'

These women, then, working within the same structure as the managers, reasoned about their work and their position in the hierarchy within the same conceptual framework. In general, they accepted the definition of themselves as not true administrators. As we shall see, however, they were far less sanguine than the managers about how they were seen and treated within the service.

As outsiders, however, we saw these women as engaged in a good deal of administration. As the most senior or sole administrator of a small hospital or centre, they were responsible for all aspects of the smooth running of their unit – the co-ordination of services and staff, direct responsibility for clerical and domestic staff, managing staff relations problems and personnel, the arrangement and supervision of building repairs and decoration, purchasing, installing and upkeep of equipment, and so on. Significantly, also, their posts appeared to require the very same sense of personal responsibility and commitment usually cited by managers as a mark of the true administrative post and the true career administrator. This is an important point to which we shall return.

There are, none the less, some striking features of these posts by which they can clearly be contrasted with the 'real administration', the mainstream posts. The first two will be discussed briefly; the remaining three will be developed further in the following sections. First, these posts were isolated from their own function, administration. The site administrators were geographically distant from their immediate superiors in administration. Both they and those servicing a professional department were, in practice, independently responsible for all aspects of the running of their unit and the servicing of their professional bosses such as doctors, pharmacists, and social workers. One woman, indeed, was unable to identify an administrative superior at all – she had no regular contact with general administration and did not know whether or how she fitted into the hierarchy. An exception to this, however, is the HCO or GAA 'general office' in a hospital. Someone in this post is obviously within general administration and has an administrative boss on site. Second, there is, as the managers said, a large clerical and secretarial content to the job – *in addition to* the heavy administrative load. Some of the women did not see any contradiction here at all. Others pointed out that the logic of including both kinds of work in the one job was not always clear, but because they had secretarial skills it was assumed that they would cover both. Thus, one woman recalled that she thought that she had applied for a secretarial post until she began the work; only then was it clear that she would also be running the centre itself.

Others, who thought initially that they had applied for an administrative post, had then encountered enormous difficulties in getting secretarial or clerical assistance because it was assumed that they would use their skills in that area and in effect do two jobs. One woman came rather closer to defining her job in terms of gender and hinted at a general feature of these posts as we came to see them – that they are in some way designed for women, and that to consider men for such posts would require some fundamental redefinition:

'I'm a dogsbody really, because I'm the secretary *and* the administrator. Whereas if a man – I don't know of any men who actually run postgraduate centres – but if a man was in post I could see that *he* would be administrator/supervisor totally, and would have a secretary to do all the secretarial work.'

The third feature of these posts is that when post-holders were appointed – usually at least ten years previously, often much longer – their jobs had not been clearly defined. Some had had no formal job descriptions at all, others had subsequently discovered that there was little correlation between the job description and the actual work. Since then, the jobs had undergone considerable and *unplanned* change over the years. Any formal redefinition or upgrading due to an increase in responsibilities and duties had usually been a tardy response to requests from the occupants and, in their view, was often inadequate. It appears that senior managers are not aware of the development of these posts or are uninterested. Fourth, whilst such posts require a degree of commitment generally accepted as a feature of 'real administration' and required of those who want a successful career in administration – taking work home in the evenings, or staying behind at short notice – the jobs do not have the status of administration and their occupants are not allowed, therefore, to operate any kind of informal flexitime arrangement to compensate. The final feature of these jobs is that the work involves what sociologists have variously called 'emotion work' (Hochschild 1979), 'sentimental work' (Strauss *et al.* 1982), and 'caring work' (Finch and Groves 1983). This work is not recognized or credited in any formal way. Where it *is* recognized by managers, it is seen as a feature of the individual post-holder and not of the post itself. It is a bonus but, in effect, it is a woman's choice, rather than an integral part of the work itself. Each of these last three features will now be developed in turn.

The initial lack of job definition and the subsequent development of these jobs is worth closer inspection because it provides clues as to how the image of these women and their work is created and perpetuated. The jobs fall into two categories. There is the compact secretarial/clerical post which subsequently grew and developed into an extremely busy administrative post. Two administrators of postgraduate medical centres were good examples of this. One spoke of it as being 'a real doddle of a job', providing secretarial back-up for courses during academic terms, doing correspondence from dictation, taking minutes of meetings and helping with the organization of the odd workshop or conference. Both jobs then 'grew like Topsy' as the work of postgraduate centres grew. 'No one had realized how they would take off,' said one; 'it's just the way the job has evolved,' said the other, 'I don't think it is anyone's deliberate planning.' Today these women run the centres themselves, are responsible for the administration of postgraduate training in all its aspects, and still carry a heavy secretarial load, which has also mushroomed since the early days. Some flavour of this is contained in the following account:

'The function of the centre is further education for doctors. I have to organize lectures and discussions, run the library, inform them of meetings, etc. . . . From September to July is the lecture programme, so my function is the back-up for the clinical tutor, all the secretarial and clerical work, all the liaison with other departments. I work for all the consultants as necessary. I help out where I can, for example, typing papers for publication, and help with research, for example getting articles from other libraries. I book the speakers. . . . I can use all the AV equipment . . . [and] when we haven't got a barman or a cleaner . . .!'

The alternative pattern was that of a job which initially involved creating a smooth-running system from chaos, setting up a new department, or totally reorganizing an existing one. We found these posts in the general office of a small hospital, or of a professional service, such as works. Here the attraction of the job was the initial challenge:

'When I came here, the office was in quite a mess. I reorganized the whole office. I had to close the office and do the filing system and everything. It was very challenging. I enjoyed it. I didn't know the first thing about the health service, but it was a challenge and I went in and burned the midnight oil, and often had meetings late into the evening with some of the professionals.'

For this woman the early days were exciting; she was responsible for any administration to do with the works department across the district, and supervised the office and secretarial staff in all the authority's hospitals. Today the work is very different; it carries a great deal of responsibility but is largely office-based and is no longer seen as a challenge:

'I control all the budgets. We control about three and three-quarter million pounds a year, and I split it up personally. My function is to split it into building and engineering, and apportion them so much each year, which I always break up into months. And then I keep the expenditure monthly and produce a statement at the end of the month, giving them the red light. If they are going forward too quickly, I give them a projection. . . . I am relied upon to tackle expenditure in emergencies. . . . I get the invoices . . . then we do maintenance contracts, which is another large part of my function. We also run the X-ray maintenance contracts although it isn't our money. . . . There's a lot to the job, but you never get bored. You have to use a lot of staff discipline. There are now just three people working for me, and I am having to learn computer work in order to supervise them.'

Although the pattern of development of the jobs is rather different in these two examples, it is the *process* of accumulation of work which is similar in both cases. One senior manager was heard to remark of one of these women: 'If C has made herself indispensable, that's C's fault.' Indeed, as we have suggested, the way in which these women have accumulated work could be (and often is) seen as voluntary, not a feature of the post itself. The reality, however, is rather more complex. The FOMF women described how they had taken on work over time on their own initiative because they could not run the office, centre, or clinic efficiently without doing so. One woman explained:

'He didn't *tell* me to take on the things I took on. I did it over a slow time, about six months, because I found that Mr — was doing some part and I was doing the other. Either I had to go chasing him – I mean, when a relative rings on the phone, or when a Sister rings me, I want to have the information at my fingertips, I don't want to say, "Ah well, I only do part of it." So, therefore, I did it because it was easier.'

Another put it differently:

'I've been very flexible in the hours that I've worked to make the job work, and I think that is probably why I have ended up with the job description that I've got now – which bears no resemblance to the original job description, simply because I've been prepared to put in the hours and the time for the sake of the job, to build the centre up.'

So, in some part, the work has accumulated through these women's own initiative. However, the reasons for doing what they have done have been to 'make the job work', either in the face of no initial job description at all, or in the face of one which had received little thought or effort. In the main the work has grown through colleagues and superiors calling on these women and the women being reluctant to refuse, while at the same time recognizing that they are too 'available', too much the 'willing horse'.

FOMF women not only have secretarial and organizational skills, they also have extensive local knowledge, built up through long service with the authority:

'Being one of the most long-standing members of staff and being the one who set it all up, there's an awful lot of pressure on you, you know, because there's few people round the site who've been here as long as I have. And they'll ring me up and say "Ah, Mrs H, yes, ah, we knew if we could get any help *you'd* help us . . .".'

This particular woman also described how it was a common occurrence for her to find reports and papers on her desk. They were seldom related directly to her work, but 'We didn't know what it was, so we thought we'd give it to you' was the common refrain.

Over the years such women have become indispensable. On the one hand this can be very satisfying, to know that your boss thinks you are a gem and that the place falls apart in your absence. On the other hand holiday arrangements are a problem because 'No one else knows what I do.' Significantly, in jobs such as these it is difficult, if not impossible, to pursue further training. 'He's only happy if I do it in my own time,' said one woman, 'he doesn't like me to be away.' 'Being a single-handed administrator, I can't justify going off,' said another. There were even a couple of instances where the women said that their bosses, not wanting to lose them, had blocked their chances of being appointed to a new post. Through these experiences some, particularly those nearing retirement, felt disaffected and disillusioned. Asked if she had a job description, one replied:

'No, I keep insisting I have one, and I keep submitting these things and they disappear. I'm getting a bit bloody-minded about it to be honest. . . . I give them what I think they pay me for and I think they should in return give me a guideline. . . . I do work hard, I don't particularly mind working hard. If I was asked to do something that wasn't on the job description I'd be the last person in the world to say, "I'm not doing this because it's not my job." . . . And I sometimes, when I'm a *little* bit uptight, I think, well, they won't give me one because I wouldn't be doing as much as I am.'

In theory, then, there are certain jobs in NHS administration which are fairly routine and simple. In practice, such posts capitalize on the considerable organizational skills of the women in them, and their willingness to utilize their skills while receiving little recognition for doing so. Vital services have depended on these women defining their own areas of responsibility and accepting the challenge of administering and developing the service. The women seldom complain about the accumulation of work, partly because of their personal satisfaction in achievement and partly because they gain satisfaction from the positive aspects of their reputation in the service. Such a woman knows she is described as indispensable, responsible, dependable, 'worth her weight in gold'; complaint would jeopardize that image. It is only those nearing retirement, whose work is no longer challenging and who have experienced the power of the negative aspects of the in-service view of them – that they are not worth training, promoting, or guiding in a career, for example – who feel able to risk their reputation by complaining. One, somewhat younger, woman vividly described her dilemmas and her reluctance to complain when her professional colleagues (medical practitioners) were assigning more and more work to her and she felt that she was 'sinking under the table', as follows:

'I felt it was so petty to have to point out that I'd got no help and really I am only one part-time little lady who is struggling along trying to fit a fifty-seven-hour job into twenty-odd hours. When you're dealing with professional people I think you've got to approach them in a professional sort of way, and I felt that was a little bit unprofessional in a sense, pointing out all my problems, which maybe they might have thought I should have resolved myself without sort of involving them.'

This comment links with the fourth distinctive feature of these posts – the unstated requirement, without recognition, of total commitment to the health service.

The women we interviewed tended to work through their lunch breaks, they sometimes stayed late, they took work home or even came in at the weekends to keep abreast of the job. For some, it was clear that the job could not be done in the hours allotted and therefore such 'overtime' had become routine:

'I don't think I've ever taken time off . . . I was off sick last year. I was 'phoned at home every day. There's lots of overtime in this job. They used to pay overtime: now I can't fit in time off in lieu – they probably owe me a lot of hours.'

It is ironic that within the service one of the most commonly cited explanations for women's failure to succeed in career terms is their inability or unwillingness, because of their domestic commitments, to put their work first. If you want to have a career in administration, we were told, you must be prepared to work late, take work home, give up precious leisure time. These women do just that; they take on the responsibilities of administrators, but are not recognized as doing so. More than one of the women interviewed had formally requested compensatory arrangements and had felt humiliated and angry at the treatment they received. Since they were not administrative staff, FOMF women were called on to explain their behaviour and to account in detail for the extra time they had worked. Their requests were refused and they had to seek support from their non-administration bosses; and when they were finally granted their requests, they were told 'never to do it again'.

The final component of FOMF work to be considered here is 'emotion work'. Much of the detail of such work came out when we asked whether a man could do the job. As most of the FOMF women are at the 'sharp end' of the NHS, they often find themselves dealing with patients and their relatives, people often in confused or anxious states. They counsel them, interpret medical practices and routines for them, mediate between them and professional practitioners, clear up misunderstandings and offer a sympathetic ear. In addition, as the central point of their units, they are the sounding-board for everyone in disagreements or misunderstandings between professional colleagues, between junior and senior staff, and, in multidisciplinary teams, between the different professions. They commented:

'[A man] wouldn't have the tact! You're walking on eggshells the whole time. He could do the shorthand, the typing, etc. but I also have to smooth ruffled feathers. . . . They come to me because I'm older and a woman; each department, the staff, men and women, want a motherly person to go to.'

'I think you need feminine intuition for the job I'm doing. In this team atmosphere, because they're all different disciplines, and there's often a lot of imbalance – and you can be very constructive in smoothing things over without doing or saying very much – saying nothing at the right time.'

It was noticeable that almost all the descriptions of this kind of 'emotion work' came from this group of women. Interviews with career administrators and with other staff yielded little on this front beyond reference to specific personnel tasks, such as career counselling. Both the sex and maturity of the FOMF women seem to be significant in their adoption of this role. If their age and their sex endow them with particular skills in this area, then obviously managers are making wise decisions in appointing them to posts which require such skills. What is significant, however, is that the work involved and the skills required are not formally recognized or acknowledged as an integral part of the job; they are accorded no status. In another setting, perhaps, such work would be seen as personnel work. Yet no one has suggested to these women that these are marketable skills, that they could make a career in personnel for example. Such work, if acknowledged at all, is seen as incidental, a bonus, but not an essential part of the job.

From these accounts, then, we are faced with two rather different views of the work involved. Senior managers see it as vital, but largely routine with a narrow focus. The skills required are seen as mainly clerical/secretarial, and both posts and post-holders are not regarded as being in 'real' administration. Listening to the holders of these posts describing their work, however, we find extremely busy, varied work involving a good deal of administrative duties and responsibilities and requiring, most particularly, organizational and personnel skills. We also find that the women in these posts are conscious, but only in a fragmented and partial way, of exploitation of themselves as workers, and of the role of gender in that exploitation. In addition, we find it well-nigh impossible to discuss the work these women perform without reference to their personal biographies, and it is to these we must turn to complete the picture.

NHS administration

Who are the FOMF women?

The biographical details of the women in FOMF positions bear many similarities. Their ages range from early forties to late fifties, nearing retirement. They are mothers who followed clerical/secretarial careers, not necessarily in the NHS, before their children were born. Their time outside paid employment, following the birth of their children, varied from just one year to over fifteen years, although all but one had in excess of five years at home. Most re-entered paid employment at a lower level than that achieved prior to the break, some beginning with casual and temping jobs before entering the health service. One woman, for example, spent eleven years in the health service before leaving to have her first child. In that time she progressed from office junior to medical records officer in the same hospital. While her children were small she worked two evenings a week at the same hospital on the switchboard at the request of the matron. Nine years later, having also done part-time bottle-washing and floor-cleaning at a local chemist, she returned to the same hospital as a ward clerk. None of the women saw such drops in status as unjust; they accepted it as inevitable, given their time outside paid employment. Most reacted as did this particular woman – 'I jumped at it,' she said. Most of the women, particularly those nearing retirement, did not have formal educational and professional qualifications, having been in full time education at a time when girls received little encouragement and were given few opportunities. Any professional qualifications they had gained tended to be secretarial and, as we have shown, opportunities to gain further qualifications or training once in post were minimal.

At the time we spoke to these women they had all been in the NHS for many years; the shortest time was eight years, the longest twenty-two, with most in excess of ten years. In that time, they had climbed through one, two, maybe three grades up to HCO or GAA. Often their 'promotion' was due to the regrading of the post they already occupied. None had changed jobs more than twice. Thus, for example, one entered her present post thirteen years ago at HCO; ten years ago it was upgraded to GAA and she has been there ever since. Another began as a clerical officer fifteen years ago; she applied for and got the more senior post, at HCO, in the same office a few years later and again has been there at that grade ever since. The process of upgrading of their own posts was invariably a result of their own initiative and could be a long and disillusioning process. One, who has been in the

77

same post for the past sixteen years, described the process by which she obtained a higher grading: 'After several years it dawned on me – it was a little silly; I was doing more than any CO, far more. I suggested HCO to Mr H [her immediate non-administrative boss].'

She was told that she could not be upgraded because she did not supervise other clerical staff. She left the matter for a year and then raised it again:

'He suggested I go on to secretarial level, so I was made a secretary. . . . Between us we drew up the job description. It was clear that personal secretary didn't cover it, no way, but it did entitle me to more money.'

A few years later, having seen other staff achieve upgradings, she brought her union into it and finally achieved her HCO grading. Another fought for two years for an upgrading. She added:

'And I'd never want to go through that. I'd never ask for a regrading because I'd have found it demoralizing, quite frankly. If they don't think you're good enough without going begging, I would never be the one to go and put it forward.'

FOMF women, then, had progressed through several grades since entering the NHS, some reaching the lowest rung of the administrative ladder. Their progress had been slow, however, and had usually taken place within the same job or at least in the same office or site. This pattern of 'promotion' clearly was not that of the elite career administrators. Earlier we touched on the in-house view of FOMF women's ambition and career prospects. Their posts were seen as outside mainstream administration and, in the main, as dead-end or ceiling posts.[9] Managers, therefore, looked for recruits for such posts whom they saw as lacking career potential and/or ambition; they volunteered that these would probably be women – and in describing the women in post they were fairly sure of the accuracy of their judgement:

'She's very sound, very able, with a wealth of health service experience. . . . She won't leave until retirement and happily so. It's a job which enables her to increase her family income. No, perhaps I do her an injustice . . . she gets some very difficult patients to deal with so there must be something more [in her] . . . [but] she's not likely to move on.'

78

NHS administration

The women themselves were aware, in part, of this senior management view of them. Few had ever been given career guidance; and opportunities to gain further training were minimal and not encouraged. Also, as we have shown, some knew that their chances of being appointed to other jobs had actually been blocked by their present superiors. Their attitude to this was ambivalent. On the one hand there were some strong expressions of resentment; on the other they were philosophical, expecting little else. One woman, within five years of retirement, had applied for a job because the challenge of that particular post excited her. She discovered subsequently that her chances of appointment were very high until her immediate superior intimated that he did not want to lose her. She was now expected to supervise her office junior on a newly installed computer without any training herself. In order to do the work properly, she taught herself in the evenings, by reading books and consulting her son. It was a laborious process which she found, in her words, 'very scary'. On the one hand she felt a great sense of achievement; on the other she felt hurt and angry that she had not been offered training when her male non-administrative bosses, who had considerably less direct contact with the computer, had received training. Typically, she had mixed feelings about this – 'I sometimes think they don't want us to know too much. . . . They only want us to know the bits that are going to be useful to them' – but immediately she qualified this by referring to her age as a reasonable justification for her treatment:

'I think the present boss is very keen on training. None of it's ever come my way, but then I'm older, you see. I mean I don't see the point, frankly, myself, in training anybody my age. Let's face it, I'm over the hill now. I'm all for "Let's get the kids as much as they can", I'm all for it. I wouldn't want to take anything off them. I just feel a bit peeved about the computer.'

Did these women see themselves as ambitious? If ambition is taken to mean a will to reach the most senior positions in the organization, then they clearly were *not* ambitious. If ambition includes a wish to develop, to be stretched and challenged in work, then all had ambition. Some had entered the health service hoping for a career. Not being one of the elite, however, and not being privy to knowledge of the system – which posts to move into, how long to stay, etc. – they had come to realize only slowly that they were not being offered a career. Others had begun looking for the 'doddle of a job', as indicated earlier. But as their jobs grew and responsibilities widened, so their interest in their own development also grew. Yet others had never seen themselves as wanting a career but had applied for their posts because of the challenges they posed – building up a new service, setting up a new office. Once they had done this and all was running smoothly, jobs could become routine and they sought others which posed a new challenge. With little guidance or encouragement, however, often working in isolation from mainstream administration and facing an in-house image of themselves as worthy but relatively unskilled and unambitious, they faced considerable barriers to their own personal development.

In both the discussion of FOMF work and of the women themselves we have seen that these staff were far less sanguine than were their managers about the in-house definition of their work and themselves. There was no groundswell of opposition to management definitions, however, either individually or as a group. Most, when they first re-entered paid employment, were grateful for any opportunity. Their devotion and commitment has stemmed from that gratitude and from the sense of personal satisfaction of 'a job well done'. The younger women, whilst voicing specific complaints, still gained satisfaction from their indispensability and their sense of 'running the show'. The older ones have accumulated too many experiences which illustrate to them their true lack of recognition and status when it comes to tangible demonstration. They were far more likely to feel bitter and disillusioned. None, however, had an alternative frame of reference for defining their work and themselves. Their complaints, therefore, about an unfair system, about elitism, sexism, and ageism were often qualified by self-blame, alternative justifications for their treatment, and by a lack of confidence about the relevance of their skills and experience outside of their present post.

Conclusion

In this chapter we have described a conceptual scheme developed since the creation of the NHS which defines the nature of an administrative career and the characteristics of a career adminis-trator. This divides the administrators into high-fliers and the rest *at recruitment*, and identifies the pathway appropriate for the former. We have argued that despite in-house concern over the years that this system does not operate well in practice, it *does* work in the sense that it effectively renders invisible and silent the vast majority of administrative and clerical staff. We have isolated one group of workers among the invisible many, and these we have labelled FOMF women. They are not of interest to senior management, to the National Staff Committee, or to the professional associations. Their work is seen as largely clerical and secretarial, as narrow in focus and as routine. They are appointed to these jobs because they are seen as lacking career potential and, once in post, are expected to sit there happily until retirement. They are all women, middle-aged and older, who have returned to work after a break for child-bearing. These features of their biography are clearly relevant to management assessment of them as lacking career potential.

The women's own accounts of their work clearly illustrate the administrative content and the wide range of organization and personnel skills required in their posts. They also counter the view of the work as routine and narrow. The changes and developments over the years have demanded the development of skills in the post-holders which have gone unrecognized. FOMF women, moreover, are intelligent and highly committed and, although they have few formal qualifications, would have welcomed opportunities to stretch and develop their abilities more. When discussing themselves and their work these facts sit uncomfortably with the in-house view. The women have a sense of injustice, which can sometimes be quite strong, and their complaints about the system begin to suggest alternative conceptual frameworks and the possibility of a grassroots challenge to the in-house view. Yet they also accept the logic of the in-house view and in the main see as immutable the administrative hierarchy and career structure and their position in it.

What would be the implications for the NHS of including FOMF women in the definition of administrator, and their work as administration? There are a number of practical implications. Job descriptions would need to be rewritten to represent truly the work done; both managers and staff would need educating on the transferability and relevance of these skills to other posts in administration, particularly in mainstream administration. The criteria for identifying 'stepping-stone' and 'dead-end' posts would need to be re-examined; the grading and salaries of the posts would require attention, and so on. The implications are rather more profound than this, however. These women make possible the professional administrative career as it is conceived today. They provide the stable base without which the present structure of a career could not operate. The history of the administrative career, as we have seen, has been based on the assumption that the NHS is run by those at the top of the hierarchy. Virtually all attention has focused on defining, recruiting, and developing those with potential to reach such posts. It is clear, however (and acknowledged by some managers) that the normal administrative career of planned movement and occupancy of stepping-stone posts is only possible if certain other posts are stable with very little turnover – and in most instances these are the FOMF posts. Having identified one of these key posts as the HCO, general office, one manager commented: 'It causes far more confusion, far more chaos, to have somebody like the HCO, general office leave than it does to have the hospital administrator leave, which is an interesting irony.' Redefining FOMF posts as administration and therefore as potential stepping-stones would require some dramatic restructuring of administration itself.

Following through this last point another serious implication emerges. If the posts were recognized as being administrative, and therefore the skills as relevant for a career in administration, the range of applicants for these posts would presumably expand. Would men, and women without the personal biography of the present incumbents, be able to perform these jobs? We believe that there would be major problems. We suggested earlier that the jobs seem to be designed for women. This has not been a deliberate plan, but has evolved largely because of the *lack* of planning for work at this level. The individual jobs have grown and developed through the inter- action of the growth of the particular service and the skills and approach of the particular women in post. These women have obviously played an integral part in defining their work, in taking seriously and expanding those aspects of the work at which they excel. In the meantime, the NHS has been structured around the assumption that women *will* develop those aspects of the work, and now depends upon it. Job descriptions capitalize on these women's professional skills – most notably, on their secretarial skills. The jobs also capitalize on the considerable skills these women have acquired through living their lives as women, notably as women with children. Their experience in taking responsibility for the smooth running of a family, of household management, of handling emotions, are ex- ploited in these jobs without being formally recognized, valued, developed, rewarded, or seen as an integral part of the jobs themselves. Elsewhere we have called these 'gendered jobs', for they have gender written into them (Davies and Rosser 1986).

Here we have concentrated rather more on the consciousness of the women and the ideological context in which they work. If either men, or women at a different stage in their domestic life-cycle or with different personal biographies, entered these posts, what would happen? The individuals themselves would be seen as at best competent but uncommitted. At worst the administration of the unit or centre in which they worked would collapse – for the unrecognized work requiring the unrecognized skills would not be performed. The jobs would have to be radically redefined and that which is invisible or seen as incidental would have to be specified. The skills required would have to be formally acknowledged and taught to the new incumbents.

Finally, we will return to our initial observation that the vast majority of administrative and clerical staff in the National Health Service have been ignored in career terms and in discussions of sex discrimination and equality of opportunity for women. None of the discussions of the fate of the women in the elite group does much to enlighten us on the fate of the vast majority of women workers. The key point about the FOMF women, and perhaps also others, is that they are the unacknowledged base for the career administrators, whether men or women. To recognize these women as administrators requires a challenge to the basic conceptualization of career, to the identification of the elite in the first place, and to their grooming thereafter. Equalizing opportunity for the elite women may be a matter of introducing more flexibility to the current system. Opening the doors to the women in the Female Office Management Function, however, would require something rather more radical. It is possible that such change may be forced upon the service as the present occupants retire and are replaced by a new generation of women with rather different personal biographies – higher educational qualifications and shorter career breaks – who may not accept the current denigration of women's skills and contribution with such equanimity. Only if change is initiated and perhaps forced in this way will the NHS truly be able to claim that it is tackling the problems of sexual inequality in administration.

In A Man's World

Acknowledgement

This chapter is based on research carried out with the support of the Department of Health and Social Security, and the Economic and Social Research Council – ESRC Grant No. RDB/1/19/2. We are grateful to the many staff in the two health authorities who made this research possible, particularly to the steering groups who tackled the topic of equal opportunities with us with interest and concern, and to both managers and staff who consented to be interviewed.

The views expressed in this chapter are, of course, those of the authors and not those of the ESRC, DHSS, or members and staff of the health authorities concerned.

Notes

1 The DHSS in conjunction with the Social Science Research Council (now Economic and Social Research Council) funded three projects on sex discrimination in the NHS – a large-scale econometric study focusing on statistical indications of discrimination, based at Nottingham University under Professors Chiplin and Sloane; an investigation into staff wastage due to maternity and into childcare provision, based at North London Polytechnic under Christine Farrell; and the project from which this chapter stems – a largely qualitative investigation focusing on policies, procedures, and practices within district health authorities.

2 It is, in fact, notoriously difficult to give accurate manpower (sic) figures for the NHS. The figure quoted for 1980 is taken from statistics published in 1982 (Department of Health and Social Security 1982) and pertaining to the numbers of administrative and clerical staff at 30 September, 1980. For a clear exposition of the problems involved in establishing staff figures see Chiplin and Greig, who have written: 'We have, in fact, attempted to construct a table of numbers employed in the NHS in England by broad occupational group from the published statistics and have been unable to do so' (1984: 4).

3 For a full description of the data collected, see Davies and Rosser (1985).

4 A National Staff Committee for Administrative and Clerical Staff was first recommended by the Lycett Green Committee (Ministry of Health 1963) in an attempt to centralize and make uniform the system of recruitment, selection, and training within the NHS. By 1978, such committees had also been established for other staff groups requiring professional training.

5 Age limits have never been obligatory, but there has been an assumption that has been compounded with each successive report. For example, when the Junior Administrative Training Scheme was extended from graduates to 'A-level or equivalent' entrants, the National Staff Committee, outlining the extended scheme of planned movement, wrote: 'This period of training would bring the typical 18 year old recruit to 22, the average age of the trainee in the graduate or equivalent level entry' (1971: Appendix 1).

6 They have not been totally ignored, of course. Each report makes some gesture toward these 'others' – stressing that training should be 'open' to all

staff, for example, or that entry requirements should not be rigidly applied, to allow for the few exceptions among the 'others' to pursue a career. Among the numerous reports on career development for administrators, the NSC produced a consultative document and then a final report for managers on the recruitment and development of clerical and secretarial staff (National Staff Committee 1981, 1983). These documents, however, work on the assumption that the vast majority of such staff lack ability or ambition for a career in health service administration.

7 The data for this paper came from two district health authorities in England. Although they are markedly different – a large, urban teaching district and a much smaller, rural, non-teaching one – the overall structure of their administrative hierarchies and the patterning of men and women within them were very similar and mirrored the national picture. For a detailed account, see Davies and Rosser (1985).

8 Our fieldwork was conducted in district health authorities only. We do not have information, therefore, on whether similar posts might be found amongst regional health authority staff. We suspect that there would be fewer, given that 'facework' administration, direct service delivery, is not a common feature of regional level work.

9 There were, of course, exceptions to this view. One personnel officer, for example, saw the health centre administration post as admirable experience for someone wishing to enter administration from a clerical/secretarial career. Another career administrator recounted entering one of these posts for a short period while waiting for a more suitable post to become vacant. Where a career administrator, privy to knowledge of the system, chooses to use such a post or a senior manager takes a specific interest in the career of someone initially recruited as 'other', dead-end posts may be used as temporary stepping-stones.

References

Brooks, J. (1979) Women in NHS Management. *Health and Social Services Journal*, 19 October: 1354–356.

Chiplin, B. and Greig, N. (1984) *Staffing and Manpower Planning in the NHS.* DHSS/ESRC Research Project on Equal Opportunities for Women: the NHS (Working Paper No. 1). Department of Industrial Economics, Accountancy and Insurance, University of Nottingham.

Davidson, N. (1979) Prejudice That Faces Women as Managers. *Health and Social Services Journal*, 8 March: 232–35.

Davies, C. and Rosser, J. (1985) *Equal Opportunities in the NHS.* Final Report on an ESRC/DHSS Project. Department of Sociology, University of Warwick.

——(1986) Gendered Jobs in the Health Service. In D. Knights and H. Willmott (eds) *Gender and the Labour Process.* Aldershot: Gower.

Department of Health and Social Security (1982) *Health and Personal Social Services Statistics for England.* London: HMSO.

Dixon, M. and Shaw, C. (1985) *Maximising Management Investment in the NHS: A Study of National Management Trainees.* London: Kings Fund College.

Drummond, P. (1981) Health Service Women Want More Than Ties. *Health and Social Services Journal*, 24 April: 464–65.

Finch J. and Groves, D. (eds) (1983) *A Labour of Love: Women, Work and Caring*. London: Routledge and Kegan Paul.

Hochschild, A.R. (1979) Emotion Work, Feeling Rules and Social Structure. *American Journal of Sociology* 85: 551–75.

Institute of Health Service Administrators (1983) *Women in NHS Administration*. London: IHSA.

Ministry of Health, Central Health Services Council (1954) *Report of the Committee on the Internal Administration of Hospitals* (Bradbeer Committee). London: HMSO.

— (1956) *Report of the Committee of Enquiry of the Cost of the NHS* (Guillebaud Committee). London: HMSO.

— (1957) *Report on the Grading Structure of Administrative and Clerical Staff: the Hospital Service* (Hall Committee). London: HMSO.

— (1963) *Report of the Committee of Inquiry on the Recruitment, Training and Promotion of Administrative and Clerical Staff in the Hospital Service* (Lycett Green Committee). London: HMSO.

National Staff Committee for Administrative and Clerical Staff (1971) *A Further Report by the NSC on Recruitment and Management Development of Administrative Staff in the Hospital Service*. London: NSCACS.

— (1979) *The Recruitment and Career Development of Administrators*. London: NSCACS.

— (1981) *A Handbook for Managers on the Recruitment and Development of Clerical & Secretarial Staff*. London: NSCACS.

— (1983) *A Guide to Managers on the Recruitment and Development of Clerical and Secretarial Staff*. London: NSCACS.

Stewart, R. and Smith, P. (1982) *Review of the National Administrative Training Scheme*. London: NSCACS.

Strauss, A., Fagerhaugh, S., Suczek, B., and Wiener, C. (1982) Sentimental Work in the Technologised Hospital. *Sociology of Health and Illness* 4: 254–78.

© 1987 Jane Rosser and Celia Davies

5

Man-made Myths:
The Reality of Being
a Woman Scientist in the NHS

Hilary Homans

This chapter explores some of the dominant ideas surrounding women working as scientists and technical staff in the National Health Service (NHS). Some of these ideas are related to women's supposed 'natural' abilities and are associated with sexuality, pregnancy, and parenting. Others assume that certain characteristics are innate and that 'masculine' and 'feminine' skills are predetermined and inevitable. Women's skills are regarded as different from those held by men, which is to their detriment in the sphere of paid employment where male values dominate and are regarded as the norm (Kanter 1977; Marshall 1984: 7). This line of reasoning assumes that the workforce is male and without domestic responsibilities (Gill and Whitty 1983: 9; Novarra 1980: 102). Moreover, women in paid employment outside the home find that their femaleness is a disadvantage when their status and opportunities are compared with male colleagues of similar standing.

Some women passively accept these male myths about their role in the workplace (for example, women at work may be seen as 'matter out of place', particularly if they are mothers, since 'women with children should not work'). Other women experience discrimination at work as an extension of what they encounter in their day-to-day lives; some are justifiably outraged by the unequal treatment they receive. The women referred to in this chapter did not possess a developed awareness of the discriminatory forces shaping their work experience. They tended to relate problems at work to their own personal inadequacies rather than locating them in the structure and

87

ideology of the organization they worked for. It is hoped that the careful documentation of these women's experiences will illustrate the pervasiveness of patriarchal ideology which sustains myths about women – myths which in fact do not stand up to scrutiny, as the following account shows.

Background to the research

The data for this exploration into social mythology (Janeway 1971) about women comes from a study of 193 women and men currently employed in NHS clinical chemistry laboratories in a regional health authority, and a further 191 women and men who had left NHS employment with the same regional health authority in the five years preceding the study.[1]

The choice of subject is important for two reasons. First, feminist researchers have drawn attention to the relevance of looking at *both* women and men at work. They argue that studies which focus solely on woman's experiences – whilst illuminating in their own right and providing a redressing of the balance away from previous work in which women were invisible (Lockwood 1966; Stewart, Prandy, and Blackburn 1980) – do not go far enough in exploring the complex social interaction between women and men at work. Moreover, as Beechey (1983) has argued, many recent studies of women's employment do not compare women's experiences at work with those of men in similar occupations. It is therefore argued that in order to understand women's position in the labour market more research is needed which is inclusive of both women and men (Beechey 1983; Crompton, Jones, and Reid 1982). Studies of professional occupations show that women who have similar qualifications to their male colleagues fare worse, for example, in terms of promotion and pay (teaching is a good example of this; see National Union of Teachers/Equal Opportunities Commission 1980). A detailed analysis of women and men in the same occupation can challenge myths about inherent natural gender differences, as the staff concerned have already been selected as suitable for the posts in question. However, as this chapter shows, discriminatory forces are at work to ensure that women and men in the same jobs do *not* have equal opportunities. The main explanations for these differentials given by male managers relate to patriarchial beliefs about women's 'natural' and biological inferiority.

Man-made myths

The second justification for studying NHS scientific staff is because they are a good example of public sector work which contains a large number of women in scientific grades. The NHS itself is one of the largest single employers in Europe, containing about one million workers; 75 per cent of these are women and 26 per cent of NHS employees work part-time (concentrated mainly in nursing and ancillary work). NHS laboratories constitute one of the major employment outlets for women with scientific training. Currently, over 18,000 people are employed in NHS laboratories – in 1981 the figures for each group of staff were: 14,213 medical laboratory scientific officers (MLSOs); 1,196 graduate biochemists, and 2,841 hospital medical staff.[2] Statistics on the numbers of hospital scientific staff by sex and grade have only been collected by the Department of Health and Social Security since 1979 (see Homans 1984: 7–8), but an analysis of the membership returns for the Institute of Medical Laboratory Sciences shows that roughly equal numbers of men and women have been recruited into the MLSO grade since 1956 (Johnson 1969: 17).

The research was conducted at a time when there was considerable interest in women in scientific occupations. 1984 was designated 'Women into Science and Engineering' (WISE) year. Additionally, previous research and training initiatives had focused on the fact that women are poorly represented in scientific careers. This has been accounted for by the relatively low percentage of girls taking science subjects at school and even lower numbers pursuing science in higher and further education (Kelly 1978; 1981; 1982). Positive measures have been taken to counter this and encourage girls into science subjects through making the subjects more attractive and appropriate to them, whilst also presenting a positive image of women scientists (see Smail 1982 for a discussion of the 'Girls in Science and Technology' (GIST) project). Studies have shown that women are as capable as men of following scientific careers (Curran 1980; Newton 1981), although they are still considerably under-represented in these careers (Ferry 1982).[3] Initiatives have also been taken to monitor the number of women in scientific occupations and to explore the effects of employment and training policies on women in these occupations (see Brayshaw and Laidlaw 1979 for a discussion of women in engineering). From all of these studies it emerges that it is not only important to examine the reasons why girls tend not to pursue scientific subjects at school, or why women are not encouraged into scientific careers, but it is also necessary to examine the structural impediments present in these careers – in particular the failure of previously male-dominated careers to accommodate to the needs of women (Saraga and Griffiths 1981).

About 10,000 women work as scientists in the NHS and most of them are employed in departments of pathology.[4] When the regional picture for women in each of the scientific grades in clinical chemistry laboratories is considered, they are clearly under-represented in senior positions and over-represented in the lower grades.[5] The unequal representation of women in medical laboratory sciences cannot be solely attributed to their lower participation in science subjects at school, although if more girls were encouraged into science subjects a corresponding increase in the number of women entering the profession might be expected. The data suggests that women qualified in science subjects are more likely than men who are similarly qualified to choose a career in medical laboratory sciences. Just over half (55 per cent) of the national recruits to the MLSO grade are women, despite the fact that fewer girls than boys have GCE 'O' and 'A' levels in chemistry (Department of Education and Science 1981). The small number of women in managerial positions[6] cannot be attributed to their under-representation in the profession as a whole. Rather, factors in the organization itself must be looked at in the search for an explanation.

The research focused on various aspects of the organization of clinical chemistry laboratories. Recruitment, selection, and promotion practices were examined, together with the differentiation of laboratory tasks by grade and sex and the opportunities for further training. Other factors considered were the flexibility of working hours (including the availability of part-time work), maternity leave and childcare provision, the possibility of resuming a laboratory career with adequate retraining after a break in service for reasons such as child-rearing, and the sexual division of labour at home. A full discussion of the findings can be found in Homans (1984), but for the purpose of this chapter the emphasis is placed on selected aspects of work organization together with a discussion of managerial attitudes which affect quality of opportunity for women at work.

Social mythology v. reality

Several myths about women emerged from the study. The most dominant theme expressed by male managers was an assumption that women scientific workers will leave on pregnancy and not return. Women were therefore considered to be something of a liability, with high turnover rates. The reality of the organization of hospital laboratories is such that women who do leave on pregnancy find it difficult to return and combine motherhood with a career. A second theme to emerge from the data was that women and men possessed different skills. Perceptions of male and female 'natural' skills have often been used to provide a justification for gender differences at work (Coyle 1982; Hartmann 1979; Homans 1984; Phillips and Taylor 1980) so that jobs become 'stereotyped', (Hartnett 1978) or 'gendered' (Davies and Rosser 1986). This theme about 'natural' ability becomes conflated with the previous point about women's biology making them less reliable, and it was generally regarded as unproblematic that men should be dominant in managerial jobs and women predominate in the more menial posts. This was seen to reflect the 'natural' order of things, since women would 'naturally' get pregnant and leave.

This chapter therefore concentrates first on the extent to which women's perceived proclivity to pregnancy influences selection and promotion practices and to a lesser extent the organization of laboratory life. Second, it draws on data to question the validity of the pregnancy myth. Third, naturalistic arguments to do with gender differences in skills, or the social construction of skills (Coyle 1982), are explored and the implications for women outlined. Finally, the chapter concludes by showing how the cumulative effect of these facets of patriarchal ideology produce a hostile working environment for women.

The myth of pregnancy

This study found clear evidence that selection and promotion practices are based on certain myths about women, the most pervasive myths being that all women will leave to have babies and that wastage due to pregnancy is greater than for any other reason. The pervasiveness of these myths was shown by the way in which they influenced practices at selection (for instance, only women were asked questions about marital status and dependent children). They also influenced notions of who can be a manager. It became clear that there were certain qualities which were judged necessary for staff wanting promotion. These qualities were not only to do with scientific or technical competence, but also related to notions of who would 'fit in' (Homans 1984: 75–6) and who was 'worthy of promotion' (Homans 1984: 91–101). Two themes ran through managers' reasons for asking women questions at interview about marital status and number of dependent children: (a) women with children may require extra time off for school holidays and children's illnesses, and (b) responsibility for childcare is seen as a mother's problem, not a parental one:

Q. 'Is that question asked at the interview then, if she would want to start a family?'

A. 'I don't know, I'm not a female who's been interviewed but I think at interviews, even at the MLSO level, I think I have asked questions like "Are you married, do you have a family?", but I think my main reason for asking it at that level was to see how much time they might need off with school holidays, and possibly with children people would need a morning off to go to the doctor's, that was the only reason for asking it at that level.'

(male, chief MLSO)

This statement may be regarded by some as an example of a 'caring' manager concerned with the domestic commitments of his female staff. This view is not unique, as similar comments were voiced in the research conducted by Curran (1985: 19). However, these views are highly paternalistic and heterosexist and perpetuate beliefs about women's primary role being to do with childcare:

'It's a bit of a personal question, I appreciate that, but I think it's something that has to be considered. It's something that can't happen to a man really, but I suppose in that sense it's unfair – it's not equal opportunity there because the man could never find himself having a family as such.'

(male, chief MLSO)

Whilst men cannot biologically 'have a family', there is nothing to prevent men being fully involved in and responsible for child-rearing. This factor was not apparently taken into consideration by any of the managers interviewed. It was always assumed that women of certain ages were potentially at risk of pregnancy. One manager, who did not ask direct questions himself about intended maternity, made his own assessment:

Q. 'Is that question asked, whether people will have children or not?'

A. 'No, well, it is asked; not asked by me. On the other hand, I can usually make a fairly intelligent guess of how long it will be, because it nearly always is a factor sooner or later.'

(male, chief MLSO)

Women who encountered these attitudes found that they did not always tally with their own future career plans. One woman who was annoyed at overhearing a conversation about the wastage of women staff on pregnancy, drew up her own list of reasons for wastage amongst *male* staff:

'A few times I've been in the staff room or just lingering about, we've heard chiefs saying, "Well, I wouldn't give a woman a job, she is likely to leave and have a baby." And to me that is the wrong attitude, but that is the attitude that most men seem to take around with them. It was on the cards that I wouldn't get a job because I was going to get married and I would probably get pregnant within three months and leave.'

Q. 'Was that said to you?'

A. 'It was said to someone in front of a friend of mine which obviously came back to me. So there is a lot of "Oh well, the men will stop here. The women won't, the women will all have babies and they'll all be off, but the men won't, they will stop." They don't seem to believe that men are more prone to heart attacks. They are also more prone to ulcers if they are in top jobs. They are also more prone to leave for promotion elsewhere, if they are fed up. Whereas the women usually stop where they are because they have got a job. It got me extremely mad some time ago thinking that you are only in a job at the moment to save up to have a baby. It isn't my idea at all. People just don't believe you, though.'

(female, MLSO)

This point was also made by Ferry and Moore in their study of women in science. They noted that 'time and again they [highly qualified women] have found themselves pulled apart on the subject of whether or not they are likely to leave soon in order to marry or have children' (Ferry and Moore 1982: 28).

Women's potential to have children was seen to disadvantage them

93

in terms of promotion. In discussions of selection and promotion, many managers subscribed to the belief that women would leave the service and not return – and it was therefore assumed that they did not want promotion. One manager considered that women 'retired' when they left the service on pregnancy. Some managers cited the extra responsibility involved in more senior grades as the reason for not appointing women, who may leave to have children after a few years' service: 'I think when given the responsibility of running a department day-to-day you don't necessarily want to employ a female who may leave to have a family and I think that's probably the only reason' (male, chief MLSO).

Breaks in service for child-rearing were also seen to disadvantage women, not only with regard to promotion chances, but also in returning to work and competing against men with similar qualifications:

'If you take the health service as a whole, I think the fact that women are liable not to be working constantly – they are liable to go off and have babies – is something that makes appointing commit-tees more reluctant to appoint them, and I think it is a factor, and it is not the only factor, it is not an absolute factor, but I think it comes into it. And I am sure, if you had two absolutely equal people, which is impossible, if it were possible to have absolutely equal people, one male and one female, you would appoint the male. Not *me*, but *they* would appoint the male, and I think it is this factor, the break in service.' (emphasis added)

(Male, top grade biochemist)

For most managers, the fact that women fail to gain promotion because they may drop out is not seen as problematic, but as a 'fact of life' which cannot be changed:

'Generally at the basic grade levels it is probably 50:50. Males tend to dominate the higher levels because simply the women drop out to get married, have babies and that sort of thing – there are no sort of sex bars, that is just the *fact of life*.' (emphasis added)

(male, senior biochemist)

'Quantitatively, one doesn't discriminate between men and women coming in as technical staff. Most often, certainly, I tend to see in my working life most of the technical grade staff, which comprises a lot of the MLSOs and the juniors. It is women that outnumber men and it is only later, really, that you see men taking quite a number of senior posts. Now I don't think that is necessarily selective promotion but just the *facts of life* that women tend to go off and get married and have their families and therefore they have a fragmented career. They come back and have a gap in experience or training and when you come down to it and you are selecting candidates, it is not the sex of the candidate but what they can contribute to their job, and you've got the candidate who is perhaps a woman who has been three years out of a job for family reasons and a chap that has been in the job. It is fairly evident that he is likely, given that the rest is equal between the candidates, that he is likely to get the job.' (emphasis added)

(male, top grade biochemist)

It thus appears that women who want to be promoted have to choose between motherhood and their career. Neither of the two full-time women in management positions had children and those in senior posts who planned to have children in the future said they intended leaving the service completely for a few years, or retraining as a teacher. For a woman to be successful in medical laboratory sciences it seems that she has to be childless; but this does not apply to men.

Q. 'And in your experience do women have equal chances of promotion?'

A. 'No – yes and no. No instantly, because women have this *terrible biological hazard* of going off and having children and the women I know that have got to the top have either been single or not had children. By inference obviously they haven't had the opportunity. Also if you count the number of, in MLSOs, the number of senior chiefs or principal MLSOs as men or women, or top grade biochemists as men and women, there are almost no females at the top in the MLSOs, and I keep trying to think of women who've reached the top who've got children – I don't know any.' (emphasis added)

(male, senior biochemist)

Such examples illustrate the problem faced by women who want to make a career in hospital laboratory sciences. They have to indicate their 'dedication' (Homans 1984: 95–6) by somehow showing that they do not intend to marry or have children. Women who do have children are disadvantaged by some managers who express strong resistance to mothers *working*, let alone being considered suitable to hold a managerial position.

Several managers expressed 'personal views' that women with babies should *not* work in the 'social interests' of the country and family life. Rosser (1984) similarly saw managers in the health service as 'guardians of morality' because they took it upon themselves to ensure that mothers were taking their 'rightful' place at home looking after the children. Managers' personal views seem to permeate the organization of the laboratory to ensure that it is difficult for women with babies to take maternity leave:

'All the laws on equal opportunity don't work if you've got someone who basically feels that women should stay at home and look after the baby. And that is quite regular in our profession.'

(male, biochemist)

'As I say, it boils down to personalities and he doesn't like the fact that women can work now with babies, and, you see this is the trouble, it's always at the discretion of the head of department.'

(female, MLSO – leaver)

Two cases were quoted where verbal maternity leave agreements were either changed or disputed. In the one case, the woman was unable to dispute the loss of her job as she had not informed her employer in writing of her intention to return to work (as required by the Employment Act 1980). However, it was inexcusable that she did not have her maternity rights correctly explained to her. In the other case a woman had a verbal agreement with her head of department that she could return part-time after maternity leave. This decision was later reversed by a temporary head of department and a personal grievance had to be taken up through the union to maintain the verbal agreement.

The belief that women with children should not work can also be related to the scarcity of part-time opportunities. Less than 10 per cent of the total sample studied worked part-time and they were *all* older married women with children. No men studied worked part-time (Homans 1984: 15, 18, 21, 129–37). The resistance to women with children working was also expressed in the context of a discussion about the feasibility of setting up a retraining programme:

'Well, I am thinking about whether people *ought* to return after they have had children, whether they have some sort of right to resume

their career, in the same way that a man who would be uninterrupted – not in the same way, but recognizing that a man will be able to carry on a career uninterrupted. Then, weighing that against people who are just getting mortgages etc., and being employed, weighing that against women who have left to have children. If they return they presumably have chosen to do that on the basis of an economic calculation, the whole social thing comes in there. You are starting to make some sort of social evaluation.'
(emphasis added)   (male, policy-maker)

This sort of reasoning ignored the plight of single parents and women who had unemployed husbands (as did two of the women studied). The myth of the male breadwinner has been challenged effectively elsewhere (Coote and Campbell 1982; Phizacklea 1982) and will not be discussed further here.

The argument so far, according to the male managers interviewed, goes something like this: women are not a reliable source of labour because they leave on pregnancy; as women are at risk of pregnancy they should not be promoted; women who are mothers should not work in the 'best social interests' of the country. In addition to assuming compulsory heterosexuality and that all women want or are able to have children, the effects of these dominant patriarchal views are quite profound. For instance, because women may become pregnant there is little incentive to encourage them to follow training courses (a point also made by Mackie and Pattullo (1977) in relation to marriage), or to ensure that they develop the skills necessary for higher grade posts (Homans 1984: 107–16). Moreover, if there is an implicit assumption that mothers should not work, then there is no incentive for policy-makers to ensure that there are adequate creche facilities, flexible working hours, and the opportunity for part-time work. In fact, within the regional health authority studied, only one-third of the health districts provided some sort of crèche or day nursery facility and only two health districts had crèches which took children at the age of six months or under (i.e. the age a child would be if the mother wanted to return to work after taking maternity leave). Out of the thirteen laboratories studied eleven had set working hours including an hour for lunch; staff in only two laboratories were able to vary their hours either on a weekly or daily basis. The overall inflexibility of working hours was found to be a particular problem by a pregnant woman who wanted to vary her hours in the early stages of pregnancy because she was suffering from morning sickness. She was not allowed to make a change, but in the same laboratory I encountered one of the male senior staff leaving early one day. He was going out to buy some wood for his garage; and because of his senior position in the organization, he did not need to ask for permission to do so!

Blowing the pregnancy myth

The pervasiveness of the myth held by male managers that women will leave on pregnancy and some of the implications of this thinking have been outlined. One of the implications that this research has been concerned with was the belief that *because women may leave to have children they should not be promoted*. When data on wastage rates was examined together with the information collected from women themselves, three major reasons emerged for disputing this assumption: (a) not *all* women leave to have children; (b) *any* member of staff is likely to leave after two years, particularly the male careerist; (c) women are assumed to want to *leave* when they have children, not stay on or return at a later date. (Women who take maternity leave and return challenge the myth that all women leave in pregnancy and do not return.) Each of these three reasons will now be considered in turn:

REASONS FOR LEAVING CLINICAL CHEMISTRY LABORATORIES

When the *actual* numbers of men and women who left NHS clinical chemistry laboratories in the region were studied over a five-year period and their reasons for doing so were examined, pregnancy did *not* emerge as the largest cause of wastage (see *Table 5.1*). The most common reason for many was 'promotion and sideways move to another department', followed by 'change of career', which for many staff involved further education. 'Pregnancy' was the next most common reason, although Siltanen (1981) has suggested that data giving pregnancy as a cause of leaving work may be over-represented and masks other reasons for leaving.[7]

For most of the staff the reason for leaving was voluntary, but nine (4.7 per cent) staff were on short-term contracts and left when the contract terminated and six (3.1 per cent) were dismissed. Edwards and Scullion have argued that women who leave work for family or

Man-made myths

Table 5.1 *Numbers of leavers from NHS clinical chemistry laboratories in the region, 1978–1983, by reasons for leaving*

Reason for leaving	Total		Male		Female	
	no.	%	no.	%	no.	%
Promotion/sideways move	52	27.2	37	50.0	15	12.8
Change of career	39	20.4	16	21.6	23	19.7
Pregnancy	33	17.3	—	—	33	28.2
Change of location	20	10.5	6	8.1	14	12.0
Short-term contract	9	4.7	5	6.8	4	3.4
Dismissed	6	3.1	3	4.1	3	2.6
Maternity leave[1]	5	2.6	—	—	5	4.3
Other[2]	5	2.6	—	—	5	4.3
Insufficient information	22	11.5	7	9.5	15	12.8
TOTAL	191	99.9	74	100.1	117	100.1

Notes
1 2 women intended returning to work after maternity leave and 3 women did not. The total number of women who left the service completely on pregnancy was 36 (18.8 %).
2 'Other' includes marriage, nursing sick relative and working fewer hours.

domestic reasons should be classified as voluntary leavers since 'women may have some choice over staying at work or "putting their families first"' (1982: 292). However, this can be contested, as I argue later; some of the women did not *want* to leave on pregnancy, but wished to remain at work in a part-time capacity after the birth of their baby.

The main reason that men left the NHS was to accept employment in a laboratory-related job with better pay and perceived enhanced career prospects. Men were more likely to go into an industrial laboratory, whereas over half the women going into laboratory-related jobs became company representatives. The main reason women left hospital laboratories was to go into further education and training. The subjects studied by men and women leaving laboratories were, with one exception, in related medical and scientific areas. For those staff who transferred to another NHS laboratory, either on promotion or a sideways move, promotion was the main reason for leaving and this was clearly related to gender – 22 men compared with 5 women. The most common reason for women leaving was to move to another laboratory in the same grade (a sideways move). Half of the women who left did this compared with 38.5 per cent of the men. (Sideways moves are usually made when staff move house and want to work in the laboratory nearest their new home, or when it is felt that experience of working in another laboratory may be useful before applying for promotion.)

In summary, change of career was the most common reason for leaving NHS laboratory work completely (20.4 per cent) but 27.2 per cent of staff transferred to other laboratories on promotion or sideways moves. Twice as many men as women left on promotion, whereas women were more likely to make a sideways move. A total of 18.8 per cent of all staff wastage was due to pregnancy, and about one-third of women left for this reason. The women who left the NHS for reasons other than pregnancy were most likely to go into further education and training (25.5 per cent), while the main reason for men leaving was to accept employment in a laboratory-related job with better pay and enhanced career prospects. This data about wastage is further substantiated by the crude labour movement rate.[8] For all staff the crude turnover rate was 10.7 per cent which is comparable with other studies of laboratory workers (Roberts et al. 1972). The turnover rate was analysed by the different reasons for leaving clinical chemistry laboratories and it was found that the rate for women leaving on pregnancy was lower for each of the grades than was the crude annual turnover rate for all reasons for leaving (see Homans 1984: 59). This is an important point for, as was shown earlier, many male managers considered that pregnancy was one of the main reasons for high staff wastage levels.[9]

THE LENGTH OF SERVICE OF LEAVERS

The average length of service of all leavers for whom information was available was 6.4 years, and the largest number of leavers left with between four and five years' service. *Table 5.2* shows the length of service of all leavers expressed in five-year periods and it is apparent that there were slightly more long-service and fewer short-service women than men, the converse of the situation of staff currently in employment (see Homans 1984: 35).

By breaking down the length of service of leavers by reason for leaving, some interesting findings emerge. The group of leavers with the shortest length of service were those who left for promotion or sideways moves. Half (49.2 per cent) of these leavers had less than five

100

Table 5.2   *Length of service of all leavers from NHS clinical chemistry laboratories in the region, 1978–1983 (expressed in 5-year periods)*

	Total		Male		Female	
	no.	%	no.	%	no.	%
Less than 5 years' service	64	33.5	27	36.6	37	31.6
5–9 years' service	47	24.5	19	25.8	28	24.0
10–14 years' service	20	10.5	7	9.4	13	11.1
15–19 years' service	1	0.5	—	—	1	0.8
Not known	59	30.9	21	28.4	38	32.5
TOTAL	191	99.9	74	100.2	117	100.0

years' service and men were more likely (53.8 per cent) to be early leavers than women (40 per cent). Leavers on pregnancy spent the longest periods of time in the NHS before leaving. Of the women who left because of pregnancy, 44.4 per cent had between five and nine years' service and only 19.4 per cent of them had less than four years' service, compared with 28.3 per cent of leavers for reasons other than pregnancy, and 49.2 per cent of leavers on promotion/sideways move. By looking at the average lengths of service by reason for leaving it is apparent that women who left because of pregnancy had the *longest* average lengths of service (7.6 years compared with 6.3 years for all leavers and 5.3 years for those leaving on promotion and sideways moves).

LEAVERS' PLANS TO RETURN TO NHS LABORATORY WORK

Earlier I described how one manager considered that women 'retired' when they left on pregnancy, and that other managers felt that women with children should not work. In fact the organization of clinical chemistry laboratories, with inflexible hours, scarce part-time posts, and limited childcare facilities, makes it very difficult for women to take maternity leave and return to work full-time. Of the thirty-six women who were pregnant during the period 1978–83, it was possible to trace only six women who took maternity leave and returned to work – three in a part-time capacity and three in a full-time capacity.[10] A further six women said they would have returned to work if part-time opportunities had been available. Not all women wanted to return to work immediately after having children and seven (19 per cent) said they thought it best that they stayed at home

Table 5.3   *Desire to return to NHS laboratory – all leavers*

	Total		Male		Female	
	no.	%	no.	%	no.	%
No	25	43.1	8	53.3	17	39.5
Yes	20	34.5	3	20.0	17	39.5
Perhaps	13	22.4	4	26.7	9	21.0
TOTAL	58	100.0	15	100.0	43	100.0

and looked after the children until they were of school age. After this they anticipated wanting to return to work, preferably part-time. Five women (14 per cent) did not anticipate returning to hospital laboratory work because they felt they would have to return to a lower grade or more menial jobs, particularly if they worked part-time (see Homans 1984: 129–37).

When male and female leavers' plans to return were compared, thirty-three out of fifty-eight (56.9 per cent) of all leavers interviewed said that they would consider returning to the NHS after a break in career (see *Table 5.3*). Women who had left were more likely (60.5 per cent) than men (46.7 per cent) to consider returning to NHS laboratory work, and twice as many women (39.5 per cent) as men (20 per cent) said they definitely wanted to return to the NHS.

Women who wanted to return to the NHS typically thought that they would return at the same grade or lower, and that they would require some form of retraining because of the move towards computerization and introduction of new equipment. However, at the moment no retraining course exists and women who had returned after a break in service had to pick up the job as they went along, or came in on a voluntary basis for several days before taking up appointment.

Arguments about women who leave on pregnancy being a wasted resource cannot be substantiated. Nineteen out of the thirty-six women (53 per cent) who left on pregnancy hoped to return to laboratory work in the future, if they had not already done so. Women leavers were twice as likely as men definitely to want to return to NHS laboratory work. Whether these women *do* return or not will depend on structural factors, such as the flexibility of working hours, part-time opportunities, crèche facilities, and retraining programmes, more than anything else.

Man-made myths

Myths about natural aptitudes

Pregnancy was accorded primacy in the explanations given by male managers for women's absence from managerial positions. However, it was not the only reason and other equally invidious explanations relating to natural capabilities were called upon. One of the benefits gained from looking at the position of women and men in the same occupation is that comparisons can be made and some of the more subtle factors affecting equality of opportunity at work exposed. Concepts of 'femininity' and 'masculinity' have from time immemorial been used as excuses for women being deemed unfit for certain types of work. The argument assumes that women are less suited to managerial and prestigious jobs because they lack drive and ambition (Homans 1984: 96–9) and are more suited to 'less glamorous work' (Marshall 1984: 31). 'Natural' aptitudes and abilities are used to justify women's disproportionate participation in those jobs which express aspects of 'femaleness', for example, nursing, caring, and service to others (Garmarnikow 1978; Hearn 1982; Statham 1978). Simultaneously, these jobs are devalued because they *are* women's work and they become 'gendered' (Davies and Rosser 1986).

When a profession in which women and men are represented in roughly the same numbers is examined it becomes more difficult to argue that the job *per se* is gendered. What happens is that certain *components* of the job are viewed as more appropriate to women or men depending on the precise nature of the task. It is quite difficult at a distance to observe these gender differences in task allocation and many people working within the profession of NHS scientist would argue that there is no gender differentiation – they are all doing the same job. However, drawing on data obtained in interviews with basic grade MLSOs (thirty-five men and forty-two women), gender differences were found in the work done within the same grade. All respondents in current employment were asked to rank certain aspects of their work from one to seven according to the amount of time they spent on each aspect. Overall, there were gender differences in terms of these tasks, women spending more time than men on the least desirable components of the job and men spending proportionately more time on the more prestigious tasks. For the basic MLSO grade there was statistically significant evidence that men spent more time than women on research, staff management, and administration. The interview data provided an illustration of the

103

informal way decisions were made to move men into certain areas: 'I found some to be more privileged than others, it just depended. There was one lad who started there just before I did and he was moved on to more sort of research work, but I wasn't, there was no sort of rotation' (female, MLSO).

Women were more likely to spend more time on clearing up, clerical work, and diagnostic work. Clearing up, in particular, was the least desirable of the tasks, though an important component of the job: 'Our lab is pretty equal, but I do find sometimes that women tend to get left the cleaning and clearing away' (female, MLSO).

The activities men spend more time on obviously enhance their promotion prospects and are regarded by some as central to the process of being 'groomed for management'.

'He [the head of department] tends to push the men, which I suppose in a way is fair enough.'

(female, senior MLSO)

'. . . you think, "Maybe is a male colleague getting a bit more than I am?"'

Q. 'In what sense?'

A. 'Well, maybe a bit more research work.'

(female, senior MLSO)

Naturalistic explanations were used to justify why women should spend more time clearing up (i.e. it is similar to the domestic labour which women are so 'suited to'). Moreover, innate 'masculine' qualities were given as the reasons why men make better managers. It was not, therefore, that men were *better* at the tasks which led to promotion, but that they possessed qualities which male managers already in post regarded to be essential to management. Potential managers should possess 'drive', should 'push themselves forward' and 'press their claims'. These qualities were typically seen to be possessed by men, but not by women. Moreover, certain managers tended to select candidates with characteristics similar to their own (i.e. some kind of mirror image).[11] 'It may have just happened to be that *the men who were short-listed had the attributes I was interested in*, they had shown themselves worthy at an early age, they put themselves forward'. (emphasis added) (male, chief MLSO). Selecting staff because they possess 'masculine' qualities serves to perpetuate what many men consider to be the 'natural' order of things – i.e. men in dominant positions.

There is evidence to suggest that men do not like working for women because this upsets the patriarchal order. Torrey referred to this in relation to male sexuality, and argued that male notions of 'virility' are bound up with their work and male sexuality is traditionally expressed through occupying 'dominant' positions. Men are thus socialized to feel emasculated 'by any sign of competitiveness or lack of submission by a woman' (Torrey 1976).

Sexuality, and ideas about the 'natural' order of things, assume greater prominence in work relations than is generally recognized. The widespread incidence of sexual harassment at work is only now becoming recognized (Cockburn 1985: 59; Sedley and Benn 1983), and there are other areas where women are not taken seriously because of their sex (Collinson and Knights 1985: 36). Two examples will illustrate this pervasive phenomenon in the context of hospital laboratory work. They both indicate the difficulties some men have in relating to women as equals or colleagues rather than as sexual objects. The first example comes from this research, when one male manager was asked what he thought could be done to improve the situation so that women are appointed to more senior posts. He replied by saying: 'I don't think that anything can be done. . . . Quite frankly I wouldn't mind a woman boss. I would like to be able to think that she could sexually harass me, but I don't think that is ever going to happen!' (male, chief MLSO). The other example comes from Sophie Laws's research into male views of menstruation. In her study she interviewed a man who had previously worked in a hospital laboratory and he told the following story about his boss there:

> 'there was a female toilet outside the lab so we could always see the women going to the toilet and he [boss] actually used to time them and if they were taking a long time he used to say, "Oh well, they've got the rags up, there's no point chatting her up."'

> (Laws 1985: 20)

Is change possible?

This chapter concludes by looking at the cumulative effect of these myths about women and the extent to which it is possible to change the situation. What is so depressing about all of this is that many of the men interviewed did not seem aware of their own sexism and the effect it had on women. Admittedly, for some, the asking of questions about equal opportunities caused them to reflect on women's position in the hierarchy and to consider how selection procedures, organization of work, lack of crèche provision, and male attitudes in general did lead to discrimination against women. Others, though, detailed examples of discriminatory practices without considering their implications. For such men these practices merely reflect the 'natural' order of things, an order which is (of course) patriarchal and permeates every aspect of women's (and men's) lives. In its most crude form this 'natural' order was referred to in terms of genetic differences between the sexes and therefore immutable:

'I don't think the opportunities [for women] are lacking, I think it's the women who are lacking themselves.'
Q. 'And could you think of anything that could be done to improve the situation?'
A. 'No, because I think it's genetic, I think it's hereditary, I do seriously.'

(male, chief MLSO)

For those who do not believe that inequalities are naturally or biologically determined but, rather, are socially constructed, there is a considerable task ahead – particularly when the fact is taken into account that many women do not see their experiences in collective terms. Throughout this chapter I have stressed the merit of studying men and women together; whilst there have been numerous quotes from individual women and men it is also possible to draw on data which reflect how women and men as a group assess certain issues.

All respondents were asked to rate the NHS as an employer for nine areas, ranging from salary to job satisfaction. There was general agreement between women and men on five out of these nine areas. However, there was considerable disagreement between the sexes in their ratings for (a) equal opportunities, (b) the opportunity to use one's initiative, (c) the opportunity to undertake further training, and (d) job satisfaction. In each of these areas women staff were more likely than men to rate the NHS poorly. The area of most disagreement was that of equal opportunities, with 45.2 per cent of women compared with 25.8 per cent of men rating it as 'poor or reasonable'. This difference was further substantiated when respondents were asked if they thought it was possible to improve equal opportunities in their work. Over half the women (58.5 per cent) compared with 37.7 per cent of men thought improvements could be made. The women studied were therefore much less likely than men to view the NHS as an equal opportunities employer. There are several possible explanations for the fact that about half (53.4 per cent) of the women thought equality of opportunity in the NHS was good. First, the NHS may in many respects (for example, pay and holidays) be a better employer than many others, particularly in the private sector. Second, women themselves may accept that they are discriminated against and consequently have low expectations in relation to equality of opportunity. For example, women who view cleaning duties as part of their role do not automatically see the relationship between spending more time than male colleagues in these tasks and a restricting of their own promotion prospects.

Much feminist writing has explored the marginalization of women's experiences. De Beauvoir in the 1940s wrote of women as the 'other' in relation to men (de Beauvoir 1972) and numerous other writers have illustrated that the male world is taken as the norm to which women are expected (and sometimes coerced) to conform. Marshall argued that women 'are outside the social construction of meaning' (1984: 55) in linguistic terms, and Spender (1980) used the concepts of 'dominant' and 'muted' to explain how women have to translate and transform their experiences to a form intelligible to men. As a consequence women often feel they do not 'fit' into the male world and may consider their experiences to be unique.

Consciousness-raising in the 1960s and 1970s provided some women with an awareness of the generality of their experiences, but for many of the women referred to in this study there certainly was an undeveloped collective consciousness. Whilst this remains, women working in hospital laboratories will view their experiences in individual rather than collective terms. Involvement in trade union activities may help to raise women's awareness of their situation, but it is not likely to resolve the problem completely unless the structure and organization of unions change. Of the women studied, 59 per cent belonged to a union but their active participation was low and they were absent from office-holding positions. This reflects the situation nationally. The union that most MLSOs belong to is ASTMS, and at a national level only 9.5 per cent of full-time officials are women as are 8.3 per cent of executive committee members (Coote and Kellner 1980). Women's issues, therefore, are not often on the agenda and it may be difficult to implement equal opportunities policies (see Homans 1984: 167–73). Women active in trade unions may end up supporting male views of priority issues, while matters to do with equal opportunities are viewed as 'the icing on the cake' (Homans 1984: 170).

Workplace-based women's groups have an important role to play in raising awareness, giving staff information about entitlements and the laws relating to sex discrimination and equal opportunities, as well as providing training in skills which would enhance career prospects (assertion training may be particularly relevant here). But it is not enough for women to change; there has to be an accompanying change in male attitudes and the organization of hospital laboratory work itself. In most instances these changes will only come about through trade unions and other bodies, such as the Equal Opportunities Commission, taking the initiative in ensuring that equality of opportunity is available to all and guaranteeing that the Sex Discrimination Act (1975) is observed. Other changes may occur through individual men becoming aware of how their practices affect women at work. However, the evidence collected in this study suggests that change at this level is likely to be negligible. It is not in the interests of many men to promote equal opportunities and, as I have shown, patriarchal beliefs about women's place are deeply held and firmly entrenched even among supposedly rational men in scientific occupations.

Notes

1 The research derives from an Equal Opportunities Commission project (funded for six months), which in turn developed out of a larger study of career opportunities for staff in National Health Service Laboratories funded by the Economic and Social Research Council.

2 Only three members of the medical profession were interviewed in connection with this study. Due to their lack of representativeness this data has been omitted from the analysis. The chapter therefore focuses only on data obtained from biochemists and medical laboratory scientific officers.

3 Elston (1980) and Day (1982) have looked at the position of women in medicine, MacGuire (1980) at women in nursing, and Ward (1980) at women in physiotherapy.

4 Hospital pathology laboratories can be divided into several divisions: chemical pathology or clinical chemistry, haematology, histopathology, immunopathology, medical microbiology, and general pathology. The data in this chapter relates only to clinical chemistry laboratories.

5 Within clinical chemistry laboratories there are often both biochemists and MLSOs working alongside each other. The biochemists have five grades of staff – probationary, basic, senior, principal, and top grade: whilst

Man-made myths

the MLSOs have seven grades — junior A (non-career), junior B, basic, senior, chief, senior chief, and principal. The probationary biochemist and junior MLSO grades are the training grades. According to the data collected in this study, 50 per cent of women and 20 per cent of men in biochemist posts were in the basic and probationary grades. Only half the women biochemists compared with 80 per cent of men had therefore obtained promotion since completing their training. Women MLSOs fared worse – only 10 per cent of women MLSOs compared with 61 per cent of men MLSOs had achieved promotion beyond the basic grade. *None* of the women MLSOs held a post above that of senior MLSO (women were therefore absent from the top three MLSO grades).

6 The management structure of the thirteen clinical chemistry laboratories studied varied tremendously. Three laboratories did not have a MLSO in post above the grade of chief MLSO and two laboratories did not have *any* biochemists in post. However, in the majority of the laboratories, grades of senior biochemist and above and chief MLSO and above carried some degree of managerial responsibility. Out of the 193 staff interviewed only nine women (i.e. 12 per cent of all female staff) compared with sixty-one men (51 per cent of male staff) had any management input, in the form of involvement in fiscal decisions and recruitment and selection of staff. All of the nine women in senior posts were biochemists and seven were employed in a part-time capacity, thus having limited managerial responsibility as management was viewed as a full time occupation.

7 Siltanen argued that women consider pregnancy to be a legitimate reason for leaving employment and one which is more acceptable than for them to tell their employer that they were leaving because of 'intolerable working conditions' or 'low pay' (Siltanen 1981: 39–40).

8 The crude labour turnover rate was calculated by taking the total number of leavers for the five-year period 1978 to 1983 and dividing this by five. This figure was then expressed as a percentage of the total number of staff in post in 1982. It is recognized that the rates achieved were very crude indicators, but no other figures were available. Usually labour turnover rates are calculated by taking the number of leavers in a given period and dividing that by the number of workers in post at the start of the period.

9 Hartnett has suggested that 'managerial judgements' about women's dependability are 'unsound': 'Evidence from this country and the USA indicates the following about turnover: high turnover rates are true of all employees, irrespective of sex, who are under 25 and in low-income clerical jobs' (Hartnett 1978: 81). Unfortunately, there was insufficient information about the ages of laboratory staff who had left to be able to make comparisons with Hartnett's assertion. However, it is clear that the highest turnover is in the basic MLSO grade.

10 Insufficient information was available for twelve out of the thirty-six women (33 per cent) who left on pregnancy. It may be the case that some of these twelve women have since returned to laboratory work in another regional health authority.

11 This notion of 'fitting in' and having similar interests is what Kanter (1977) calls 'homosocial reproduction' and applies mainly when selecting

staff at more senior levels. At the junior MLSO levels, dexterity and organizational skills are seen as the most important criteria and this is where women were in the majority.

References

de Beauvoir, S. (1972) *The Second Sex*. Harmondsworth: Penguin.

Beechey, V. (1983) What's So Special about Women's Employment? A Review of Some Recent Studies of Women's Paid Work. *Feminist Review* 15: 23–45.

Brayshaw, P. and Laidlaw, C.J. (1979) *Women in Engineering*. Engineering Industry Training Board Reference Paper 4/79. Watford: EITB.

Cockburn, C. (1985) Technology as a Factor in Occupational Segregation. In EOC Research Bulletin No. 9, *Occupational Segregation by Sex*. Manchester: Equal Opportunities Commission, pp. 45–61.

Collinson, D. and Knights, D. (1985) Jobs for the Boys: Recruitment into Life Insurance Sales. In EOC Research Bulletin No. 9, *Occupational Segregation by Sex*. Manchester: Equal Opportunities Commission, pp. 24–44.

Coote, A. and Campbell, B. (1982) *Sweet Freedom: The Struggle for Women's Liberation*. London: Pan Books.

Coote, A. and Kellner, P. (1980) *Hear This, Brother: Women Workers and Union Power*. London: New Statesman Report No. 1.

Coyle, A. (1982) Sex and Skill in the Organisation of the Clothing Industry. In J. West (ed.) *Work, Women and the Labour Market*. London: Routledge and Kegan Paul, pp. 10–26.

Crompton, R., Jones, G., and Reid, S. (1982) Contemporary Clerical Work: A Case Study of Local Government. In J. West (ed.) *Women, Work and the Labour Market*. London: Routledge and Kegan Paul, pp. 44–60.

Curran, L. (1980) Science Education: Did She Drop Out or Was She Pushed? In Brighton Women and Science Group (ed.) *Alice Through the Microscope*. London: Virago, pp. 22–41.

Curran, M.M. (1985) Recruiting Gender Stereotypes for the Office. In EOC Research Bulletin No. 9, *Occupational Segregation by Sex*. Manchester: Equal Opportunities Commission, pp. 1–23.

Davies, C. and Rosser, J. (1986) Gendered Jobs in the Health Service. In D. Knights and H. Willmott (eds) *Gender and the Labour Process*. Aldershot: Gower.

Day, P. (1982) *Women Doctors: Choices and Constraints in Policies for Medical Manpower*. A study commissioned by King Edward's Hospital Fund for London. London: King's Fund Project (Paper No. 28, January).

Department of Education and Science (1981) *Statistics of School Leavers, CSE and GCE England 1981*, tables C25, C28, C29. London: HMSO.

Edwards, P.K. and Scullion, H. (1982) *The Social Organisation of Industrial Conflict*. Oxford: Basil Blackwell.

Elston, M.A. (1980) Medicine: Half Our Future Doctors. In R. Silverstone and A. Ward (eds) *Careers of Professional Women*. London: Croom Helm, pp. 99–139.

Ferry, G. (1982) How Women Figure in Science. *New Scientist* (1 April): 10–13.

Man-made myths

Ferry, G. and Moore, J. (1982) True Confessions of Women in Science. *New Scientist* 95 (1 July): 27–30.

Garmarnikow, E. (1978) Sexual Division of Labour: The Case of Nursing. In A. Kuhn and A.M. Wolpe (eds) *Feminism and Materialism*. London: Routledge and Kegan Paul, pp. 96–123.

Gill, T. and Whitty, L. (1983) *Women's Rights in the Workplace*. Harmondsworth: Penguin.

Hartmann, H. (1979) Capitalism, Patriarchy and Job Segregation by Sex. In Z.R. Eisenstein (ed.) *Capitalism, Patriarchy and the Case for Socialist Feminism*. New York: Monthly Review Press, pp. 206–47.

Hartnett, O. (1978) Sex Role Stereotyping at Work. In J. Chetwynd and O. Hartnett (eds) *The Sex Role System*. London: Routledge and Kegan Paul, pp. 76–92.

Hearn, J. (1982) Notes on Patriarchy, Professionalisation and the Semi-Professions. *Sociology* 16: 184–202.

Homans, H. (1984) *Career Opportunities for Women in Clinical Chemistry Laboratories*. Report submitted to the Equal Opportunities Commission. Manchester: EOC.

Janeway, E. (1971) *Man's World, Woman's Place: A Study in Social Mythology*. New York: Dell Publishing.

Johnson, A.P. (1969) *Organisation and Management of Hospital Laboratories*. London: Butterworth.

Kanter, R.M. (1977) *Men and Women of the Corporation*. New York: Basic Books.

Kelly, A. (1978) *Girls and Science: An International Study of Sex Differences in School Achievement*. Stockholm: Almqvist and Wiksell.

—(ed.) (1981) *The Missing Half: Girls and Science Education*. Manchester: Manchester University Press.

— (1982) Why Girls Don't Do Science. *New Scientist* 94 (20 May): 497–500.

Laws, S. (1985) Male Power and Menstrual Etiquette. In H. Homans (ed.) *The Sexual Politics of Reproduction*. Aldershot: Gower, pp. 13–29.

Lockwood, D. (1966) *The Blackcoated Worker*. London: Allen and Unwin.

MacGuire, J. (1980) Nursing: None is Held in Higher Esteem . . . Occupational Control and the Position of Women in Nursing. In R. Silverstone and A. Ward (eds) *Careers of Professional Women*. London: Croom Helm, pp. 140–64.

Mackie, L. and Pattullo, P. (1977) *Women at Work*. London: Tavistock.

Marshall, J. (1984) *Women Managers: Travellers in a Male World*. Chichester: Wiley.

National Union of Teachers/Equal Opportunities Commission (1980) *Promotion and the Woman Teacher*. London: a National Union of Teachers research project published jointly with the Equal Opportunities Commission.

Newton, P. (1981) Who Says Girls Can't Be Engineers? In A. Kelly (ed.) *The Missing Half: Girls and Science Education*. Manchester: Manchester University Press, pp. 139–49.

Novarra, V. (1980) *Women's Work, Men's Work: The Ambivalence of Equality*. London: Marion Boyars.

111

Phillips, A. and Taylor, B. (1980) Sex and Skill: Notes towards a Feminist Economics. *Feminist Review* 6: 79–88.

Phizacklea, A. (1982) Migrant Women and Wage Labour: The Case of West Indian Women in Britain. In J. West (ed.) *Work, Women and the Labour Market.* London: Routledge and Kegan Paul, pp. 99–116.

Roberts, B.C., Loveridge, R., Gennard, J., and Eason, J.V. (1972) *Reluctant Militants: A Study of Industrial Technicians.* London: Heinemann.

Rosser, J. (1984) Personal communication.

Saraga, E. and Griffiths, D. (1981) Biological Inevitabilities or Political Choice? The Future for Girls in Science. In A. Kelly (ed.) *The Missing Half: Girls and Science Education.* Manchester: Manchester University Press, pp. 85–97.

Sedley, A. and Benn, M. (1983) *Sexual Harassment at Work.* London: National Council for Civil Liberties.

Siltanen, J. (1981) A Commentary on Theories of Female Wage Labour. In Cambridge Women's Studies Group (ed.) *Women in Society: Interdisciplinary Essays.* London: Virago, pp. 25–40.

Smail, B. (1982) Changing the Image of Women Scientists. *Women and Training News.* NALGO 9 (Winter): 11.

Spender, D. (1980) *Man Made Language.* London: Routledge and Kegan Paul.

Statham, D. (1978) *Radicals in Social Work.* London: Routledge and Kegan Paul.

Stewart, A., Prandy, K., and Blackburn, R.M. (1980) *Social Stratification and Occupation.* London: Macmillan.

Torrey, J.W. (1976) The Consequences of Equal Opportunity for Women. *Journal of Contemporary Business* 5 (Winter).

Ward, A. (1980) Physiotherapy. In R. Silverstone and A. Ward (eds) *Careers of Professional Women.* London: Croom Helm, pp. 165–84.

© 1987 Hilary Homans

6

Women Lawyers –
Marginal Members
of a Male-dominated Profession

Anne Spencer and David Podmore

Introduction

Although at present about 40 per cent of law students at university and polytechnic are women, the number of women practising law is low – only about 12 per cent in both the barristers' and solicitors' branches of the profession.[1] The number of women entering the legal profession has, however, steadily increased in recent years (thirty years ago only two or three per cent of practising lawyers were women). The profession remains, nevertheless, both male-dominated and male-orientated (Podmore and Spencer 1982a). This is true not only of the law, of course. Management is characterized by a similar 'masculine' ethos and orientation (Kanter 1975), which is equally strong in engineering (Robin 1969: 210) and in medicine (Lorber 1975; Quandango 1976).

The 'masculine' ethos and orientation of the law has a number of damaging consequences for women entering and working in the profession. Epstein (1974, 1981) has observed how the marginalization of women in male-dominated professions has much wider implications than the imposition of 'quotas' for new groups of entrants. Women practising law find that they are not very welcome and that the ways in which they can use their knowledge and abilities are controlled and channelled by a variety of mechanisms, often insidious. For example certain areas of work will be relatively inaccessible to them; other areas will be foisted upon them as 'appropriate' to women. Women lawyers frequently find themselves denied full participation in professional life because of their exclusion from informal (and sometimes from formal) activities.

For most women in the legal profession there are limits to the type and quality of work available to them and in consequence limits to their remuneration and promotion opportunities (Podmore and Spencer 1982b). As members of a visibly 'deviant' status group, women are pushed to the margins of the profession. This marginalization is accomplished via a more or less conscious and explicit set of assumptions held by the dominant male sector of the profession about (a) the nature of the profession, and (b) what women are like. These two stereotypes are manifested in modes of operation within the profession which ensure that, in the majority of cases, women are marginal members. In this chapter we examine these two forms of stereotyping employed by men in the legal profession and argue that they constitute most important factors contributing to the marginalization of women.[2] Data collected in the course of interviews with thirty-two men barristers and solicitors are used to examine these stereotyping activities, and interviews with seventy-six women lawyers are also drawn upon.[3]

The nature of the legal profession – as male lawyers see it

The interviews with male barristers and solicitors provided a clear indication of what they considered the profession to be like. Since they are the majority gender within the profession and are dominant within it, men's ability to define the situation and 'write the agenda' as far as women are concerned is very considerable. Attempts by women lawyers to redefine their situation in a male-dominated profession usually have to be at a subversive and covert level. If professional life is regarded as a 'game' (Long 1958) bounded by rules, it is very much a man's game in which the rules are man-made rules. This, of course, creates very considerable problems for women because the qualities which are looked for in men lawyers arouse intense suspicion when encountered in women. We now consider some of the main features of the legal profession and the position of women within it, as defined by the men interviewed.

IT'S AGGRESSIVE – AND IT'S MALE

The aggressive and 'masculine' nature of the law is a view which emerges very clearly from the interview data, when men lawyers were discussing the nature of the work that they did. One barrister who worked in a set of chambers with no women tenants (colleagues) at all – said that the law: 'is a career based to some extent on competition and hustling and hitting people on the head and so on. Old-fashioned people like me tend to think that's more the masculine rather than the feminine role.' The aggressive imagery used to describe his occupation ('hitting people on the head'!) is revealing, as is the view that professional life involves being competitive. Practice at the Bar is therefore seen as being inherently unsuitable for women or at least for 'feminine' women, an issue to which we shall return.

Interactions with clients was one focus for these qualities of aggression. A perceived need to be 'hard' with clients because they sometimes behaved aggressively towards their lawyers was indicated in some of the interviews with solicitors. One described these problems and how to cope with them as follows: 'Sometimes I have to tell clients to jump in the lake, because they sometimes think we're here to be whipped and kicked up the arse, and God knows what.' The use of the metaphors of actual physical violence are quite telling in this context, as an expression of the extent to which male lawyers really *do* perceive the legal profession as being, occasionally, an arena for quite high levels of aggression.

For the barristers, the courtroom and the process of undertaking advocacy also represented an expression of aggressiveness. A barrister, discussing why he chose to work in this branch of the profession, explained: 'Also, doing advocacy represents a means of channelling and disposing of aggression in a controlled setting . . . you can take out your aggression in cross examinations, and so on.' This view of advocacy was not echoed by the women barristers, who tended to emphasize the dramatic aspects, the status and prestige, and the financial rewards as being their motivation for undertaking this kind of work.[4] However, this male barrister, although mentioning other reasons for his choice also, put the greatest emphasis on what he regarded as the highly aggressive nature of doing advocacy.

In a similar vein a solicitor commented: 'I can fill a court, I can make the magistrate listen . . . I suppose my size helps there.' He added: 'But it's much more difficult for a woman.'

This is, of course, not quite such an overt statement as that of the barrister, nevertheless the ability to dominate a situation, to 'make the magistrate listen', is mentioned as an important aspect of the solicitor's task. That this solicitor directly mentions his physical size in this context is, we think, significant. It seems to have links with the argument, frequently advanced by men, that their greater size and superior physical strength are reasons why they should be regarded as innately superior to women. The reference to 'filling the court' and the view that a woman would find this more difficult to achieve, acknowledges a view commonly held by people of both genders in the legal profession. This is that women are disadvantaged in terms of undertaking advocacy by their higher and often softer speaking voices. We would by no means wish to take for granted that this proposition is correct; nevertheless, in an already male-dominated profession, advocacy and court work is even more a masculine preserve and women specializing in this work are even more disadvantaged and marginalized.[5]

ITS OBJECTIVE, LOGICAL, AND PRAGMATIC – AND IT'S MALE

The male lawyers interviewed clearly identified objectivity, and a rational, logical approach as key features of the legal profession and key attributes that members should possess for the competent performance of their role. As one respondent said: 'The most important attributes in my view [are] *objectivity*, ability to listen, and the ability to be *logical* and *pragmatic* and also *not to lose your objectivity*' (emphasis added). These are very much attributes linked to the 'masculine' stereotype[6] and, given the male-dominated nature of the profession, identification of competence with 'masculinity' is to be expected. The problems this generates for women are explored later in this chapter but it is important to note that these characteristics are believed by the dominant male members of the profession to be essential requirements for competent membership. 'Objectivity' is believed to be particularly important, in the sense of maintaining a proper, professional detachment from the client and the case or problem. One of the interviewees described the key attributes for professional competence in terms of: 'your ability to master facts and present arguments, and your *logical deductive approach* to the problem' (emphasis added).

The message, we feel, is essentially the same.

PREJUDICE IS JUST A FACT OF LIFE

This feeling was reflected strongly in the interviews with male lawyers. They seemed agreed that the law is indeed a male-dominated and male-orientated arena and it was accepted that the entry of women will be to some extent resisted and resented for this very reason. A solicitor commented:

'I think that there is still rather an assumption that it's a male profession and I think a lot of people – particularly, probably, the older and more traditional elements – deep down think things would be a lot better if they didn't have so many women coming into the profession.'

As well as suggesting that 'a lot of people' (i.e. men?) are worried about the increased entry of women into the profession, it is implied here that this is likely to be detrimental to the profession's status and prestige.[7] In a similar vein another solicitor said:

'I think that solicitors as a whole are inclined to be at the end of the scale which I think the Equal Opportunities Commission described as male chauvinist, and a woman, therefore, to succeed has in some way got to respond in those circumstances. . . . What I would call a gentle type of lady would in my view find it rather difficult.'

This comment not only makes the point clearly that there is prejudice within the profession against women, but also suggests that this will 'inevitably' create difficulties for women entrants. There is no sense of any feeling that the profession should adapt its norms to accommodate women, but rather that it is up to women to cope with the situation as best they can. This kind of complacent admission of prejudice was very common in the interviews.[8] The use of the term 'male chauvinist' and similar terminology of this kind is also recurrent, perhaps as a demonstration that these men feel they are 'up to date' with the issues. For example, from another interview: 'I suppose they [women] do inevitably come up against the sexist joke and there are still quite a lot of men who regard it as not being a woman's place to do these things.' What comes out most strongly here is the *inevitability* of women being discriminated against. Kennedy (1978: 151) has described how: 'Many [barristers'] chambers openly admit a "no women policy" whilst others hide their discrimination behind all sorts of excuses.'

The problems of discrimination and prejudice are by no means restricted to women in private practice. A justice's clerk commented as follows: 'The selection of justices' clerks, the selection of all senior appointments in the magisterial service, is left to committees of magistrates. I would be fairly sure that the majority of those committees would be prejudiced against women.' In a similar manner a lawyer working in a public sector organization said: 'We are a very male-oriented organization. There are a few women coming up into the middle echelons but mainly I deal with [the organization's] managers at a senior level and I can't think of one woman, quite frankly.'

What came over throughout the interviews was the level of complacency about the situation. The small number of women lawyers, their under-representation in the senior ranks of the profession,[9] and the high degree of prejudice against them are simply accepted as 'facts of life' by most male lawyers.

WE'RE NOT PREJUDICED, IT'S THE CLIENTS

When asked to comment on the possibility of prejudice against women in the legal profession, some respondents laid this at the door of their clients. One solicitor, when asked about women in private practice, commented: 'I think there are certain areas of work, particularly in the company, and commercial field, where the clients might raise an eyebrow.' Company and commercial law is high-status, high-prestige work, highly 'visible' and amply remunerated. Not surprisingly, few women work in this field (Podmore and Spencer 1984). It is convenient for men to attribute the exclusion of women laywers to the assumed prejudices of clients. There is no suggestion that such assumptions are actually checked out with clients. Another solicitor remarked, more generally: 'I think many clients are suspicious of women [solicitors], certainly men [are] . . . that's the first thing, that *natural* suspicion' (emphasis added). It is worth noting here that we are being told that the problem is one of client prejudice, *but* the solicitor himself sees such suspicion as 'natural'!

Whilst a number of male solicitors referred to prejudice against women on the part of the lay client, we found a different pattern amongst barristers. Barristers, because their client is the solicitor, were able to produce 'explanations' involving quite complex and sophisticated layers of possible prejudice against women. One said: 'The clerks would tend to be wary of giving her [a woman] work. This is not because the clerks are prejudiced, but because of what they think are the prejudices of the solicitor.' Others used the straight-forward excuse of lay client prejudice: some clients, especially criminal case clients, find it difficult to accept women barristers.[10] Another barrister laid the blame on solicitors, saying: 'I think that some solicitors would be slightly wary of instructing a woman to do certain types of cases, whether from their own personal prejudices or because they feel that their clients might be prejudiced, confronted with a woman barrister.'

The circle of prejudice and discrimination against women is thus neatly closed. However, these accounts, which centre on 'client prejudice', fail to convince. They have an air of offloading blame whilst attempting to keep oneself, and, indeed, one's entire branch of the profession, pure. At the same time the *de facto* situation is accepted in the same way as it was by the male lawyers quoted earlier, who quite straightforwardly conceded that there was prejudice and even that they themselves were prejudiced.

SINCE PREJUDICE IS A FACT OF LIFE, IT'S WOMEN'S PROBLEM, NOT MEN'S

The interviews with the male lawyers indicated, time and again, similar attitudes towards women in the profession. The commonly expressed view was that it was women who were expected to make the accommodation and to conform to the generally 'masculine' ethos of the law. There was no suggestion that this ethos should be questioned or subjected to change. One solicitor said: 'bearing in mind the world in which we live, a woman probably needs to be far more extrovert, in order to be as successful as a man. Undoubtedly we . . . the male species expect more of women than we do of other men.' This contains several interesting assumptions. First, the 'world in which we live' is something simply to be taken for granted. If prejudice is a fact of life, this should not be challenged in any way. It goes without saying that 'rocking the boat' would not be in the interests of men generally and men lawyers in particular. Second, though the problems which women face in operating in a man's world are recognized, these problems are just noted. It is women who will need to work much harder, be 'more extrovert', and generally strive to conform to the male model of how the profession operates. Third, the reference to men as a 'species' is telling with regard to this male lawyer's world view. If men are a species, what then, are women?

Another respondent commented that: 'male chauvinism is bound to affect some women. Some women, not all, find it difficult to compete with men in terms of expressing personality, being forceful.' Once again we have a clear indication of the supposed aggressive and competitive nature of the profession, the inevitability of prejudice against women, the recognition that this causes problems for women and the expectation that women must modify their behaviour in order to conform.

WOMEN TAKE WORK AWAY FROM MEN AND THEN JUST LEAVE IN ORDER TO MARRY AND START A FAMILY

This view was articulated by a number of the men interviewed, who made no secret of their feelings against women practising in the legal profession. One of the respondents said:

> 'I think men, if they were honest enough, resent women coming along and doing work which they might otherwise do, when they say to themselves, you know, "What's she taking this work away from me and building a practice [for], she's only going to go and leave in five years' time."'

This respondent was suggesting that male lawyers – if only they were prepared to admit it – view women lawyers as competitors. We are not sure how general this man's resentment against women is, but it seems to echo some of the sentiments opposed to women entering the profession which were so strong in the early years of this century.[11] A second aspect of the resentment of the solicitor quoted above is specifically located around the belief that women will not continue to work, probably after they marry and certainly after they have children. The notion that women will drop out of the profession constituted, in the minds of some of the men interviewed, a rationale for prejudice. They seemed to feel that it was pointless for women to have competed with men, to have built up their practices and then not to have continued to practise over the course of a 'normal' (as defined by men) working lifetime. Another solicitor commented:

> 'As far as I'm personally concerned I'm bound to say that if I'm honest, yes, that I am prejudiced against women solicitors. . . . With women solicitors, and particularly women partners, you're always concerned in the long term whether they're going to stay with you.'[12]

The alleged 'unreliability' of women seems to be no more than a convenient rationalization on which to hang a more thoroughgoing prejudice. The 'problems' caused by women as colleagues and partners in firms of solicitors are so widely believed by the men who dominate the profession that women find it extremely difficult to obtain partnerships (Podmore and Spencer 1982b). The notion that women are 'problematic' acts as a useful rationalization for keeping women in positions of subordination within the profession. Similar prejudices also make difficult women's entry to the profession in the first place.

On the subject of gaining entry, the potent stereotypes concerning women's unreliability because of the supposed primacy of their domestic and family lives are often used by the male 'gatekeepers' as a means of denying access to women in the first place. Consider this remark by a man solicitor: 'I certainly wouldn't take on a woman articled clerk. [Why not?] For that reason – most of them *do* end up getting married and you've got to win clients over a ten-year cycle, and you can't do it, it's too much of an investment in an articled clerk.' Our research has demonstrated that women have much greater difficulty in obtaining articles than do men (Podmore and Spencer 1982b). Many of the women respondents described interviews for articles where detailed information was sought as to their future marriage and family plans. These kinds of prejudices clearly affect the chances of women's entry to the profession, as well as their progress to partnership status once they have entered. The assumption that, where women are concerned, marriage (possibly) and family responsibilities (certainly) automatically equate with leaving work would seem to have a somewhat limited basis in reality.[13] It is worth noting that this assumption never needs to be tested for veracity; the holding of the assumption means that it is unlikely that the men solicitors concerned will accept women as articled clerks. Women's alleged lack of commitment to their legal careers is merely a convenient rationalization which gives the actions of male gate-keepers who discriminate against them a cloak of legitimacy.

Assumptions about the primacy of women's domestic and family commitments and the use of these assumptions to deny or limit the access of women to the legal profession or to circumscribe their careers are by no means confined to the solicitors' branch. Barristers' chambers are equally reluctant to take on women.[14] Our research suggests that women experienced the worst problems at the point where they were trying to obtain pupillage, though most who had completed pupillage actually obtained tenancies without too much difficulty (Podmore and

Spencer 1982b). When the men barristers interviewed discussed this, however, they tended to locate the problem around giving women tenancies. One barrister said:

> 'I think probably there is a reluctance to take a woman on as a tenant in chambers still. . . . Even in these chambers the general view is that you have a woman every so often to be slotted in. You wouldn't normally have a run of three or four women as you do men.'

The reason for this reluctance to accept women is of course the alleged 'unreliability' of women because of their assumed domestic commitments. From another interview:

> 'one of the objections to it [taking in women] in chambers is that it creates a difficulty that if you do have children, you leave the Bar. One girl who was a pupil here . . . she went off to other chambers and about three years later she had two children and left the Bar. Now that leaves a void.'

It is revealing to note that knowing of *one* woman who left the Bar to have children has given rise to the implied generalization that *all* women at the Bar will leave if they have children! However, this kind of assumption is superficially attractive because it sounds like a reasonable justification for refusing to have women at all or, in some cases, perhaps one or two women in sets of chambers containing twenty to thirty barristers. Many chambers now have what one respondent referred to as 'the statutory woman'; however he went on to allude to the limited openings for women:

> 'That was a factor in their decision on whether the ladies got tenancies. I know that certain members were saying, "Well, we'll have to watch the proportion, basically, of ladies to gentlemen", even though their numbers were significantly less than the males. And of course it would not be a factor if any man applied – basically, no one says, "Well, there's fourteen men and three ladies." It's just another man.'

These kinds of rationalizations and justifications for discrimination against women constitute a problem of considerable proportions for women in both branches of the profession.

What male lawyers feel about women lawyers

The interviews provided a considerable amount of information on male lawyers' attitudes and opinions regarding their women colleagues. Although some respondents took a neutral or positive view, many men expressed thinly veiled or open hostility and prejudice towards women in the profession. It was clear that many men lawyers saw women as a very different species whose personal qualities rendered them 'unsuited' to legal practice. A less extreme version of this view held that women were particularly suited to certain areas of legal work but not to others.

WOMEN AS SEXUAL OBJECTS

There was evidence in the interviews with men lawyers of a tendency on the part of some of them to evaluate women colleagues in terms of their sexual attractiveness and personal appearance, rather than as fellow professionals. For instance, a man solicitor commented, on the idea of a woman practising in the profession:

> 'The advantage that she may have is that she may be quite pretty and therefore have a mild sort of sexual attraction to the tribunal that she's appearing in front of. If you've got a young twenty-five-year-old [woman] barrister in that position, with a judge in his fifties . . . it may appeal to his almost paternal instincts.'

This is an evaluation based on the age and sexual attractiveness to men of particular women, rather than on professional competence. It also contains the implication that men in general will evaluate women in this way and that professional advantage will accrue to women whose attributes as sexual objects are positively evaluated. This set of assumptions contains at least two problems for women. First, if they are perceived as gaining professional advantage by being 'attractive', the advantage gained is bound to be regarded by men as unfair, resulting in further resentment of women in the profession and perhaps as a justification for discrimination against them. Second, what of the women who fail to conform to the male criteria for successful sexual objectification, because they are not young enough to be so regarded, or because they are not deemed to be 'attractive' (or whatever)? Surely the implication here is that such women might be

123

professionally disadvantaged by their lack of 'success' as sexual objects?

Another solicitor remarked:

'In certain sorts of cases I would think a woman is helpful. In court work occasionally she's useful because if you get somebody who's a good-looking lady then, unfortunate though it might be, they can often get a better deal . . . if they go about things correctly and they look smart.'

This embodies the same kinds of assumptions referred to above. The resentment expressed here is quite explicit, however, and does not need to be implied from what is said. This remark goes somewhat further as well, in the sense that it is suggested that not only may women (or, rather, 'good-looking ladies') be treated better by courts and tribunals, but also that they may be more likely to achieve their desired legal outcomes as a result of their personal appearance and (by implication) sexual attractiveness to the largely male judiciary. The extent to which men in the profession believe this to be the case will obviously have an effect on the extent to which women lawyers are accepted or rejected by their male colleagues. A male barrister said, of his female colleagues: 'In crime, if you're well turned out and you're a nice looking female, then you tend to attract the customers because of what you look like, as opposed to how good you are.' The perception of this man was, therefore, that 'nice looking' women will be better treated in court, and not only are they thus likely to achieve better outcomes, but it is their sexual attractiveness that enables them to obtain the work in the first place! On this view, however the work of women lawyers is evaluated – whether it is on quantity, quality, level, successful outcome, or whatever else – it can always be written down or written off by men as a product of women's success as sexual objects rather than as legal professionals. This seems to represent a no-win situation as far as women are concerned. It also has the air of being an extremely useful form of defensive reasoning for men, particularly men who might not be as successful as they would wish.

One of the barristers interviewed dismissed the whole subject of women colleagues by saying: 'Well, it's always nice to have a pretty face around.' This represents total devaluation of women lawyers, reduced to the status of 'a pretty face', welcomed in offices or chambers for their decorative qualities rather than their professional competences and abilities. Such attitudes serve to marginalize women as much as any of the factors we discuss in this chapter. These attitudes are encapsulated in the following quotation from an interview with a solicitor, who was discussing the nature of his work:

'You're in the sort of job where you can work eighteen hours one day and if you pinch a couple of hours off the next afternoon to meet some bird in a wine bar, then, you know, you can generally – you'd better edit that bit – you can generally organize things, I think.'

Where men hold and express such attitudes towards women in general, it is extremely difficult to believe that they will regard women colleagues as competent professionals who are equal to themselves.[15]

WOMEN AS DIFFERENT KINDS OF BEINGS

Many of the interviews suggested that the view was prevalent amongst men lawyers that women are in some quiet way entirely 'different' from men, as a function of their gender. The idea that women are somehow 'different' from men continues to survive, despite considerable evidence that there is a large amount of overlap between women and men in terms of personal qualities, abilities, and so forth (King 1974). A typical remark came from one of the solicitors: 'I do think that . . . their [women's] emotional make-up is so different. It isn't just sort of a physiological thing . . . it's a whole make-up which is entirely emotionally different, it operates completely differently.' This is not just a discussion of differences of biology. The belief here is in some kind of gendered difference – innate and very considerable – in thought processes and mental responses between women and men.

How does this alleged gender difference manifest itself? A solicitor observed: 'I think there's a tremendous potential there [if] solicitors would allow it to be developed, for the feminine perspective to be put across which is often warmer and softer and more concerned for people than perhaps males are.' We found this to be an extremely prevalent stereotype amongst men lawyers. It is widely held by men generally.[16] There is an assumption that women are innately gentler, more caring, and more 'people-orientated' than are men. This seems to be a comprehensive derivation from the kinds of unpaid domestic servicing activities of men, children, the elderly, and the ill traditionally undertaken by women in the home, what is assumed to be 'innately' women's work. In another interview we were told:

'that men and women see things from a different perspective and I therefore try and make allowance for that and am more tolerant to women, whereas with men I'm probably more impatient with them when they don't really seem to understand what I'm trying to explain.'

Here is further support for the perception, by some men lawyers, that women are different kinds of beings. Here, also, there is the definite implication that women are also regarded as *inferior* types of beings. 'Different' in this context clearly does not imply 'equal' as well, because the difference is something towards which 'tolerance' and 'patience' must be extended. There is a suggestion that there is something about women which makes them naturally 'slower on the uptake'. One may also see evidence here of a belief in a basic level of shared understanding existing between men, but not between women and men.

WOMEN GET EMOTIONALLY INVOLVED

This section is relevant to the earlier discussion about the nature of the legal profession, as identified by men lawyers. We summed this up as 'objectivity, logicality, and pragmatism'. It was clear from the interviews that many men lawyers felt that women did not possess these qualities. One solicitor said of this: 'If I was going to instruct somebody I wouldn't necessarily want a woman to act for me, because I think they tend to be . . . less pragmatic about the problems and more emotional.' The term 'emotional' was frequently used by men to describe women and formed a central part of their stereotypes about what women are like, and was obviously a highly undesirable characteristic for a professional to possess.[17]

A solicitor noted that: 'It's more frequent that they [women] get tied up in the case than a man does.' This kind of 'involvement' with work is regarded as undesirable and unprofessional behaviour, although characteristic of women, as we shall go on to explore. Another interviewee remarked on this:

'In cases of rape and sexual assaults and other offences, perhaps on children, I think they find it harder than a male to remain professionally objective. . . . I would have thought that in those sorts of cases she would have greater difficulty in maintaining her independent judgement.'

Here, clearly, being 'professional' is equated with being 'objective'; so saying that women become personally involved in their work, that they become 'emotionally involved' or 'subjective', amounts to saying that women are 'unprofessional', or at least not as professional as men.

These kinds of points were sometimes made in a rather different way, which on the face of it was rather more sympathetic to women lawyers. A solicitor described the greater 'emotional involvement' of women lawyers with their work as follows:

'I suspect that in certain fields of work they may more easily strike a rapport with the client. I think particularly, obviously, divorce work where they're acting for the wife . . . in conveyancing. . . . To most solicitors it's just another file, but for most women actually involved in moving house it's a fairly traumatic experience and I think a girl lawyer is more readily able to appreciate it.'

At first glance, a greater degree of 'rapport with the client' would seem to be an advantageous characteristic for women lawyers to possess. However, as we have shown elsewhere (Podmore and Spencer 1984), many women lawyers are channelled (and indeed channel themselves) into certain areas of work deemed most 'appropriate' for them and allow themselves to be directed away from others. The 'appropriate' work tends to be of lower status, less financially rewarding, less demanding, and less 'visible'. Matrimonial and conveyancing work are good examples of legal 'women's work'. The remark quoted above may be seen as a justification for keeping women within those areas of work thought (by men) to be particularly appropriate to women by virtue of their gender, by claiming that women are particularly effective within such areas. The reason advanced for women's suitability to such work is actually the other side of the coin of the argument that women are not sufficiently 'objective'.

The tendency of male lawyers to present damaging stereotypes about women in such a way that, initially, it seems flattering to them can be illustrated from another interview, with a barrister: 'If anything I'm more cautious against women barristers because I don't have that intuitive flair, which some have . . . that sort of emotional grasp of the thing.' This statement reiterates the argument about the greater 'emotional involvement' of women which, as we have already indicated, is regarded by many men lawyers as somewhat 'unprofessional'. It also adds another familiar term to the stereotype of women –

that they are 'intuitive'. A comment from another interview develops this notion further: 'It's dreadful getting them [women] in matrimonial work . . . against you, because . . . they are inclined to be a little more subjective. Perhaps they *feel* it more, who knows?' This expresses the stereotype in more pejorative terms. After all it may be the case that if women *do* tend to be more 'involved' with their work than men, this may be due to the need for women to achieve success to a greater extent than men, in order to obtain the same degree of recognition. (A number of writers have noted that women in a 'man's world' are expected to perform much better than their male counterparts.)[18] If all this is true (and we have only the word of men lawyers on women's greater 'emotional involvement'), it might tend to make women lawyers actually more dangerous opponents in litigation. Some men might need such a convenient rationalization to explain away their own relative lack of success, either in general or in cases against women lawyers.

WOMEN AREN'T TOUGH ENOUGH – OR ELSE THEY'RE MUCH TOO TOUGH

We have argued that the legal profession is regarded by male lawyers as both aggressive and competitive. Concomitant with this is the perceived need (by male lawyers) for legal practitioners to be 'tough', together with a belief that women will not be 'tough enough'. A solicitor said of this: 'The main disadvantage is that they're generally not tough enough. Intellectually they've usually got what it takes, but not many women are sufficiently tough to stand the rough and tumble of the sort of practice that this is.' The problem here for women is that being 'tough' conflicts with being 'feminine'. 'Toughness' may well be a type of behaviour which is difficult for women to learn; 'toughness' is seen by men lawyers as essentially a 'masculine' attribute. A solicitor said, bluntly: 'Women are temperamentally unsuited to the work. They burst into tears if spoken harshly to.' It is implied here that 'toughness' is not a learned behaviour anyway, but a temperamental predisposition, the lack of which automatically disqualifies women from practising as lawyers.

It is instructive to go on from this to consider how men lawyers react when women *are* seen as being 'tough' or otherwise not conforming to the 'feminine' stereotype. A solicitor told us about his experience with a woman articled clerk: 'I had a woman articled clerk two years ago who was a bloody pain in the neck and in fact we had to ask her to transfer her articles. . . . She was rude and didn't realize that I was the boss . . . she was a right little madam.' What seems to have happened here is a breakdown in the 'dynamics of deference' (Bell and Newby 1976), with the male solicitor unable to accept any challenge to his superordinacy. This reaction might be based on hierarchy rather than gender, but we find the use of the phrase 'right little madam' to describe the woman as an indication that it was *as a woman*, as well as an articled clerk, that she had failed to 'know her place'. A barrister said, indicating the effects of a legal career on women: 'It has the effect of hardening women up. It must do, I mean it does. It produces its little numbers of tough spinsters, I think.' This is not an edifying image and it cannot be reassuring to women lawyers to be regarded in such a derogatory light. This is a particularly unflattering appellation, given the evidence from the interviews with women lawyers of a fairly high level of preoccupation with the maintenance of a 'feminine' identity as a response to working in a 'masculine' profession.

The comments of a male barrister on the subject of women judges (that is, women who have been outstandingly successful in their legal careers) serve as a suitable conclusion:

> 'The lady judges I've been in front of . . . have all been on the hard side. . . . Perhaps they had to work bloody hard . . . to get there, so they had to be hard as nails to get there in the first place and, well, some of them are mothers so they can't be bereft of all emotion. . . . In my experience . . . the lady judges have always been harder than the men.'

Conclusion

This chapter has tried to capture the classic 'double-bind'[19] for women working in a male-dominated and male-orientated profession and the basic incongruity between their personal identity as 'feminine' and their membership of a profession which is strongly 'masculine'. Women lawyers are essentially marginal members of their profession and can find themselves in a 'no-win' situation. If they attempt to conform to the dominant male norms of the profession, they will be regarded as 'unnatural' women;[20] while if they distance themselves from professional norms they will not be accepted by men as competent professional colleagues. In the last resort, however, whatever women actually do and however they behave, they are still left with the problem that some men will persist in evaluating them only as sexual objects, as we have shown.

This rather depressing picture represents what we captured in the early 1980s when the interviews were carried out. At that time only one practising lawyer in ten was a woman. In the mid-1980s one lawyer in eight is a woman and the proportion is increasing at the rate of about three-quarters of a percentage point each year. At this rate, by the mid-1990s over 20 per cent of practising lawyers will be women. We have argued elsewhere (Podmore and Spencer 1982b: 31) that as women enter the legal profession in increasing numbers they are likely to be less and less willing to accept consignment to a marginal status. If we are correct in this assertion then male attitudes and actions will be under increasing pressure to change. We recognize that change in the deeply held assumptions which this chapter has highlighted will be a lengthy, difficult, and conflictual process.

Acknowledgements

The support of the Economic and Social Research Council and of the Department of Management Studies, Sheffield City Polytechnic, is gratefully acknowledged.

Notes

1 In 1984 there were 5,497 practising women solicitors in England and Wales (12.3 per cent of the total) and 641 practising women barristers (again, 12.3 per cent of the total).

2 We recognize that there are other factors which contribute to the marginal status of women (see Spencer and Podmore 1983).

3 Over 80 per cent of these lawyers were in private practice and the remainder worked in local government, commercial and business firms. All of the solicitors were located in the West Midlands; many of the barristers were from the Midlands but some practised in London and elsewhere.

4 Women lawyers experience a considerable 'deficit in rewards' compared with their male counterparts. Ten years ago women barristers' earnings were only 50–60 per cent those of men, even when barristers of similar seniority and doing similar work were compared (Royal Commission on Legal Services 1979: 444).

5 The whole atmosphere of the courts is unsympathetic to women:

'There is a tendency to ignore women lawyers, to suggest their invisibility by using the collective "gentlemen" when addressing counsel, even if it includes a woman. Judges may also invoke a sort of sexual or frivolous imagery which can unnerve women lawyers. One judge, seeing a group of women counsel waiting to go into court, said: "I see we've got the chorus girls here today."'

(Pattullo 1983: 7)

6 We have argued elsewhere that society is pervaded by a set of 'taken for granted' beliefs about the characteristics and qualities of men and women. Men are characterized in terms of objectivity, logicality, independence, competence, etc.; women in terms of warmth, sensitivity, expressiveness, and compliance (Podmore and Spencer 1982a: 22–3).

7 More than one writer has suggested that the increased entry of women into an occupation or profession lowers its prestige and desirability as a career for men. See Touhey (1974).

8 Some male lawyers scarcely bother to conceal their prejudice against women, as the work of Kennedy (1978) and Pattullo (1983) similarly indicates.

9 In 1984 only thirty-two of the 940 appeal, High Court and circuit judges and recorders were women, and only seventeen out of the 809 Queen's Counsel. In fifteen leading London solicitors' firms, there were only thirty women amongst a total of 711 full partners!

10 A woman barrister gave this example of a male client's attitude:

'I remember having an absolutely hopeless case once. I had to defend a careless driving. . . . There were four prosecuting witnesses against him and three passengers in his own car who wouldn't give evidence for him. He insisted on pleading not guilty and, not surprisingly, was found guilty and afterwards he said to me: "Everyone told me I'd lose if I'd got a dolly bird as my barrister"!'

11 See Podmore and Spencer (1982b) and, for a full discussion of the opposition to women's entry to the profession, Sachs and Wilson (1978).

12 There is, presumably, no certainty that a *man*, once he has joined a firm of solicitors or a set of barristers' chambers, will remain *in situ* until retirement age. This does not, however, seem to render men 'unreliable' by virtue of their gender!

13 See Spencer and Podmore (1984: 48).

14 On this see Kennedy (1978).

15 It is not just junior lawyers who refer to women colleagues in so derogatory a manner. As suggested in note 5 above, judges do likewise. Some male lawyers reveal their sexism in the opposite way (which can be equally frustrating for the recipients), by excessive 'courtesy' and 'chivalry' towards their women colleagues – see Cheeld (1976).

16 And by women too? – see Broverman *et al.* (1972).

17 This quality is said to render women unsuitable for management positions, too (Kanter 1977: 201–05; Seear *et al.* 1964: 92).

18 See, for example, Dinerman (1969: 952), Fogarty *et al.* (1971:48).

19 On the 'double-bind' situation, see Prather (1971) and Chapman (1978).

20 As Margaret Mead observed: 'Each step forward in work . . . means a step backward as a woman' (1962: 289).

References

Bell, C. and Newby, H. (1976) Husbands and Wives: The Dynamics of the Deferential Dialectic. In D.L. Barker and S. Allen (eds) *Dependence and Exploitation in Work and Marriage*. London: Longman, pp. 152–68.

Broverman, I.K., Vogel, S.R., Broverman, D.M., Clarkson, F.E., and Rosenkrantz, P.S. (1972) Sex-role Stereotypes: A Current Appraisal. *Journal of Social Issues* 28 (2): 59–78.

Chapman, J.B. (1978) Male and Female Leadership Styles – the Double Bind. In J.A. Ramaley (ed.) *Covert Discrimination and Women in the Sciences*. Boulder, CO: Westview Press, pp. 97–123.

Cheeld, D. (1976) The Rise of an Angry Young Woman. *The Law Society's Gazette* 73: 634–35.

Dinerman, B. (1969) Sex Discrimination in the Legal Profession. *American Bar Association Journal* 60: 951–54.

Epstein, C.F. (1974) Ambiguity as Social Control: Consequences for Women in Professional Elites. In P.L. Stewart and M.G. Cantor (eds) *Varieties of Work Experience*. Cambridge, MA: Schenkman, pp. 26–38.

— (1981) *Women in Law*. New York: Basic Books.

Fogarty, M., Allen, A.J., Allen, I. and Walters, P. (1971) *Women in Top Jobs: Four Studies in Achievement*. London: Allen and Unwin.

Kanter, R.M. (1975) Women and the Structure of Organizations: Explorations in Theory and Behaviour. In M. Millman and R.M. Kanter (eds) *Another Voice*. Garden City, NY: Anchor Books, pp. 37–74.

— (1977) *Men and Women of the Corporation*, New York: Basic Books.

Kennedy, H. (1978) Women at the Bar. In R. Hazell (ed.) *The Bar on Trial*. London: Quartet Books, pp. 148–62.

King, J.S. (1974) *Women and Work: Sex Differences and Society*. London: HMSO.

Long, N. (1958) The Local Community as an Ecology of Games. *American Journal of Sociology* 64: 251–61.

Lorber, J. (1975) Women and Medical Sociology: Invisible Professionals and Ubiquitous Patients. In M. Millman and R.M. Kanter (eds) *Another Voice*. Garden City, NY: Anchor Books, pp. 75–105.

Mead, M. (1962) *Male and Female*. Harmondsworth: Penguin.

Pattullo, P. (1983) *Judging Women: A Study of Attitudes That Rule Our Legal System*. London: National Council for Civil Liberties, Rights for Women Unit.

Podmore, D. and Spencer, A. (1982a) The Law as a Sex-typed Profession. *Journal of Law and Society* 9: 21–36.

— (1982b) Women Lawyers in England: The Experience of Inequality. *Work and Occupations* 9: 337–61.

— (1984) *Gender in the Labour Process – the Case of Women and Men Lawyers*. Paper presented to a conference on the organization and control of the labour process, University of Aston.

Prather, J. (1971) Why Can't Women Be More Like Men: A Summary of the Sociopsychological Factors Hindering Women's Advancement in the Professions. *American Behavioural Scientist* 15: 172–82.

Quandango, J. (1976) Occupational Sex-typing and Internal Labour Market

Distributions: An Assessment of Medical Specialities. *Social Problems* 23: 442–53.

Robin, S.S. (1969) The Female in Engineering. In R. Perrucci and J.E. Gerstl (eds) *The Engineer and the Social System*. New York: Wiley, pp. 203–18.

Royal Commission on Legal Services (1979) *Final Report*, vol. 2. London: HMSO.

Sachs, A. and Wilson, J.H. (1978) *Sexism and the Law*. London: Martin Robertson.

Seear, N., Roberts, V., and Brock, J. (eds) (1964) *A Career for Women in Industry?* London: Oliver and Boyd.

Spencer, A. and Podmore, D. (1983) *Life on the Periphery of a Profession: The Experience of Women Lawyers*. Paper presented to British Sociological Association Conference, University College, Cardiff.

—(1984) Women in a Male-dominated Profession in England: Pressure and Strain in Family and Domestic Life. *International Journal of Sociology of the Family* 14: 47–66.

Touhey, J.C. (1974) Effects of Additional Women Professionals on Ratings of Occupational Prestige and Desirability. *Journal of Personality and Social Psychology* 29: 86–9.

© 1987 Anne Spencer and David Podmore

7

The Fifth Dimension –
Gender and General Practice

Barbara Lawrence

This chapter is based on a study of single-handed women general practitioners, carried out in Birmingham and the Midlands. It acts as a case study to illustrate how aspects of general practice are organized in relation to issues of gender. In order to set the study in its appropriate context, I begin by considering the role of the 'family doctor', the development of group practice, women in medicine, and women in general practice.

The 'family doctor'

General practice in recent years has come to be viewed as a specialism within medicine and has consequently evolved out of the embodiment of the old 'family doctor' ethos. The term 'general practitioner' still evokes images of traditional general practice, despite significant changes in its organization. Historically, the GP or family doctor (who was almost invariably male) worked completely alone. In some cases the services of a receptionist were employed, although this position was usually filled by the doctor's wife (Finch 1983). In fact, with the surgery being so often attached to the GP's home, his professional and home life were inextricably intermingled. It was not only the doctor's wife who was so important to the smooth running of the practice; his whole family were incorporated into and bound up in this demanding 'life' profession, a profession which was part of life and family. The term *'family* doctor', then, was evocative not only of the man who cared for and treated whole families and became a part of his community's family life, but also of a man who brought his whole family into the forefront of this caring role. He was himself the epitome of the good 'family' man, father to his own children and 'father' to his community of patients. His wife, too, was the community's 'mother' and confidante, as well as mother to her children and organizer of both home and (to some extent at least) practice. The doctor's family was the model for family life and his own life was that of the family man in all senses of the word, both professionally and domestically. In the fashion of the good father he altruistically 'sacrificed' himself to his own family and to his professional 'family'.

The concept of the 'family' doctor as depicted in the ideal type thus had considerable implications for the life of the traditional GP and for the development of the present general practitioner service. In looking at how the traditional single-handed GP ran his practice, it is clear that the concept of 'organization' in general practice did not exist as such. The GP ran morning and evening surgeries for five days a week, plus one on a Saturday, and between surgeries visited patients in their homes – being on call seven days and seven nights a week. This 'total' profession, as it could be called (similar to the idea of 'total' institutions),[1] became for many an intolerable pressure – GPs were never able to go home and just shut the door. There was clearly a need for rethinking and reorganizing general practice, which could both increase efficiency and improve the general practitioner service for the benefit of the doctor, his family, and his patients.

Appointment systems were rarely found in traditional general practices (some GPs still prefer not to use them (Cartwright and Anderson 1981)) and there was a much greater amount of home visiting of patients, a factor which has diminished through the much wider use of cars and telephones and the nature of illness and treatment. There have been other changes, too, which have affected the nature of general practice – such as the creation of the National Health Service, which altered fundamentally the system of remuneration despite GPs retaining their independent contractor status. So, the recent organization of general practice has been characterized more and more by alternatives to the traditional single-handed GP and 'family' doctor.

The development of group practice[2]

The discussion of possible changes to the traditional family doctor method of practising and the discouragement of single-handed practice goes back many years. As long ago as 1920 the Dawson Report favoured the concept of group practices operating out of health centres and this idea has been followed by a number of other committees and advisory groups subsequently, who have argued the case against single-handed practice. The case against single-handed practice has stressed such issues as the advantages of peer influence and informal learning within groups to raise the standard of care, and hence the status of the general practitioner, leading to more satisfaction in their work. In addition, financial arguments have been advanced, concerning the ability of group practice to provide better premises and equipment and more ancillary help. A more varied professional life is possible too, it has been claimed, since more opportunities exist for GPs to hold outside appointments, with the greater flexibility which becomes possible in the management of time. And group practice, it has been suggested, provides a more realistic method of organization for the development of primary health care teams (Bowling 1981). In effect there has been an increasing weight of argument positively to promote group practice as beneficial for both doctors and patients, while single-handed practice has been negatively assessed as out-moded and detrimental to both.

The watershed in the change from the great majority of doctors practising single-handedly to a majority practising in groups and partnerships (of whatever size) seems to have been the 'Doctors' Charter' of 1965 (Fry 1979). This came as a result of considerable unrest on the part of general practitioners over the status of GPs in comparison with hospital consultants, arising from the system of remuneration in general practice. General practitioners threatened to withdraw from the NHS in 1965 in response to what they saw as the government's inaction regarding their case. The threat of mass resignations from the NHS brought the government into direct negotiations with the profession over the Charter, resulting in a contract which included some, but not all, of its demands. The new contract which emerged forms the basis of the present structure of general practice. The contract consisted of a basic payment available at the full rate to doctors with at least 1,000 patients who provided full services for a minimum period in each week, available at proportionally reduced rates to other doctors. Additional payments were made in respect of group practice and practice in deprived areas. There were distinction awards depending on doctors' attendance at postgraduate training courses. There were additional services remunerated on an item of service basis, capitation fees with an age allowance for patients over sixty-five of 30 per cent higher than for other patients, and night and weekend work were remunerated as were home visits between midnight and 7 a.m. Six weeks' paid holiday and a notional five and a half day week were established, on condition that doctors arranged for patient care in their absence (Bowling 1981).

Most significant in the present context was the establishment of financial incentives for group practices. The movement towards group practice between the early 1950s and the early 1970s was very considerable; in 1951, 80 per cent of GPs practised single-handedly whilst by 1971, 80 per cent practised in partnerships of two or more. This figure has remained more or less stable since the early 1970s and a large proportion of the doctors who do not work single-handedly still practise in small groups or partnerships. Bowling (1981) has suggested that this could possibly be because the concept of group practice and the primary health care team are anathema to the traditional notion of independence still respected by many doctors.

In their study of general practice, Cartwright and Anderson (1981) looked at doctors' and patients' perspectives of partnerships/groups and single-handed practice, and compared these with Cartwright's earlier study published in 1967. Their findings are particularly interesting in relation to debates about size of practice and the advantages and disadvantages embodied in partnership size. They concluded that: 'people's relationships with and opinions about their doctor vary remarkably little with the number of doctors in the practice' (Cartwright and Anderson 1981: 17).

The authors picked out a number of ways in which practising single-handedly or in partnerships affect the quality of practice and of life for both doctors and patients. For example, doctors in partnerships are on call at night less than those working single-handedly, have more ancillary help, better facilities, and carry out more procedures themselves. Single-handed GPs rarely take GP trainees into their practices for a period of training under the Vocational Training Scheme. Despite these differences the study suggested that there seems to be little relationship between GPs' enjoyment of their practice and whether or not they practise single-handedly or in a partnership. There was, however, somewhat more frustration experienced in practising in partnership, but no difference in frustration levels caused by lack of leisure or free time. Of significance was the fact that satisfaction with the care given to patients increased with the length of time patients had been with their doctor, and not with the size of practice partnership.

In summing up the findings of their comparison between single-handed GPs and those in partnerships, Cartwright and Anderson suggested that the decline in single-handed practice and increase in partnerships with three or more doctors appears to have had little effect on the nature of general practitioner care or on patient–doctor relationships (1981: 40). Changes in the organization of general practice since the 1967 study were considerable, while those in the basic relationship between patients and doctors were small and mainly insignificant.

Such findings are interesting if one considers the reasons behind the initial impetus and subsequent moves towards partnerships and away from single-handed practice. They suggest that the advantages claimed for partnerships and group practices have been over-stated. This study similarly shows some of the benefits of single-handed practice as far as GPs (and, in particular, women doctors) are concerned.

Women in medicine

There is an extensive body of literature illustrating the male-dominated nature of many of the professions, and medicine is a good example of such a profession. Elston (1977, 1980) has provided an historical analysis which illuminates the strategies by which male supremacy has been built up and maintained within the medical profession. She has also documented the steps by which women have now become a substantial proportion of medical school intakes and also made it clear that there are a number of other factors which need to be considered when looking at the position of women in medicine. Perhaps, though, one factor in the increase of women in medicine is that it has been seen as a more suitable 'science-based' career for a woman to pursue than pure science or engineering (Kelly 1975). Women who go to medical school are more likely to be drawn from higher-status backgrounds than are men, and are also less likely to fail examinations. But, as Elston (1980) has remarked, this early promise is not on the whole reflected in later working life. The early promise which gains entry into medical school is quickly and adversely affected (however successfully a woman performs in that context) by a background of a student culture which is predominantly male and which is continued into the professional career (Becker 1961; Young 1981).

Academic success is only part of the key to a successful medical career, of course. Elston (1980) has cited studies which demonstrate that women in a number of professional fields are excluded from key learning contexts – informal settings such as clubs, changing rooms, and bars – and thus may not learn the importance of informal contacts, and therefore fail to develop them (Lorber 1975, 1984; Smith 1976). Domestic commitments, too, can limit out-of-hours interaction with peers and prospective patrons and women are consequently either formally or informally excluded from this 'inner fraternity', thus circumscribing their career opportunities (Epstein 1970; Lorber 1975, 1984). Several studies of the medical profession have shown that, despite women having better academic records, men progress further and more quickly through the various grades to consultant levels and have more postgraduate qualifications (Aird and Silver 1971; Beaumont 1978; Jefferys and Elliott 1966).

There has been a change in the nature of the objections made by men to women entering the medical profession. In the nineteenth century objections typically focused on the 'unsexing' effects of exposure to anatomy; now they concern the question of 'wastage'. According to Elston (1977, 1980) this objection is couched in the terms that it is undesirable to waste scarce and expensive resources on training women who, ultimately, will give priority to domestic commitments (or, as Leeson and Gray (1978) have phrased it, the view that women keep prospective male colleagues out of medical school by selfishly occupying 'their' places!). The discussion of 'wastage' is linked to the question of women's 'domestic' role and the problem of reconciling professional and domestic lives (Lawrence 1984). For present purposes it should be recognized that this problem of reconciliation has a profound effect not only on how women's loyalties and commitments are distributed between work and home life, but also in expectations of their achievements, possibilities, and even the medical speciality they follow.[3]

In medicine (as in other male-dominated professions) there is a decreasing proportion of women at progressively higher levels of the training ladder. In addition, there is a low percentage of women at consultant grades and an uneven distribution of women consultants across the specialities. It is evident that any growth in numbers of women consultants is only likely in those specialities where women are already comparatively well represented at more junior levels. The uneven distribution of women across the fields of medicine is not solely the outcome of 'choice'; that is, the exercise of personal

139

preference is not the main factor in determining where women (and indeed men) work. Women are most heavily represented in community medicine and school health services, in general practice, and in certain hospital specialisms such as anaesthetics, radiology, mental illness, and children's mental illness (Mackie and Pattullo 1977). These are areas which typically have more flexible working arrangements and which permit resolution, or partial resolution, of the real or potential role conflicts between work and home. Another reason sometimes put forward for the high proportion of women in such specialties is, of course, that women have the 'appropriate' personal characteristics for such work. However, some of women's supposed 'innate characteristics' – such as manual dexterity, for example – do not seem to lead to many women specializing in plastic or neuro-surgery, nor does their supposed 'special knowledge' lead to many being employed in obstetrics, gynaecology, or paediatrics! (Young 1981).

Women in general practice

General practice is viewed as particularly suitable for married women and those with children because of its possibilities for flexible working arrangements. Rhodes has claimed that more and more women are working in general practice because work in it is 'sometimes easier to arrange to suit a variety of circumstances, including running a home, than work as a consultant in hospital' (Rhodes 1983: 964). Despite this, in 1985 women made up only 18 per cent of all GPs in England and Wales. The fact that women working full-time seem to have less chance of finding a partnership than their male colleagues, and the lack of part-time jobs in those areas where part-time training schemes are well established, could be major factors in preventing more women from entering general practice in the first place (McPherson and Small 1980).

It has been suggested that women have a special role to play in general practice as a result of their 'nurturative female mentality', which is seen as particularly desirable in general practice (*Journal of the Royal College of GPs* 1979). Most authorities, however, challenge such a suggestion. According to Cartwright and Anderson's study, there is no evidence that women GPs adopt a more expressive role than their male colleagues. They observed that what was noticeable was the general *lack* of differences between men and women GPs. The main difference seemed to be that women doctors had rather fewer patients than male doctors (Cartwright and Anderson 1981).

Others have discussed in some detail the advantages and dis-advantages for patients in having a woman GP, as well as the particular attributes women may bring to general practice, especially in relation to women patients. Sex-stereotyping appears to be an explanation for the present gender distribution of patients (Jefferys and Sachs 1983; Leeson and Gray 1978; Marinker 1975). The suggestion is that most women patients prefer women GPs, because they are thought to be more sympathetic and more caring, better communicators, and well qualified for dealing with women and children because of a supposed common experience. Bhargava has drawn a distinction between sex-stereotyping and sex congruency, defining the latter as 'perceived compatibility between sex-role expectations and the demands of a specialty' (1983: 1020). Sex congruency is rooted in and stems from sex-stereotyping, the nature of which varies, of course, from society to society. This leads, for example, to women hospital doctors in India specializing largely in obstetrics and gynaecology because of strong norms concerning women's modesty. Thus, ethnicity and culture can play a part in the consulting patterns and expectations of patients.

The question of patient preferences has been examined by Gray (1982), who looked at the effect of the doctor's sex on the doctor–patient relationship. She concluded that communication is easier, more time is given, drugs are less frequently dispensed, and women patients are treated more seriously if the doctor is a woman. Barrett and Roberts (1978) and Roberts (1985) have shown how middle-aged women patients often are not taken seriously by male GPs, being treated as intrinsically 'sick' rather than as being, in many cases, victims of having to conform to a female stereotypical role in the home.

Finally, Young looked at the dichotomy that exists between being a woman on the one hand and being a doctor on the other, arising from the male orientation of the medical profession (although this is less noticeable in general practice than in hospitals and other areas of medicine):

'This is because the relationship between doctor and patient is more intimate, more trusting and more lasting, and because GPs work one-to-one with their patients and are asked to meet very real demands day-to-day, whether "trivial" or not, whether emotional, social or physical.'

(Young 1981: 155)

She suggested that there is less possibility of hiding behind a mythical image or a totally physically orientated way of thinking. It is apparent, though, that many GPs maintain in their relationships with their patients much of the distance imbued by hospital indoctrination at earlier stages of their careers.

The contention of this chapter is that gender is a crucial factor in understanding doctors' orientations to general practice. The studies discussed above form the background against which I will consider the experience of single-handed women GPs.

Single-handed women GPs – a case study

Single-handed women general practitioners are an example of a minority group choosing to operate in a particularly difficult and demanding area of professional practice. With growing government pressure to discourage single-handed practice (this was reviewed in some detail in the Acheson Report (1981)), there is some justification for studying this small group of doctors. In particular, as will become evident, a study of single-handed women GPs highlights more clearly the problems and pressures faced by *all* women doctors and, on a wider scale, by all women in male-dominated professions.

In this research, interviews were carried out with twenty-nine single-handed women GPs in the Midlands.[4] Single-handed GPs made up 14.7 per cent of GPs nationally in 1981, largely concentrated in inner-city areas. There were considerable variations between cities in the proportion of single-handed practitioners – in London the figure was 34.4 per cent and in Birmingham 22 per cent. Of the single-handed GPs in Birmingham, 20 per cent were women, although women only make up 8 per cent of all Birmingham GPs (compared with 18 per cent nationally).[5]

The main thrust of this chapter is to examine the reasons why the single-handed women GPs decided to practise on their own. All the changes that have occurred in the organization of primary health care provision (appointment systems, bleeps, deputizing services, greater emphasis on partnerships, health centres, and so on) have been designed to ease the pressure on the GP and to increase efficiency in the delivery of services to patients. However, some GPs reject some (and in a few cases practically all) of the advantages and facilities of group practice in favour of working single-handedly. It will be argued that the reasons for this are structural, personal, and interpersonal and that there are specific reasons related to gender which encompass these.

Group practice came about as both a negative and a positive reaction to single-handed practice, as has been indicated. The recommendations of the Acheson Report (1981) were unfavourable to the concept of single-handed practice and favoured the use of incentives to encourage GPs to practise in partnerships and groups. However, many of those who now choose to practise single-handedly do so as a negative reaction against group practice and partnerships and because of a positive attraction towards single-handed practice. It is this negative/positive dichotomy that will now be explored empirically. It will become apparent that some of the important negative reactions against group and partnership practice are gender-specific. These negative and positive reactions to group and single-handed practice are highly interrelated. They are discussed under four headings – financial grievances, personal relationships, continuity, and independence. A fifth dimension which interacts with the other four categories, gender and 'ghettoism', forms the concluding section in which the importance of gender influences throughout the chapter are brought into focus.

Financial grievances

The financial grievances expressed by many of the women GPs were directly attributable to the structure of general practice and had contributed to their decisions to leave partnerships and groups for single-handed practice. Several respondents mentioned financial exploitation by male senior partners, this was particularly difficult to tackle because of the unequal status between the partners. Such grievances were closely related, also, to the problem of personal relationships which arise in many businesses and partnerships (this is discussed below). Financial problems were often linked with 'personality clashes', exacerbated by the unequal status which in many cases amounted to blatant exploitation, in that the women GPs felt that they had to shoulder the greatest burden of work for the least reward. Some saw their male senior partners putting little effort into the practice, but reaping the greater financial benefits. Several women stressed how the 'financial hardship' (*Pulse* 1983) which single-handed practice undoubtedly imposes was, in most cases, *less* onerous than past experiences of financial exploitation by seniors in group practices.

Several different aspects of financial exploitation were raised. One woman, whose previous experience of practice had been solely with her husband, had steered clear of joining a partnership after his death even though, as she remarked, 'Financially I would have been much better off.' Another experienced great difficulty in getting a single-handed practice, had been particularly keen to do so, and had not been disappointed when she achieved it because:

'Whatever you do you are doing for your choice, and whatever you get, you get it in your hand. . . . There [in a group practice] you worked and you *didn't* get anything in your hand . . . you just did what the senior partner . . . what he wanted, you did.'

Another GP described at length the financial aspects of her disillusionment with group practice, which she believed was crucially related to her two months' maternity leave. She explained 'a blow-up about money' as follows:

'Just before New Year's Day they informed me that they didn't want me as a partner any more. . . . I'd been a partner in a partnership of three with a list of eight and a half thousand. I'd been a partner for three years and should have got parity at the end of that. . . . The other thing I found out was one of the partners was paying himself £50 a month . . . for doing the practice accounts. He never bothered telling anybody.'

The notion discussed in the Acheson Report (1981), that general practice is a business, found substantial agreement amongst respondents. For instance, one practice was:

'just a standard general practice, run sort of as a business to make money, that was the attitude, you know. You look after the patients but it was to make money, it was looked on as a sort of livelihood rather than just done for the good of the patients.'

It was apparent that financial problems within general practice for the women GPs were related to their junior status at the time they practised in partnerships. However, there were aspects which were clearly gender-related. For example, one woman talked about her many years of boredom as a doctor in public health[6] (an area in which many women work, to fit in with marriage and childcare) and her excitement at getting out of public health and into general practice, which she had long wanted. Her initial experience was very disappointing: 'it was pretty awful there. I knew I was being underpaid, but I wanted to get out of public health into general practice and that was the way I could do it . . . but I continued to be underpaid.'

Evidence from the interviews, then, showed a considerable amount of financial exploitation within group practices. Obviously, such exploitation of one doctor by another does not occur in single-handed practice. But there were other factors which made single-handed practice appear attractive. The matter of personal relationships in group practice was frequently referred to by the women interviewed.

Personal relationships

Practising alone means never having practice quarrels or disagreements (*Pulse* 1983). Many of the women interviewed referred to episodes involving disruptive personal relationships with their partners. While there was agreement that there are sometimes very positive facets to practising in partnership with others, many respondents were relieved, once they had gone into practice on their own, at not having to cope with their partners. The suggestion was made that group and partnership practice is in some senses the 'perfect set-up' – as long as you can cope with colleagues! As one woman said: 'The disadvantages are, for me at least, the people you work with, obviously. You have to, for it to work, you have to find colleagues who you can get on with.' She had found that in her experience there had been 'a lot of animosity in the practice' where she had been previously.

The problem of unequal financial status within general practice discussed above impinged on the personal relationships between GPs. There was much discussion of partners putting different amounts of effort into their work, so that some respondents talked of the pressure engendered by lazy senior partners. One woman expressed this in the following way:

'I mean I had this feeling that – which may have been slight paranoia, because we were so busy and I was very, very tired by then – it was like a paranoiac feeling that I was doing more work than anybody else. In fact I was just beginning to feel for the first time resentful that I was doing a man's job and doing everything at home as well.'

145

A successful partnership needs to be based on shared aims and values – it is more than just a financial arrangement. One woman felt that in the practice where she had worked, they all 'got on well together, we were all people who cared about people, and that was the principal thing'. This comment was later qualified, however, as follows: '[They] reckoned to try and do a good job [but] one had to agree with the senior partner. . . . Provided you were sort of prepared to do what he wanted . . . if I had stuck my neck out it wouldn't have worked.'

Practice relationships can go wrong between any partners, men and women, and one respondent who had practised with another woman had relationship problems too: 'It was very, very difficult and, increasingly, it became evident that . . . we couldn't work together.' The idea of a 'personality clash' was given on several occasions as the main reason for changing practices: 'eventually we decided that we'd have to split up.' Another woman interviewed, who had only ever practised in a group practice as a locum for three months, put the idea succinctly when she said: 'I mean having partners is very much like having a husband or a wife, you know, it's a lot of hassle. . . . You spend a lot of energy sort of coping with a partner, whereas you could be using that energy elsewhere.'

Five of the women interviewed had in fact practised in the past with their husbands. One had some particularly interesting things to say about that arrangement. She found that:

'more and more I was allowed to do more of the work. . . . He took a lot of time off, and because I was his partner, and couldn't really object because I was his wife, I ended up doing more and more work. And I suppose I got resentful.'

The literature on husband/wife partnerships in the professions tends to suggest that this is for the most part a supportive and positive way of working. In most of the professions it is not easy to draw a line between where professional and home life begin and end. In medicine, and very much so in general practice, professional and home life are closely interwoven, as has been noted above. For this reason a husband and wife working in the same profession – and, particularly, together – will offer understanding and be supportive of each other. However, this ignores the potential for exploitation inherent in such an arrangement and there were several stories of problems. As one woman concluded: 'it's not a good idea, husbands and wives working together, unless they've got a very firm partnership agreement drawn up before they go into partnership.'[7]

Problems involving personal relationships often concern the exploitation of one partner by another. This exploitation is sometimes intrinsically related to issues of gender, which are considered later. Along with financial exploitation, problems of personal relationships are negative reactions against partnership practice. Continuity and independence, which are discussed next, act both as positive attractions to single-handed practice and as negative reactions against partnership practice.

Continuity

The notion of continuity refers to continuity of treatment from the point of view of both the patient and the doctor. The problem of lack of continuity for doctors involves not getting to know patients, or not being able to see through a course of treatment. For patients, the problem is of the difficulty of having to start anew with each visit to the surgery and thus never forming a relationship with any one doctor. In Cartwright and Anderson's (1981) study of general practice patients' and doctors' attitudes, issues of continuity in both partnerships and single-handed practices were compared. A high proportion of both patients and doctors believed that continuity was often lacking in partnerships but practically assured in single-handed practice. Both felt that continuity was highly desirable.

The women GPs interviewed were agreed that the problem of continuity was quite successfully overcome in single-handed practice. As one woman said: 'It's a different quality of medicine I practise now than I did in the partnership.' The question of quality and continuity is plainly apparent from her explanation of a group practice she had been in:

'the 8,000 patients that the practice had saw three partners and a trainee. . . . Although they were registered with certain people, obviously they didn't see that person, they saw whoever was available, or whoever they chose if they were lucky. . . . There was no continuity of care, really.'

Single-handed practice is often criticized because of the absence of possible consultation on cases between partners. There is, obviously, no possibility of referral of patients within the practice. However, the advantages of continuity for the doctor are considerable: 'it's treating the unit as a whole that's enjoyable . . . in the partnership I didn't get that sort of enjoyment.' Continuity can be viewed not only in terms of the treatment offered; the whole environment and doctor–patient relationship is affected: 'In a lot of ways it's easier because I know everybody in this practice, and I know exactly what's going on . . . they didn't come and see somebody else last week.' Continuity and relationships within the practice can also be related to size of practice and list. From the doctor's point of view it is preferable for her to feel in touch with all her patients, which is not possible in a large practice with several thousand patients on its list. Comments from three women illustrate this:

'I think by having a small practice you can get sort of fairly chatty with patients.'

'I would really rather . . . keep the practice small, so that we know everybody.'

'I think satisfactions are, making friends with the patients.'

It is apparent, then, that the comparatively small lists in single-handed practices allow GPs to know their patients and patients to know them, to build up a good relationship with patients (and vice versa), and to follow through a course of treatment from beginning to end, or until referral to hospital is necessary. These are all very positive functions of practising alone. One doctor spoke in terms of the satisfaction she had achieved through the continuity of care in single-handed practice: 'You have the satisfaction of following something all the way through and making a diagnosis before you send them off to hospital.' Continuity of treatment and care is important for both doctor and patient, but the question of independence is crucial from the doctor's point of view.

Independence

The notion of independence suggests two opposing theories. First of all, the desire for independence can be viewed in terms of doctors' positive entrepreneurial desire for their own practices. In this sense single-handed practice can be compared to the idea and attraction of owning and running a small business. Indeed the two have many common facets. The data from the interviews with the women GPs pose a second and opposing theory, which comprises both negative and positive aspects. The negative reactions against partnership/group practice and the positive attractions to single-handed practice which are linked with the desire for independence concern the individual herself, rather than her immediate relationship to capital and entrepreneurship. It will become clear that this desire is also related to gender issues.

The desire for independence which the women GPs discussed was directly related to experiences of different aspects of exploitation in general practice and is closely connected with the frequently expressed wish to 'practise in the way they wanted'. For example: 'I decided that I'd like to run a practice in the way I thought it should be done.' And: 'I've got what I want . . . from the point of view of the practice, a practice I started myself, and I organize and run in the way I like.'

The wish for independence was a negative reaction against past practice experiences and made single-handed practice appear attractive. A woman who had previously been in a large group practice with her husband demonstrated the dichotomy: 'when the opportunity for this practice came up I accepted it mostly because I wanted to be independent and do things my way.' She explained how working single-handed can make a difference in the organization of a practice:

'It's a different system of working. I think if you work on your own, you can choose to do things as you want, like I have a special baby clinic, I have a special ante-natal clinic, all coming separately for different clinics. . . . Being independent you can organize your own timings and you can run things exactly as you want it.'

The notion of independence and being able to 'run things exactly as you want it' in single-handed practice facilitated the resolution of what had been problems in past practice experience:

'There used to be a gynae session with the other practice where all the women with gynae problems were seen on a Friday morning. . . . Now I do it all, but it's the attitude that is different because you're not sort of coming in on a Friday morning thinking "God . . . I've got thirty women!" The quality, I'm sure, it must be better at the end of the day . . . it feels easier anyway.'

Independence and freedom in organization were all expressed in terms of 'being the boss' which was described as an important element of satisfaction: 'It's a great satisfaction being my own boss, I mean I can do exactly what I want to do; I like that, I like that aspect of it.'

Independence and the individual's positive/negative attraction to single-handed practice have so far been described in terms such as being 'freer' and being able 'to do my own thing'. Control, though, was another term used in explaining independence:

'I wanted to have *control* over the rest of my working life, which I in a large practice was not going to have. The person who was senior to me in the practice was younger than me in years, so no way was he likely to retire before me, and I just felt that I wanted to have control over what happened.'

'Wanting to control' is important. It can be related to the norms of professional training which stress not only independence but embody also the concept of superior knowledge gained in the process of training which is both highly specialized and of considerable length. The model of the traditional GP portrayed earlier embodies such ideas. Here the GP worked independently and, through maintaining such independence and along with his professional training, was assured of a degree of deference from patients based on a supposed superior knowledge. Partnership practice necessitates relinquishing some of the ideas of 'independence' inherent in the medical socialization process, in favour of norms of both co-operation and hierarchy between partners. These can also affect (possibly for the better?) the deferential nature of the patient–doctor relationship which is so apparent in the traditional single-handed practice. Changed ways of practising are anathema to the traditional concept of the professional, while single-handed practice is its tangible expression. The desire for control expressed by the single-handed women GPs can be understood in relation to such a background, in its being the best way they can express their professional socialization. When feelings of lack of autonomy and impotence were mentioned, these were very much in opposition to the 'professional' norms which they had internalized. For example:

'when I was there I realized I was treated more like an employee. . . . None of my ideas or nothing was needed there, I was just pushed around and felt I was doing all the work there, so I thought I'll move out and have my own practice.'

So a desire for independence and control over their working lives was in many cases a result of and a direct response to negative past experiences in partnerships, as well as of a positive attraction to the independence and individualism instilled by professional training which is satisfied by practising single-handedly. This positive/negative dichotomy in the explanation of the desire for independence is in opposition to the entrepreneurial thesis, which discusses independence and control in terms of capital and which has been explained elsewhere in terms of as a desire 'to paddle their own canoes' (*Pulse* 1983).

Conclusion – gender and ghettoism

The reasons for practising single-handedly discussed in terms of financial grievances, personal relationships, continuity, and independence have shown that there are positive attractions to single-handed practice and negative reactions against partnership. In the discussion so far the issue of gender has been considered only peripherally. However, gender is an important aspect of the decision taken by women to go into single-handed practice. This 'fifth dimension' of gender can be looked at from two perspectives. First, gender is a central consideration in interpreting the four areas already discussed. It can be demonstrated how explicit examples of the exploitation of women doctors have an overall part to play in the 'discriminatory environment' of general practice (Bourne and Wikler 1978) which shapes the decisions and actions of women GPs. Second, there is the issue of what can be termed 'ghettoism', which is a feature of the discriminatory environment. This means that women are 'ghettoized' within general practice into certain areas of general practice in much the same way as they are channelled within medicine generally.

Cartwright and Anderson have noted that: 'In general it is the *lack* of difference between men and women general practitioners which is most notable' (1981: 127–28). While the present study is not of a comparative nature, the women GPs interviewed suggested many instances where gender was a definite factor in their experiences. This was discussed as a general issue as well as more specifically and personally:

'If I had gone into partnership, financially I would have been much better off, but I thought about all these upsets . . . and especially for the lady doctors, I hear that men doctors, they exploit a lot, so I was not prepared for it.'

A GP, in talking of her difficult practice experiences – which she attributed to being a woman – suggested that it was not a personal problem but one of gender generally: 'they've taken on a lot of lady doctors since and bullied them terribly.'

Through a consideration of the notion of 'ghettoism' it becomes apparent that gender-associated problems pervade each of the four categories discussed above. While women are channelled into certain areas of medicine generally, they are channelled *within* general practice too. Ghettoism occurs when women doctors find themselves seeing specific categories of patients in a group practice – many of the women, especially for specifically 'women's problems' (gynaecological, obstetrics, and family planning), many of the psychiatric cases (a large proportion of whom are women) (Young 1981), and the paediatric cases, especially when children are brought along to the surgery by mothers.

There were endless examples of this sort of ghettoism:

'[In] the practice that we joined, there were four men so . . . I was doing mainly gynae and maternity and paediatrics and seeing children.'

'we had got the midwife to give a little bit of help in ante-natal but I was doing the whole lot, all day I was doing it.'

The notion of ghettoism implies not only that women doctors see particular categories of patient, but that this is *imposed* on them to a large extent. In discussing reasons for becoming GPs, it was clear that many women chose positively to follow a career in general practice. They had for the most part become general practitioners in preference to specializing in hospital medicine (although Turner (1979) has suggested that general practice is often second choice to hospital medicine). The specific choice, for the majority of respondents, had thus been *not* to specialize. General practice implies offering the full range of medical care; that is one of its principal attractions. So while interests and specialisms within general practice may naturally arise, these should not be imposed but followed through choice. In the case of the ghettoized women GPs in this study, choice was not a factor in their past experience whilst they were working in group practices. The imposition of ghettoism came from several sources; first, in respect of assumptions which were made about the sort of medicine they should, and would like, to practise. These assumptions were made by male colleagues and seniors, by some female colleagues, by themselves, by other practice personnel (e.g. receptionists, nurses, midwives, etc.), and by patients. Assumptions were made that because they were women doctors, they should *want* to treat women and, particularly, 'women's problems'. The normative expectation was that women doctors should treat women patients. This arose out of their supposed common experience as women and the supposed innate 'feminine' characteristics of women doctors (discussed earlier) which include being more 'sympathetic'. These views are shared both by health professionals (male and female doctors and other practice personnel) and by patients.

The supposedly sympathetic nature of women doctors can lead to patients exploiting this view: 'I think the patients talk too much to women. I often find that they'll sit here and they'll talk to me over things I know jolly well they wouldn't feel free just to bring up what they want to a gentleman.' This situation was seen as having both positive and negative aspects:

'To some extent it's nice, because it means that the patients will talk to you more freely and tell you problems earlier; on the other hand it's a nuisance when people just sit there chatting to you.'

'a lot of patients think they can take advantage of women a little easier than men.'

Respondents suggested that because many patients, particularly women, viewed them as more 'sympathetic' they were very popular, and consequently busier than male partners and this was 'because I was a woman'. In essence, however, it was because women GPs saw the bulk of the women patients and children that they were so busy. Many women patients prefer to see a woman doctor for gynaecological, obstetric, and family planning consultations not only because of their common experience and their supposed sympathetic nature, but also to avoid facing possibly embarrassing situations with male doctors (this can happen in reverse for men patients, though very much less frequently). The fact that women patients prefer to see a woman doctor came out clearly in the interviews: 'I found a lot of women came to see me. I did find I had a lot of "woman problems".'

It is evident, then, that a form of specialization within general practice is imposed on women GPs. While it must be recognized that many women doctors are happy to treat a large number of women patients, they have for the most part *not* chosen to specialize in obstetrics and gynaecology, etc., but, to all intents and purposes, find themselves doing so. This ambiguous situation must be put into context through comparison with hospital medicine. In order to specialize in obstetrics and gynaecology it would be necessary to follow a hospital career. However, these specialisms in hospital medicine are male-dominated ones, being top-heavy, at the consultant grades especially, with male doctors. Women have difficulty in progressing far, in much the same fashion as occurs in many other surgical specialties. Personal experience, along with many other alleged 'feminine/innate' characteristics such as being sympathetic and dextrous, for example, are *not* seen as valuable or helpful to a career in obstetrics and gynaecology specialisms in hospital medicine. In general practice, though, the situation is the complete reverse, and for many women GPs it is not a position of their own making or choice. The women interviewed in this study found that single-handed practice went a long way towards allowing them to practise the sort of medicine they chose. It allowed them more choice in the sorts of patients and conditions they were exposed to, so that they were able to experience a much fuller range of medical care, rather than specializing. Inevitably, these women GPs still spent a proportion of their time treating 'women's conditions' and for the most part were happy to do so, but they were *also* now exposed to a much wider range of patients and conditions and were consequently more completely 'general' practitioners.

Being a *woman* GP in a group/partnership practice affects the practice in its operation. It affects, too, the woman GP herself in terms of her financial relationship to the practice, her personal relationships with other members of the practice, how the continuity of treatment affects both doctor and patient, and the independence and control which doctors have within the practice. It also exaggerates the effect of ghettoizing doctors into certain specialities; for women this occurs in the treatment of 'women's' and children's conditions. The *gender* of the doctor (the fifth dimension) is not only a reactive force on its own, but interacts with the other four categories in contributing to decisions made to practise single-handedly. Many reasons were given for practising single-handedly, but for the single-handed women GPs in this study, decisions taken to practise alone were directly related to gender issues, though the women themselves did not always articulate their reasons in this way. In discussing gender issues in relation to choice of practice it must be recognized that career choices are not made in isolation. For women GPs, gender issues must also include the discussion of how they organize their out-of-hours cover and their domestic situations and how these different but connected areas of life are reconciled. These, too, are of relevance to practice strategies and decisions.

What I have tried to show in this chapter is that the figures which suggest a trend in general practice towards doctors practising together in partnerships and groups are gender blind. In fact this trend has moved much more slowly for women doctors than for men in general practice in Birmingham, since the proportion of women to men practising single-handedly is considerably greater than the proportion of women to men in general practice overall. It is apparent that the reasons for this are closely related to gender issues. Negative experiences of group practice have attracted women to practising single-handedly, experiences which have interacted with gender issues and the power relationship between men and women. These negative experiences are epitomized in the concept of ghettoism, the term which I have used to describe the way in which women GPs are channelled into a limited form of general practice to which, traditional stereotypes suggest, they are particularly suited. Where their roles are circumscribed in this way – usually by their male superiors and colleagues, but sometimes by their patients and themselves – women GPs may well respond by continuing to opt for single-handed general practice.

Notes

1 Such an occupation or profession is 'greedy' in the excessive demands which it makes on its incumbents. See Coser (1974) for a full discussion of this concept.

2 In the discussion which follows, a 'partnership' refers to two or more doctors practising together and a 'group' to three or more doctors practising together. The terms are thus largely interchangeable.

3 These considerations apply to women in other male-dominated professions, of course; see Podmore and Spencer (1984) for a discussion of the domestic and work roles of women lawyers.

4 The single-handed women GPs interviewed constituted two-thirds of the names which were obtained from the relevant Family Practitioner Committees. Their ages at the time of interview ranged from 29 to 68 years. The sizes of their practices were between 1,000 and 3,200 patients. The interviews were taped, semi-structured, and lasted on average about one and a half hours each. Some GPs were studied in greater depth by being observed in their surgeries and on home visits over a longer period. One important factor in this study is the ethnic origins of the women GPs

concerned. Of the twenty-nine women interviewed, thirteen were not of British origin and twelve of these were Asian. However, ethnicity will not be discussed in this chapter as a separate issue. It is intended that this aspect of the study will be written up elsewhere.

5 The proportion of women doctors is expected to increase dramatically in the near future, with the change in policy over admissions to medical school encouraged by the Equal Opportunities Commission. As a recent newspaper article observed: 'statistically at least, medicine is becoming an equal opportunities profession; in 1984, 43 per cent of the applicants were women and they filled 44 per cent of the available places.' (*Guardian* 1986).

6 The term 'community health' is now more commonly used.

7 For a further consideration of the issues surrounding husband and wife partnerships, see Lawrence (1984).

References

Acheson Report (1981) *Primary Health Care in Inner London: Report of a Study Group*. London Health Planning Consortium.

Aird, L.A. and Silver, P.H.S. (1971) Women Doctors from the Middlesex Hospital Medical School, University of London, 1947–67. *British Journal of Medical Education* 5: 232–41.

Barrett, M. and Roberts, H. (1978) Doctors and Their Patients: The Social Control of Women in General Practice. In C. Smart and B. Smart (eds) *Women, Sexuality and Social Control*. London: Routledge and Kegan Paul, pp. 41–52.

Beaumont, B. (1978) Training and Careers of Women Doctors in the Thames Region. *British Medical Journal* 1: 191–93.

Becker, H. (1961) *Boys in White: Student Culture in Medical Schools*. Chicago: University of Chicago Press.

Bhargava, G. (1983) Sex-stereotyping and Sex Congruency: Components in the Sex-role Definition of Medical Specialties in India. *Social Science and Medicine* 17: 1017–026.

Bourne, B.G. and Wikler, N.J. (1978) Commitment and the Cultural Mandate: Women in Medicine. *Social Problems* 25: 430–40.

Bowling, A. (1981) *Delegation in General Practice: A Study of Doctors and Nurses*. London: Tavistock.

Cartwright, A. (1967) *Patients and Their Doctors*. London: Routledge and Kegan Paul.

Cartwright, A. and Anderson, R. (1981) *General Practice Revisited: A Second Study of Patients and Their Doctors*. London: Tavistock.

Coser, L.A. (1974) *Greedy Institutions: Patterns of Undivided Commitment*. New York: Free Press.

Dawson Report (1920) *Committee on the Future of the Medical and Allied Services (Interim Report)*. London: HMSO.

Elston, M.A. (1977) Women in the Medical Profession: Whose Problem? In M. Stacey, M. Reid, C. Heath, and R. Dingwall (eds) *Health and the Division of Labour*. London: Croom Helm, pp. 115–38.

— (1980) Medicine. In R. Silverstone and A. Ward (eds) *Careers of Professional Women*. London: Croom Helm, pp. 99–139.

Epstein, C.F. (1970) *Women's Place: Options and Limits in Professional Careers*. Berkeley: University of California Press.

Finch, J. (1983) *Married to the Job: Wives' Incorporation in Men's Work*. London: Allen and Unwin.

Fry, J. (1979) *Trends in General Practice, 1977*. London: British Medical Journal.

Gray, J. (1982) The Effect of the Doctor's Sex on the Doctor–Patient Relationship. *Journal of the Royal College of GPs* 32: 167–69.

Guardian (1986) Careers: Fit to Be a Doctor. 21 January.

Jefferys, M. and Elliott, P. (1966) *Women in Medicine*. London: Office of Health Economics.

Jefferys, M. and Sachs, H. (1983) *Rethinking General Practice: Dilemmas in Primary Medical Care*. London: Tavistock.

Journal of the Royal College of GPs (1979) Editorial: Patients and the Doctors. Vol. 29: 195–99.

Kelly, A. (1975) *A Discouraging Process: How Girls Are Eased out of Science*. Edinburgh: University of Edinburgh.

Lawrence, B. (1984) *How to Become a Career Woman and an Ideal Wife as Well – Single-handed Women GPs' Domestic Lives*. Paper presented to the British Sociological Association Annual Conference.

Leeson, J. and Gray, J. (1978) *Women and Medicine*. London: Tavistock.

Lorber, J. (1975) Women and Medical Sociology: Invisible Professionals and Ubiquitous Patients. In M. Millman and R.M. Kanter (eds) *Another Voice*. Garden City, NY: Anchor Books, pp. 75–105.

—(1984) *Women Physicians: Careers, Status and Power*. New York and London: Tavistock.

Mackie, L. and Pattullo, P. (1977) *Women at Work*. London: Tavistock.

McPherson, A. and Small, J. (1980) Women GPs in Oxfordshire. *Journal of the Royal College of GPs* 30: 108–11.

Marinker, M. (1975) *Women in General Practice*. Proceedings of a conference organized by the Department of Health and Social Security, 4–5 July.

Pulse (1983) Singlehanded Practitioners. 26 February.

Rhodes, P. (1983) Part-time Work for Women. *British Medical Journal* 286 (19 March): 964–66.

Roberts, H. (1985) *The Patient Patients*. London: Pandora.

Smith, R. (1976) Sex and Occupational Role on Fleet Street. In D.L. Barker and S. Allen (eds) *Dependence and Exploitation in Work and Marriage*. London: Longman, pp. 70–87.

Spencer, A. and Podmore, D. (1984) Women in a Male-dominated Profession in England: Pressure and Strain in Family and Domestic Life. *International Journal of Sociology of the Family* 14: 47–66.

Turner, J. (1979) The Wrong Way to Get Better Doctors. *New Society*, 7 June: 572–74.

Young, G. (1981) A Woman in Medicine: Reflections from the Inside. In H. Roberts (ed.) *Women, Health and Reproduction*. London: Routledge and Kegan Paul, pp. 144–62.

© 1987 Barbara Lawrence

8

Women Academics:
A Case Study in Inequality

John McAuley

Introduction

This chapter takes the form of a case study which attempts to explore, through interviews and participant observation, some of the inequalities encountered by women in an institution which claims, as many do, to be an 'equal opportunity employer'. Only the problems and dilemmas of women as they affect the teaching staff are considered. This is in order to impose some boundaries upon the work, although it is realized that the experiences of all staff and students in relation to gender issues are intertwined. Although much of the material is drawn from a particular institution of higher education, data have been included from a number of sources. As the study developed it became apparent that, at a micro-level, some of the features discussed were very complex; only rarely were pure 'ideal types' of male or female perspectives about gender to be found. However, embedded in the values and attitudes of many men in the institution were strong features which militated against the development of equality for women.

In this chapter the argument is that although there is a plurality of cultures within the institution, there is a dominant paradigm which largely prescribes the relationship of teaching staff to teaching, research, and the other activities that are part of academic life.

Since the origins of many public sector institutions of higher education lie in colleges of technology or advanced technology as the dominant partners in the process of amalgamation that took place in

158

the 1970s, it is not surprising that the ethos of such institutions reflects the 'male' world-view of science and technology, carrying with it particular connotations of competence in terms of individual performance within the institution. Although both men and women are engaged in active competition within this paradigm, women – because they are seen to be 'different' from men and because they are a minority population in the institution – carry the burden of being perceived as symbolic of a different system of values and a different approach to core academic activities. It is argued in this chapter that, although *some* women in the institution do not see the issues of equality as of great importance, many are actively engaged in processes involving the shifting of men's consciousness in relation to women. Women do this through political activities within the institution (for example by gaining access to committees), by promoting the importance of gender understanding in teaching and research programmes, and by engaging in 'consciousness-raising' forms of social interaction with their male colleagues.

A man's common-sense view of the situation

Imagine, if you would, a male member of staff of an institution of higher education within the public sector. He is not unaware of the contingencies that confront his female colleagues in the institution, yet has not been in a situation in which he has had to explore these issues in any depth. He is not being represented as some sort of Weberian 'ideal type', but rather as a character from the centre of the mean curve of distribution who holds to a nest of propositions about women as colleagues.

The starting-point for his set of propositions is that there is no need for a gender-based equal opportunities group within the institution, because the preconditions for the unequal treatment of women do not exist. This somewhat provocative initial proposition could be developed in the following way. The institution is, at heart, one that values in its staff qualities that amount to 'good teaching', the ability to undertake research, and the ability to develop the self in both these roles. The institution further values displays of enthusiasm and entrepreneurial activity. These values are enshrined in the public culture of the organization; by and large the institution is not experienced by the teaching staff as one that is repressive in its demands on individuals, even though teaching loads are heavier than

159

would be common in a university. Although there is now little recruitment into the institution and although there are currently few promotions (and we – i.e. men – look back to the 'golden age' when such promotions did occur regularly), we (men) deal with such promotions as do occur with organizationally normal rancour. We say that X got his promotion by creeping his way through the system, or that Y did not deserve his promotion because he was not properly qualified. Sometimes promotions are assessed without rancour – they can be seen as deserved, as organizationally appropriate. As is common in our sort of institution, women do not get too many of these promotions – they never have done – but that lack of promotion cannot be explained by discrimination. After all, we (men) have long ago abandoned the line of argument that women are not serious members of the academic community and we have also abandoned assertions that we would find it 'impossible' to work with a female head of department.

Comfortable consensuality encounters reality

The male common-sense view outlined above relies upon an implied commonality of understanding between men and women as to the nature of the organization and its general approach to its primary activities. If, however, there really is an absence of a general gender-based duality in relation to the nature of the appropriate paradigm in which to conduct education, then we would have to look elsewhere for the source of the sense of alienation from and marginalization within the institution experienced by many women teachers. It might even be claimed, in a man's world, that any manifestations of discontent from women are merely symptomatic of the feminist urge to propaganda. This approach ignores the 'two worlds' view expressed by such writers as Kaplan (1985), which states that over a wide range of substantive areas women and men have quite different versions and understandings of the nature of reality. This view would suggest that, since the commonality of understanding as to the purposes of the institution and the means by which these purposes are to be achieved described above is in itself illusory, exploration of the sense of alienation of many women staff has to be understood from the standpoint of their interactive situation with men and also from that of their structural location in the organization. Both these items are intertwined.

Table 8.1 *Gender distribution of teaching staff in the faculties of the institution*

	Head of department and above		Principal lecturer		Senior lecturer		Lecturer grade 2		Totals	
	M	F	M	F	M	F	M	F	M	F
Engineering	2	—	24	—	55	1	11	—	92	1
Science	7	—	45	1	90	8	12	5	154	14
Building & mechanical	4	—	26	3	58	17	15	9	103	29
Art and design	4	—	10	—	26	8	5	1	45	9
Social studies	4	—	22	5	60	21	11	9	97	35
Humanities	3	1	14	3	22	14	3	1	42	19
Education	4	—	10	1	21	15	1	—	36	16
Miscellaneous	7	—	19	—	13	3	2	1	41	4
	35	1	170	13	345	87	60	26	610	127
Proportion	35 :	1	13 :	1	4 :	1	2.3 :	1	4.8 :	1

First I will consider how women are located amongst the teaching staff of the institution.

Within the institution, 'faculties' are the major subject groupings. It can be seen from *Table 8.1* that at the most senior level of faculty management – head of department and dean – there is only one woman in post. It is generally understood within public sector higher education that the 'career grade' is senior lecturer, but it is clear that the highest proportion of women to men is at the lower grade of lecturer grade 2. The status of principal lecturer is gained through promotion and is officially assigned on the basis of the performance of specific responsibilities (e.g. director of studies for a major programme). Women are considerably under-represented at this grade in relation to men. Although women do not quite reach a 1:2 ratio with men in any faculty, they most nearly do so in the faculties of education, humanities, and social studies. The implications of this are discussed later.

In understanding the implications of the number of women staff and their distribution hierarchically and between faculties and departments it has to be recognized – it is a social fact – that the institution is trapped in its own history. In many departments the age profile of staff has become one in which most are over forty years of age and have probably worked in the institution for seven years or more. The key period of appointments into the institution ended in the late 1970s; in a period of retrenchment in the education sector generally there are few possibilities for staff to seek employment or promotion elsewhere and there are few new teaching appointments made inside the institution.

The failure to appoint women – relative to the number of men appointed – in the period of growth was not out of any deliberate or focused gender bias. Rather it came out of a sort of carelessness. Dale Spender has pointed to the way in which, in higher education:

'it is the male system of values that prevails . . . it is they who decide – on the basis of their own experience and their own logic – what the form and substance of education will be. . . . Men have used this power to keep women and their concerns invisible.'

(Spender 1982: 113)

This assertion argues a purposiveness in men's actions that is not always there – even though the outcome may well be the same as if it were. Indeed if men's actions were more definitely purposive in this matter it could be suggested that they might be more capable of amelioration. The dynamics of exclusion of women are much more shadowy and may be seen to be rooted in men's common-sense assumptions about the nature of the world and in their ignorance about the differences between these and the hard truths as they are encountered by women. This proposition can be illustrated by looking at recruitment to the institution. It is expected that advertisements for posts should be, as with application forms and other information, at least neutral with regard to gender. I say 'at least' because advertisements for posts at many institutions carry the disclaimer that the organization is an 'equal opportunities employer' – though in some cases that message may have as much sincerity of intent as do health warnings on cigarette advertisements. This statement has consequences both for applicants and for existing women staff who seek promotion because, in the absence of substantive activities which lead to the implementation of policies that clearly *would* equalize the position of women in relation to men, the *claim* to practise equality of opportunity is actively damaging to women. This is because the statement comes to be accepted by men as a representation of the truth. Because many men are either not aware of, or are uncomfortable about, the implications of the establishment of equalization policies they can (and do) suggest that, since the symbolic claim to equality exists, women already have equal opportunities. If, in this situation, women are still unable to gain either appointments to or promotion within the institution, then men can suggest that women's failure is actually generated by their inability to meet the demands of the institution – they have been offered the 'helping hand' but are unable to grasp it.

It was clear that a number of the women who were interviewed had well-defined ideas about the sorts of policies that would, over time, ameliorate the disadvantaged position in which women were placed with regard to both recruitment and promotion. It was equally apparent to these women, however, that institutional policies even to *begin* equalization would be a long time coming; and further, because the majority of teaching staff and virtually all senior management are men, any policy guidelines that would emerge would be within the boundaries of reality as understood by men.

There are other aspects of both advertisements and application forms that have implications for women applicants for positions at the institution or for promotions within it. For example, if one undertakes the simple task of reading the underlying messages in the application form used by the institution, one finds a box that asks applicants to identify 'former name (if applicable)'. My understanding of the world indicates that few men have 'former names' (unless attempting to hide a past that is best obliterated), whereas women often do. Many women feel that an attempt to establish marital status before interview is potentially discriminatory. Because of pressure from various sources the institution abandoned in 1982 a categorization device that asked applicants to identify 'marital status' – but the attempt to seek out a 'former name' might be seen as perpetuating this particular discriminatory device. However, since the former device of also asking for 'number of children' has been abandoned the discriminatory element is not, perhaps, as strong as it once was. It is worth commenting that this latter device was highly prejudicial to women in that in the world of male common-sense the affirmation of children on the form indicated (in a male applicant) a desire for stability, whereas in a woman applicant it indicated the likelihood that she would be absent in order to look after them in periods of illness or holiday. These, I would argue, are taken-for-granted 'realities' in a man's world.

If the 'two worlds' view is taken seriously, there are other aspects of application forms and advertisements that can be problematic for women. It is often the case that advertisements require that applicants for teaching positions 'should have relevant industrial and professional experience'. The crucial aspect of this, for women, is that they may feel less conviction about the validity of their own background experience because a pervasive gender-related feature of many occupations is that women are accorded lower status in those occupations than are men, even where there is equality of qualification and length of time in work.[1] Institutions of higher education in the public sector have taken it for granted that industrial and professional experience is important for most teaching positions; this is perhaps natural given that the tradition of these institutions is rooted in the provision of vocational and professional education. It could be argued, however, that an unquestioning demand for this sort of experience is not always a benefit to the development of good teaching and research practices. The industrial and professional experience possessed by applicants might be essentially unstimulating and might lead to the adoption of somewhat rigid, unquestioning attitudes in relation to their disciplines. The experience which is seen by the institution to be so important may be essentially routine and practice-orientated, with a consequent neglect of theoretical and wider understanding. The full implementation of an equal opportunities policy would involve fundamental questioning of the taken-for-granted attitude that new members of staff 'should have' industrial and professional experience. Such a review might indeed lead to improvements in staff development programmes which would enable staff to gain experience in other institutions and organizations that are relevant to present teaching and research needs.

Features inhibiting the promotion of women

In the previous section I have shown some of the features which deter women from applying for positions in the institution, in that criteria presented in advertisements and application forms project images and expectations that women experience as problematic. Such features can be used by appointments panels as a means for not selecting women, because criteria such as 'experience' are accepted unquestioningly as 'appropriate'. I have also suggested, *inter alia*, that these criteria can also affect deleteriously the promotion of women who have obtained teaching posts. There are other features that impede women's access to promotion within the organization. One of the criteria that are commonly established in departments as marking a potential for promotability is access to positions of 'responsibility', although, as I have noted above, not all promotions are believed by staff to happen in this manner. The sorts of responsibility that access 'normal' promotion would include such activities as director of studies or course leadership (responsibility for a major programme of study), membership of committees, and undertaking research and consultancy.

Although the institution is officially highly committed to the teaching activity as providing the basis of its primary mission, these other activities are seen as the features that actually define promotion potential. The organizational assumption is that teaching staff are by definition 'good' at the teaching activity – it is a basic prerequisite for appointment to the collectivity – and quality of teaching cannot, therefore, be seen (in the view of the organization) as a sufficient criterion for promotion. In order for there to be promotion from the career grade of senior lecturer to that of principal lecturer, there need to be at least four conditions satisfied. One is that there is available within the 'official establishment' of the department a place for a promotee. If there is, then the would-be promotee must have displayed his/her ability to organize, to research, to be entre- prencurial, or whatever constitutes the requisite task ability for the transition to take place. The third criterion is that the promotee is able to make public that he or she has undertaken these activities. Finally and importantly, there is the discovery of some system of support or sponsorship that will make available a place in the principal lecturer grade.

In the context of their understanding of the sorts of situation that affect women members of staff in higher education, Woodall and her colleagues have written: 'the culture that pervades our higher educational institutions is one that emphasises publishing, dashing around to conferences, competitive debate, scholarly analyses and climbing an academic ladder' (Woodall et al. 1985: 22). These writers argued that, in their experience, such activities are 'buttressed and cemented' by male patterns of sociability and that the culture in which these activities is located is masculine in its ethos. If we look at the activities which they mention it would seem that, irrespective of gender, at least three of them are entirely appropriate to any higher educational establishment. To undertake work that results in the publication of papers, to attend conferences, and to participate in academic debates are important features of the academic's construction of what it is to be a competent member of the collectivity, both from the point of view of personal development and also in order to generate organizational responsiveness to change. However, what transforms these activities from benign, gender-free endeavours is the ethos within which such activities take place – the general cultural milieu. There is evidence that women see themselves as undertaking these key academic activities in quite a different spirit and in quite different modes from those in which men conduct them.

For example within the research activity, women claim that, conventionally, little account is taken of gender issues. Indeed, Stanley and Wise (1983) characterize their work as coming from a distinctive paradigm of social science, one that always respects the 'data' provided by the subject; in particular, they claim, feminist research is characterized by its essential humanness. Similarly, Maher writes that 'in every scholarly discipline wherein the female experience has been challenged' there is a need to re-evaluate radically 'the research methods by which knowledge of the field was gained in the first place' (1985: 33). The sort of general epistemological shift to which this writer is alluding is that which eschews the 'single objective, rationally derived "right" answer . . . for the construction of knowledge from multiple perspectives through cooperative problem-solving' (Maher 1985: 33).

Although many men would object to the annexation of this type of research methodology by women (in the sense that many men who are social scientists would see themselves as working out of this paradigm), the important point is that the preferred approach for women undertaking research in the social sciences is not the dominant paradigm within many institutions. Interviews with women (not in the institution) undertaking research in the natural sciences suggest that they do not have this conflict. Even where women do find themselves comfortable with the 'normal' paradigm, they have to confront the structural constraints of the research community. This community, expressed in research validating committees and funding bodies, is predominantly male in its composition. In their major funding operations the concept of 'track record' of applicants for research applies as a rational response when allocating scarce resources. In this situation there is a tendency to give awards to people who are 'known' – and these tend to be men. Furthermore because women are not, by and large, able to gain access to Reader posts (these are positions which have particular responsibility for research), women are seen as agents of implementation of research rather than agents of creation of research. (A positive aspect of the institution in this case study has been a deliberate policy in at least one faculty to promote women in the research endeavour.)

It is clear that women's image of themselves when conducting academic discussions has a very different 'edge' to it from that of men. For example, one of the women interviewed in this research, commenting on the way women typically conduct themselves at conferences and in academic debate, emphasized how women attempt to be supportive of each other in debate. She referred to ways in which comments on each others' papers are designed to be facilitative and constructive, in contrast to the way in which she saw men as behaving when commenting – that is essentially to be destructive, to be individualistic and competitive. She saw the approach of women to intellectual activity as being just as rigorous as that of her male colleagues, but that it came from a different conception of the nature of the pursuit of the scientific debate. Given the dominant paradigm of a male-dominated, individualistically orientated academic culture, a co-operative culture can be seen as institutionally problematic and cause some degree of marginalization and discrediting of people (women) who work in this way, because of men's belief that 'rigour' can only be achieved 'by the cut and thrust of academic debate' – i.e. destructive criticism.

Turning to the core activity of the institution – teaching – there are significant differences in the images that men and women hold about the ways in which this activity is conducted. Interviews with teaching staff indicated that the image that many women have of men (and many men have of themselves) is that the teacher is an expert and that his or her function is largely concerned with the transmission of knowledge; further, that the proper relationship in the classroom is based on the ideas that power is essentially indivisible, that teaching is essentially subject-based, and that it is essentially impersonal with regard to the student population. On the other hand the interviews suggested that the women staff tend to see the teaching situation as one in which there is potential for mutual learning, in which teaching is essentially concerned with the journey towards knowledge, in which attention to process issues may be more important than the subject itself (that is, the process may become the subject), and that teaching is essentially a personal, interactive matter. This approach can be illustrated in the admittedly extreme case of women involved in teaching women's studies courses. Here the underlying personal orientation implied by the model of teaching discussed above may be amplified by the teacher's relationship to the subject itself. Raymond has written that:

> 'the true aim of the teaching I have been describing [in women's studies] is not to enforce feminist ideology but rather to *empassion* students with feminist knowledge. Inquiry is a profound passion and the teaching of the male academy has most often left its female learners with a passionless knowledge.'
>
> (Raymond 1985: 57)

(As this author suggests, there may be a boundary issue from time to time in relation to 'passion' becoming 'preaching'; her felicitous suggestion is that 'preaching is passion separated from its sources'.)

Both these models of the teaching activity are, in their own ways, positive. They are affirmative of somewhat different ideals about education, but both actually have some sort of grasp of the educational task. However when teachers are in a bad temper with each other or have not given the matter too much thought, the 'shadow' elements of these models are given transcendency. Men are characterized as 'hard', 'authoritarian' characters, and women as 'emotional', 'unable to control their classes', or 'incapable of actually transmitting any knowledge'. In settings that are male-dominated these images of competence/incompetence become distributed amongst the men. To that extent they are free-floating images in relation to gender. In one department which had been almost exclusively male, two women research staff volunteered to undertake some teaching. The initial assumption made by most of the men was that they would occupy a person-centred position with regard to their teaching. As one of the women observed: 'they, the "liberal" men, took us on because they thought we'd be their natural allies; they were in for a nasty surprise.' Indeed, although the teaching style of these women was student-centred, when it came to assessment of work the women were perceived by themselves and by their male colleagues as being as 'tough' and 'rigorous' as the most 'authoritarian' men. This example illustrates the trite but inescapable difficulty that reality is very complex; both men and women may hold personal ideologies about teaching or research or whatever that are simple in their essence but complicated in their implementation.

Behind logics of teaching there may hide sentiments about the activity itself;[2] shadow and substance are actually inextricably intertwined.

Although many women teachers feel that they are ascribed teaching styles and approaches by their male colleagues that tend to be either directly discrediting or else ambivalent in their messages about total competence, the women interviewed did not feel that these ascriptions were inflexible or (even where they were powerful) that they were inescapable. The women saw the roles ascribed to them as potentially or actually negotiable, more in accord with the sort of model of role suggested by Turner (1962) – with its emphasis upon the actor's ability to understand and evaluate what is happening in the situation – rather than more deterministic and mechanistic models.[3] The women interviewed felt that, although it was arduous, they could actually negotiate with male colleagues in order to avoid being marginalized (for example by the demonstration of competence), or being placed into what men considered to be a residual status (by not taking on, for example, an institutionalized 'caring' role).

Some women commented on a continuing difficulty that they encountered in that many men had a negative view about the 'reliability' of women. This was particularly directed towards women with children, but could also be directed towards women generally on the grounds that women are 'less committed' to their careers. This characterization is, of course, undertaken without recourse to 'factual' information, such as data on absence or attendance. Men tend to perceive women as being more tied down by domestic circumstances than are men and therefore more likely to be absent from work. There is a sentient paradox here that operates powerfully to the disadvantage of women. At the heart of the paradox is that members of staff – women and men – are permitted, in the culture of colleagueship, to be absent if they are attending conferences or undertaking consultancy (although staff do operate a rough and ready model of felt equity in this matter). So it is accepted that colleagues can be absent for periods of time. However there is a transmitted feeling that absence from work for domestic reasons is a source of disapproval from others and of guilt in the self. One of the women interviewed felt that a consequence of her having children was that she had been recategorized into the status 'parent', whereas men with children were not viewed in this sort of way. She went on to say:

'We have to be really careful to be seen to be doing things. We must not bring children into the department and when things go wrong [at home] we must not show it. Men handle such things covertly – when they have to handle a crisis it is not seen in the same disparaging way!'

More generally, men still created a quite rigid separation between the life of home and the life of the institution and of work. Not only was such a clear distinction seen as 'natural', as a taken-for-granted matter of 'fact', but it was also, for most men, a convenient way of being. (In many settings it can be the cause of some embarrassment if a male colleague brings into work some tale of sadness or evidence of troubles of a domestic sort.) However, there were also women in the institution who practised just as rigid a separation and there were men for whom their domestic and work lives were inextricably intertwined. But one of the consequences of the rigid separation of home and work is that women tend to become lodged in a situation in which they over-compensate. To avoid being seen as not sufficiently 'committed' they throw their resources disproportionately into the teaching activity – a highly visible phenomenon – at the expense of, for example, research. Although men also experience pressure to take on heavy teaching loads, it seems that women are more likely to succumb to such pressure than are men. Crucially, as I have argued above, teaching is *not of itself* seen as meriting reward in promotion or status terms in the institution. Although this pressure on women (which, it must be emphasized, is generated by themselves as well as by their male colleagues) appears to be widespread, it is not necessarily a binding feature of institutional life. One of the women described the 'existential moment' when she felt able to step a little outside the teaching activity, with the realization that she did not have to undertake *every* possible teaching commitment that came her way. A great sense of release came with the realization that she would have available the sort of time and space that would enable her to undertake research and consultancy activities.

Models of leadership inhibiting the promotion of women to senior positions

In the previous section I have argued that women can undertake negotiation in order to establish co-competence with men as colleagues. At the same time women's achievement of senior positions and their movement into 'management' status in the institution continues to be fraught with difficulty. There appear to be two major features here. One concerns the characteristics which are required to be a senior manager; the other concerns the way in which the pool of women available to take on leadership/management roles is repressed.

In order to illustrate the first of these features I will explore some of the implications of the following advertisement for the position of director of a polytechnic. Although this advertisement was not in respect of the institution upon which this chapter is focused, some of the features of the advertisement have relevance for the institution – and indeed for any institution that adopts a particular model of leadership. Part of the advertisement read:

> 'The successful candidate must therefore have the proven ability to motivate and manage a large organisation and the experience in education, industry or the public service to provide convincing leadership in a period of educational development.'

From one point of view the criteria in the advertisement are self-evident; they represent common-sense, even mundane, expectations of the qualities expected in a person occupying a leadership position. Contained within the advertisement, however, is an unstated but specific concept of leadership. This concept seems to relate more to male than to female values about leadership. The expressions 'proven ability' and 'convincing leadership' are both indicative of a view that sees leaders as exerting a sense of dominance and that believes in the concept of 'captaincy' as this is conventionally understood, rather than (for example) a *primus inter pares* theory of leadership. Mant (1983) has discussed preferences for styles of leadership and suggested that most women prefer to undertake leadership roles in a manner that is rather different from that of most men. It is important to note that in his discussion Mant has taken a fairly generalized set of criteria for the assignment of the modes of leadership on a gender basis. In doing this he has taken common-sense versions of the nature of women, but has interpreted these characteristics in a benign manner (contrary to the usual negative view which men take of the characteristics of women when applied to the leadership function).

At heart, Mant's argument is that most women (and some men) have a greater interest in leadership styles that emphasize the need for both leader and led to have a close identification with the nature of the task or with the organization. Essentially a non-combative style of leadership, it calls upon qualities of co-operation and an ability to achieve identification with the mission of the organization. Mant went on to argue that most men (and some women) exercise a preference for a more direct, interpersonal style of leadership. Here there is a preference expressed by the leader either for affiliation or, alternatively, for creating situations of dynamic conflict in order that, according to the belief system enshrined in this style, the 'best' solutions to situations and problems might emerge. With its emphasis on competition and the ability to be entrepreneurial, this form of leadership, characterized by Mant as the 'raider' style, is seen by him to have become the predominant leadership style in many Western organizations. Certainly within public sector higher education it has perceived advantages. Its emphasis on personal relationships and the ability to modify organizational situations through these relationships gives to decision-making the appearance of speed and of an ability to respond rapidly to the exigencies of the environment. Furthermore, because this style generates centralization of decision-making in the organization, it gives to members, so it is claimed, a sense of certainty.

Both these styles of leadership have their 'shadow'. In the non-combative case the leader might be regarded as indecisive and in consequence may be thought to be poor with regard to crisis management. The processes of seeking commitment and organizationally directed allegiance are necessarily slow, which may not match a rapidly changing organizational environment. The 'shadow' of the 'raider' style lies in the ways in which competition can become merely combative and in which conflict may lose its positive dynamism. The leader's desire for affiliation can become seen as merely self-seeking or alternatively as compulsively rebarbative and conflict-ridden, so that other members collude to protect themselves – and in so doing place the organization into a cycle of conflict. When occupying or being considered for leadership positions women tend to be seen by many men (and some women) as incumbents of these 'shadow' styles. Women are placed in a no-win situation in which if they display strong 'raider' characteristics they are felt to be excessively hyperactive and too assertive; it may even be suggested that women who behave in this way have 'nothing else in their lives'. On the other hand, if they practice an organizationally centred style of leadership they may be characterized as too 'passive'. Even where senior management do have some understanding of the legitimate need of women to achieve leadership positions, there may be a reluctance to promote them because of the tacit understanding that in the current economic climate a head of department or dean must be able to 'fight for his corner'.

There is, of course, nothing new in the discovery that, whatever women do, it may well turn out to be 'inappropriate', given the bundle of propositions which most men (and some women) hold about women. In the field of mental health Broverman and her colleagues have written about stereotyped views of women's psychology:

'for a woman to be healthy from an adjustment viewpoint, she must adjust to and accept the behavioural norms for her sex, even though these be less healthy for the generalised competent mature adult.'

(Broverman *et al.* 1970: 6)

In other words, it is 'healthy' and 'right' for a woman to be psychologically *un*healthy – no doubt so that male-dominated society can denigrate and dismiss her *whatever* she does. If this is translated to the present context it reinforces the suggestion that women are permitted to exercise leadership only in styles that are considered to be 'appropriate' to their gender – but that when they actually do this many men (and some women) will think the less of them [4] A number of the interviews were conducted in a department that had recently acquired a male head; in this department, very atypically, the majority of staff were women. There did not appear to be any strong feelings expressed that a man had obtained the post, and indeed some of the women expressed pleasure at this appointment with the feeling that a man would be able to 'sort us out as a department'. Another woman stated that her experience of women as leaders in other organizations had caused her to believe that women had 'poor self-control and were not good leaders'.

In addition to these opposing views about the nature of leadership and management capability, it is clear that there is a profound structural barrier to women achieving promotions to the highest positions in public sector higher education. The point is simply that the general pool of women available to take up such positions is small compared with the pool of men. Unless the wording of advertisements is specific, there are likely to be very many more men applicants than women. In the absence of significant policies at a national level to begin to create equalization of opportunity (through, for example, policies of positive discrimination) it will continue to be unlikely that women will obtain senior appointments.

Fighting back – women as agents of change

In the previous sections there has been some discussion of the ways in which men can, sometimes deliberately and sometimes unwittingly, 'decompetence' their women colleagues. It is important to make it clear that this is not a consistent effort, even if it is ubiquitous. Although the culture of the institution is male-dominated it is not appropriate to regard that culture as entirely monolithic. Just as there are some women in the institution who exercise a preference for undertaking their activities in accord with the 'masculine' model, so there are men whose preferences are participative and who are co-operative in their endeavours. Although there are static elements, there is a negotiated area between men and women staff as they carry out their duties within the institution. As Strauss *et al.* have noted:

> 'when professionals are brought together and enjoined to carry out their work in the same locale, concepts of structure (formal and informal) as relatively set systems of norms and expectations are inadequate to explain resulting activity. The activity of interacting professionals is, we submit, largely governed by continual re-constitution of bases of work through negotiation.'
>
> (Strauss *et al.* 1964: 375)

Thus when staff are recruited into an organization they can alter the shape and ethos of the parts in which they are located.

I have referred above to the way in which men's expectation that women colleagues would be a 'soft touch' in terms of their assessment of students was based on an error that was bound up in men's stereotypes of women. Defeating those stereotypes represented, in itself, a shift in perspective for some of the men, so that the women were re-categorized into the status of competent colleagues – they were seen as capable of being 'just like us' in their ability to assess students. Another example of women as agents of change will now be considered.

One woman brought into her teaching in a department concerned with organization studies a central interest in gender and the implications of gender differentiation for women. The reactions of the

174

male staff to this adventure in learning were diverse. Some saw this developing situation as entirely to be welcomed on the basis of their understanding that men could not adequately undertake teaching in which the dilemmas confronting women in organizations were the central issue. The men recognized that this was an important area of concern that had not been 'undertaken properly' before. Another, somewhat less altruistic view, was that for women to undertake this sort of teaching was to be welcomed because it meant that the whole area of gender and gender relations could be relegated to women colleagues. These men recognized that gender issues were important, but a problematic area for them in the teaching situation. Most men were, however, relatively indifferent about the introduction of this subject into the teaching programmes. This indifference tended to be either slightly hostile or passively uninterested; the hostility arose out of an attitude that there was no particular issue to discuss, as attention to gender was essentially somewhat marginal in its thrust and distracted from the major issues of understanding organizations, while the passive indifference suggested a gentle puzzlement that such an area of concern could exist, together with an acceptance that it might – as long as it did not involve them. As the women involved in this teaching were research staff their period of stay in the department was limited. Their feeling was that when their contracts had been concluded and they were no longer attached to the institution, their long-term impact would be experienced as negligible. This may, indeed, have been the case, but what they did achieve within the system was a shift of awareness within the culture of the department that at least placed gender 'on the agenda' as a topic of some significance in the way that the department conducted its affairs.

This theme of culture change and the development of conscious-ness was reiterated in interviews with women in other departments. Speaking of the development of gender as a topic in syllabuses in her department, one woman teacher observed:

> 'women have to be in the right place at the right time . . . they need to be assertive. . . . You've got to struggle all the time, you can't let up. You've got to make sure that course planning committees have a gender aspect.'

This last point highlights the need to ensure that women are well-placed in the process of negotiation for the acceptance of gender as a significant area, not only at informal levels but also within the formal structure of an institution. At this latter level, women who had been involved in the establishment of a women's studies course at a postgraduate level spoke of the way in which getting that course through the institution's system had been educative for the men who sat on the committees, who had to be persuaded that women's studies represented a legitimate subject for the award of a degree. It seems clear that when women begin to articulate claims for the legitimacy of gender as an area of concern in syllabus construction they are also concerned with processes of culture change, with the potential for modification going beyond the introduction of new syllabus areas into the curriculum. In doing this, however, women may incur a high personal cost. Amongst the women interviewed there was an awareness that the 'performances' they give before committees and the like must not only be highly articulate, but also not *too* abrasive. The women saw that they must be 'committed', but not *too* much so (they did not want to be seen, as one of the interviewees put it, as being 'at it again'). One of the women commented on the cycle of stigmatization she felt that women get involved in if they express interest in raising gender issues. The cycle was such that – in a situation of male physical dominance by virtue of their numbers – women are on the one hand literally less visible (there are few of them), but when they *are* present they are very noticeable. Because their presence is noticed, because a higher profile is given to them than that of many of their male colleagues, women have to exercise more control. This applies both to their behaviour and to what they say. They are, in Goffman's (1969) felicitous expression, more 'on-stage' than their male colleagues. Women, for example, are likely to become somewhat self-conscious about the topics they choose to talk about and how they discuss them. This very self-consciousness may well be disabling in the sense that it pushes women into areas of discussion in which the affirmation of their feminist nature is assured. Although the women interviewed at the institution said that they had not personally experienced harassment, it is clear that there are circumstances in which: 'where women step out of line . . . they receive the full force of a reaction which constitutes a specific and highly effective form of intimidation' (Ramazanoglu 1985: 3).

One situation in which women are seen by many men (and some women, particularly those who do not see themselves as 'feminist') to be 'stepping out of line' is when feminist interest is understood to represent an incursion into the common-sense understandings about gender relations. This may be illustrated by what appeared to be very simple incidents that were discovered (by both researchers and actors) and commented upon (by actors) in the institution. One such incident was where hand-outs generated by staff did not always accord with the sorts of gender guidelines suggested by, for example, the British Sociological Association. (Similar guidelines have been adopted by the institution's official 'Working Party on the Place of Women' in order to assist the elimination of sexist language.) In particular instances men showed impatience when women staff indicated the need for change in such materials – men did not always understand the necessity for these changes either in practical or symbolic terms.

At another level, women in the institution encountered ubiquitous features of interaction that they felt inhibited the development of straightforward 'professional' relationships. Women were sometimes addressed collectively by men colleagues as 'the ladies' or individually as 'dear' – but men did not address each other in this familiar way! There were other examples of 'decompetencing' behaviours by men. Women experienced these practices as everyday items of common-sense culture, which Heritage refers to as: 'part of the filigree of small-scale, socially organised behaviours which are unceasingly iterated. . . . The institution of gender appears as densely woven fabric of morally accountable cultural practices' (1984: 198). Such practices render men into causes of many women's anger and despair.

The women interviewed saw men's use of language as not deliberately repressive, although a few men were identified as having malign intent. From the men's perspective it was an accepted mode of behaviour to be 'forthright' in social interaction. This can be experienced as abrasive behaviour by those who hold to a more subtle view as to the nature of everyday interaction. In a general way, forthright or even aggressive behaviour:

'tends to be regarded by men as fairly trivial and perhaps even therapeutic. . . . People who are subjected to this sort of behaviour are not expected to take offence at it, certainly not lasting offence.'
(Spencer and McAuley 1985: 5)

This does not necessarily place women in a position of weakness with regard to interaction with men; indeed, many women learn to become as abrasive as their male colleagues. But for some women this process of re-socialization brings with it a sense of separation from valued aspects of an earlier self.[5] Although most of the women interviewed did not want to be trapped in passive, 'caring' roles, some felt that, in developing themselves into (relatively) powerful professional women, they had lost touch with the positive aspects of their identity gained from earlier socialization. On the other hand some regarded the growth of abrasiveness as the development of a new area of competence, in which case they did not consider that there was a necessary loss in such qualities as sensitivity.

Beyond abrasiveness there is also the question of the use by men of sexist language. Reference has earlier been made to men's practices in this matter and an issue of some concern for women is the ability to find the appropriate response. They might, for example, choose to 'ignore' such comments, or else adopt what might be referred to as a strategy of parallelism (one woman commented: 'Every time he calls me "dear", I call him it back. That has made him stop it'). A third strategy is to make every instance of the occurrence of sexist language the occasion for a justified rebuke. Whichever of these strategies is undertaken, each has its own consequences. In the first instance the hurt is kept inside, in the second there is the possibility that parallelism can lead to a collusive trivialization of the issue, whilst in the third the women concerned were aware of the potential possibility for personal disruption and the portrayal by men of women as negative, obsessed with 'these things'. When women undertake this sort of corrective action they characteristically experience themselves as being pushed into behaviours that are essentially, as far as they are concerned, time-wasting. As one woman observed: 'It's not my job to educate men into improved behaviour.' The need to adopt *any* strategy in this matter and women's consciousness of this issue points to the requirement women feel to be placed upon them that their identities need to be very carefully managed in order to achieve a portrayal of competent institutional membership. As Epstein has noted: 'for the women professional, the working environment is always transmitting messages that she is unique, and she anticipates them' (1970: 181). Although some women may feel that the careful managing of their behaviour suggests a degree of collusion with men, most, concerned with the practicalities of making a living in the organization, saw it as a realistic strategy for bringing about change at an interactive level.

Conclusion

It has been suggested throughout this chapter that most of the women interviewed were aware of features in the institution and in their working relationships with male colleagues that were problematic, both in personal relationship and career terms. For their part, many men had a dawning awareness that there *was* an issue there that would not simply go away. (However an ability to be aware can give rise to complacency and a false optimism, e.g. that by being more sensitive to language they had then 'done enough' to remedy the situation.)

Although all members of the institution had to demonstrate at least a degree of competence – however that is to be defined – in order to legitimate their continuing participation, women, because of their minority situation, typically felt they had to make their presentation of self rather more 'effortful'. In a different professional setting Epstein wrote that gender discrimination was lower when: 'some do not permit their own self-consciousness to cause them to over-react. Women who are professional . . . and do not deny their sex, are said to be able to make the best impression on men and gain acceptance' (Epstein 1970: 195). Although this position may be ideologically offensive to some women, such a view was recognized by most of the women interviewed to be a reflection of their own understanding of the situation. In interactional terms, what many women actually have is clearly defined professional boundaries; if men offend these boundaries then women will inform them of the offence. At an organizational level, it was clear that women had taken initiatives which affected the culture and, potentially, the structure of the institution. For some, the process of gaining accreditation through the committee system for a postgraduate course in women's studies was a solidarity-creating experience for them. It was certainly an educative experience for the (almost exclusively) male members of the various committees in which the proposal was discussed. At a structural level, women had a major responsibility for the organization of a 'Working Party on the Place of Women' in the institution. As this was a sub-committee of the institution's academic board, the feeling expressed by women was that it is more likely to have some effect on the institution's policies than not. Although, like all public sector higher education organizations, the institution has had to face the vicissitudes caused by inadequate funding, its self-image in terms of its achievement of primary goals was high. There was a general feeling that members handle their work competently and that the institution has a good relationship with its environment. This was encouraging for, as Epstein has observed: 'It is not that better . . .

institutions do not discriminate, but their treatment of individuals tends generally to be considerate and more universalistic' (1970: 195). It seems that the sense of organizational maturity of the institution has, at a macro-level, brought about a heightened awareness of some of the gender issues inherent within it. A state of heightened awareness is a prerequisite for structural change to take place, although this may not necessarily lead to an attitude shift for all staff members.

There are, however, two features which continue to block the full development of equalization for women in the institution. The first is historical – that most appointments to the institution took place when there was little or no consciousness within it of gender issues. Gender awareness only really comes about for organizational members *as* members when there are numbers of women in the organization who will articulate what these issues are. It has been shown above that, where there are women who see gender issues as important (and not all women do), they have altered men's understandings of the situation. However, whether from malignancy or sloth or ignorance, many male teachers in the institution – even today, in the mid-1980s – still 'make an excuse and leave' when the topic of equality for women is raised. Second, some women suggested that access to senior positions is now *more* difficult for them than it used to be, because of the reassertion of the belief that senior managers need to be 'tough, capable of fighting for their own corner', and the concomitant belief (by men) that most women are incapable of taking on this sort of role. No doubt the desperate financial and other pressures on public sector higher education are responsible, at least in part, for this reaction.

Notes

1 As several of the contributions to this volume indicate.
2 This distinction is derived from Roy (1955).
3 This could be contrasted with experience of women teachers in schools, where it appears that women's traditional roles ('caring' etc.) are implicitly and explicitly institutionalized into status positions that have as part of their job descriptions items such as 'responsibility for pastoral care'.
4 The classic 'double-bind' situation.
5 I am persuaded by Belotti's suggestion that the self *is* socialized – she cites the experience of children in infant school where, although there is an attempt to respect the individuality of each child, teachers end up by reproducing, quite unconsciously, the habitual modes of the 'active, managerial boy and the passive, subordinate girl' (1975: 137).

Academics

References

Belotti, E.G. (1975) *Little Girls: Social Conditioning and Its Effects on the Stereotyped Role of Women during Infancy*. London: Writers' and Readers' Publishing Co-operative.

Broverman, I.K., Broverman, D.M., Clarkson, F.E., Rosenkrantz, P.S., and Vogel, S.R. (1970) Sex-role Stereotypes and Clinical Judgements of Mental Health. *Journal of Consulting and Clinical Psychology* 34: 1–7.

Epstein, C.F. (1970) *Woman's Place: Options and Limits in Professional Careers*. Berkeley: University of California Press.

Goffman, E. (1969) *The Presentation of Self in Everyday Life*. London: Allen Lane.

Heritage, J. (1984) *Garfinkel and Ethnomethodology*. London: Polity Press.

Kaplan, A.G. (1985) Female or Male Therapists for Women Patients: New Formulations. *Psychiatry* 48: 111–21.

Maher, F. (1985) Classroom Pedagogy and the New Scholarship on Women. In M. Culley and C. Portuges (eds) *Gendered Subjects*. London: Routledge and Kegan Paul, pp. 29–48.

Mant, A. (1983) *Leaders We Deserve*. London: Martin Robertson.

Ramazanoglu, A. (1985) *Sex and Violence in Academic Life, or You Can Keep a Good Woman Down*. Paper presented to British Sociological Association Annual Conference.

Raymond, J.G. (1985) Women's Studies: A Knowledge of One's Own. In M. Culley and C. Portuges (eds) *Gendered Subjects*. London: Routledge and Kegan Paul, pp. 49–63.

Roy, D. (1955) Efficiency and 'the Fix': Informal Intergroup Relations in Piece Work. *American Journal of Sociology* 60: 255–66.

Spencer, A. and McAuley, M.J. (1985) *Sticks and Stones May Break My Bones but Names Will Never Hurt Me: Verbal Violence and the Dynamics of Exclusion from the Professional Arena*. Paper presented to British Sociological Association Annual Conference.

Spender, D. (1982) Sex Bias. In D. Warren Piper (ed.) *Is Higher Education Fair?* Papers presented to the 17th Annual Conference of the Society for Research into Higher Education. Guildford: SRHE, pp. 104–27.

Stanley, L. and Wise, S. (1983) *Breaking Out: Feminist Consciousness and Feminist Research*. London: Routledge and Kegan Paul.

Strauss, A., Schatzman, L., Bucher, R., Ehrlich, D., and Savshin, M. (1964) *Psychiatric Ideologies and Institutions*. New York: Free Press.

Turner, R.H. (1962) Role Taking: Process versus Conformity. In A.M. Rose (ed.) *Human Behaviour and Social Process*. London: Routledge and Kegan Paul, pp. 20–40.

Woodall, J., Showstack, A., Towers, B., and McNally, C. (1985) Never Promote a Woman if there's a Man in Sight. *Guardian*, 10 September.

© 1987 John McAuley

9

Who Becomes an Engineer?
Social Psychological Antecedents
of a Non-traditional Career Choice

Peggy Newton

Introduction

Very few women become engineers and women who consider engineering as a career often face reactions of doubt and disbelief from their families, friends, and future colleagues. One of the questions which is often asked, either explicitly or implicitly, is about their femininity: 'How can a woman remain feminine in an environment which is so strongly dominated by men, both in numbers and in values?' A recent film about women engineers entitled 'What's a Girl Like You . . .?'[1] accurately reflects the concern that many people feel about women in engineering. There is a strong popular feeling that a woman must be very tough and masculine to survive as an engineer.

Recent initiatives designed to increase the numbers of women in science and technology have challenged this stereotype and have raised important questions about how women are represented in these fields. These programmes have generally assumed that the masculine image of science and technology is an important factor in women's career decisions about these fields. In seeking to bring about change, most programmes have been concerned with modifying this masculine image and making science and technology more relevant to women's interests and experiences. They have encouraged school pupils to question traditional definitions of sex roles and have suggested that science and technology are important to both sexes.

A key feature of two of the best known experimental programmes – 'Girls Into Science and Technology' and the Engineering Industry

Who becomes an engineer?

Training Board's 'Insight' – has been to provide attractive role models of women scientists and technologists.[2] The assumptions underlying this strategy are clear. Most people expect female scientists or engineers to be tough, aggressive, and masculine and often assume that they will have radical views about equality between the sexes. By presenting women who do not conform to these popular images, these programmes have encouraged girls to see science or engineering as possible careers for themselves. The picture of the female scientist or engineer as being rather 'masculine' and holding unconventional views about women's roles is not only widely held, but is also strongly reflected in the academic literature on women in science and technology. The female scientist or technologist has often been viewed as 'deviant', and her commitment to her work has been seen as compensating for 'problems' with feminine identity.

This chapter begins with a discussion of some of the limitations of previous research on women in engineering. It then considers the social context in which girls and boys choose engineering and the highly negative (or rather non-conforming) image of engineering as a potential career for women. Drawing on recent developments in psychological theory, known as gender schema theory, it suggests that the choice of engineering has different psychological implications for the two sexes. This argument is supported by empirical data from a group of young women entering engineering at technician level. The study cited offers comparisons between female technicians, their male counterparts, and young women entering traditionally 'feminine' fields of work. It is particularly concerned with how people in various occupational groups define their 'femininity' and 'masculinity' and how these concepts may be linked with factors in their family life and early childhood. Finally, the chapter explores the implications of this research and other studies for the recruitment and retention of female engineers. The focus of the chapter is on female engineers in the United Kingdom, though research from the USA is also drawn upon.

The limitations of previous research

Most of the research on women engineers has been severely limited by the lack of appropriate control or comparison groups and by an almost exclusive focus on highly qualified women. Until recently much of the information available was autobiographical and consisted of personal comments in conference proceedings on the 'problems' for women in engineering (Kundsin 1973; Ott and Reese 1975). Furthermore, women engineers were often included in samples of women scientists and there was no attempt to distinguish between the two groups, although there appear to be important differences in personality and values between scientists and engineers and between people in different fields of science (Bachtold and Werner 1973; Cotgrove and Weinreich-Haste 1982). Even in more systematic studies, researchers have usually focused on women studying (or intending to study) engineering at graduate level (Bryant 1984; Davis 1975; Weinreich-Haste and Newton 1983; Wolpe 1971). However, this balance is beginning to be redressed with studies of women technician trainees (Breakwell and Weinberger 1983; Newton 1981; Newton and Brocklesby 1982), though there is still very little information on women training at craft level or on women actually employed as engineers at any level (Engineering Industry Training Board 1984; Davidson 1984).

Although many of the shortcomings in the existing research stem from the scarcity of potential subjects and the difficulty of attracting research funding for the topic, the majority of studies have served to perpetuate popular images of women engineers. Without comparison groups it is easy to overestimate the difficulties faced by female engineers and to fail to recognize the problems faced by women in other fields of employment. It is an open question whether the experiences of female engineers and women in other fields are qualitatively different, or whether they simply represent a more extreme form of discrimination faced by all women in employment. Much of the discrimination experienced by women is not deliberate and overt, but stems from organizational policies that have been designed by, and for the needs of, men:

'The great weight of evidence of the research in the UK and the USA shows that it is far less likely to be overt prejudice and discrimination against women in organizational policies that works against them but rather that the systems have been designed and administered by and for men – taking men's careers and attitudes as the norm and never questioning that this is in the interests of the organization. This affects every aspect of the system and particularly every hurdle in the career ladder.'

(Rothwell 1982: 19)

Many of the difficulties faced by women are thus traceable to structural factors and to the conditions under which they are employed. However, both individual characteristics and institutional factors need to be considered in analysing women's representation in various occupations. Recent research on female engineers suggests that they differ from both their male counterparts and from women working in traditionally feminine fields in that female engineers are less concerned about distinctions based on gender and are relatively comfortable in being seen as different from others. These differences make it easier for these women to become engineers, but they also appear to distance them from their male colleagues. To understand who becomes an engineer, we need to place the issue in a social context.

The social context

In both the USA and the United Kingdom engineering has had a lower status than other scientific fields and has often had difficulty in attracting talented entrants. The problem has been particularly severe in the United Kingdom and may have been exacerbated by the fact that the title 'engineer' has been used to encompass a very wide range of occupations, ranging from craft to professional level. Yet in both countries women have viewed engineering much more negatively than other scientific careers and have seen the field as extremely 'unfeminine' (Roberts 1964; Rossi 1965).

Although there have been increases in recent years both in the numbers of women technician trainees and in the numbers of women studying engineering at polytechnics and universities, they remain a rarity. In 1982 only 2.4 per cent of technicians and 3.5 per cent of scientist and technologists in the engineering industry were women (Engineering Industry Training Board 1984). Therefore women entering most fields of engineering today are still pioneers and subject to the extra pressures associated with being token women in a strongly male-dominated industry. It will be argued that the traditional labelling of engineering as a 'man's world' makes the process of choosing engineering quite different for females compared with males. These differences have far-reaching social implications, which serve to confirm the male's choice of engineering and to confirm his career pattern as a usual one whilst at the same time labelling the female's career pattern as deficient, rather than merely different.

Because of the strong labelling of engineering as a 'man's world', the choice of engineering has different social and psychological implications for the two sexes. The boy who chooses engineering is seen as following his natural talents and interests. He is typically encouraged in a single-minded pursuit of engineering-related hobbies and his narrow interests are seen as both 'natural' and appropriate. His choice is seen as congruent with his developing 'masculinity'. In contrast, the girl choosing engineering is seen as defying gender-role expectations and as seriously lacking in 'femininity'. Rossi (1965) has speculated that the barriers to a woman's career choice in engineering operate much earlier than in her choice of medicine or scientific fields. She sees engineering as representing a complete antithesis to 'feminine' skills and interests. Engineering presents both a highly 'masculine' image, and it also suggests less prestigious blue-collar work. Rossi went on to argue that girls expect little parental support for the choice of engineering as a career, especially from their mothers, and they assume that they will meet resentment from future male colleagues. Unlike other scientific careers, many women see engineering as a job requiring skills and characteristics that women do not possess.

These speculations have received strong empirical support, especially the suggestion of the strong 'deviant' image of engineering for women. In her study of female engineering students, Wolpe found that 50 per cent of the sample felt some stigma associated with their choice of career and that they had 'sometimes felt odd rather than happy about their decision' (1971:130). This powerful negative image of engineering as a career for women serves to prevent most girls from ever considering it as a career, and may lead women who have begun a career in engineering to question their choice. In a large sample of sixth-form girls studying science, Roberts (1964) reported that only 16 per cent would consider engineering as a career. High amongst the reasons for rejecting engineering was the view that it was a 'man's field' and unsuitable for women. There was also a strong feeling amongst respondents that they were not well enough qualified or academically good enough to do engineering. Even amongst women intending to study engineering, concern about the field being a 'man's world' is strong. In a survey of 674 seventeen-year-old women considering engineering as a career, Weinreich-Haste and Newton (1983) found that the two leading concerns about working in engineering were lack of mechanical experience and discrimination by potential employers. Both findings have been widely replicated in other research (Breakwell and Weinberger 1983; Bryant 1984; Davidson 1984; Newton and Brocklesby 1982).

Who becomes an engineer?

The persistent social labelling of engineering as a career 'unsuitable' for women appears to lead to differences in the type of commitment that women and men have to engineering and in their perspectives of it as a career. These differences are reflected in their political attitudes and values, particularly in their views on women's role in society.

Career commitment, attitudes, and values

Girls and boys choose engineering for different reasons and at different points in their school careers. These differences serve to accentuate the differences between female and male entrants to the field and also appear to be linked with characteristic political attitudes and values. Typically boys choose engineering relatively early and do so out of a fascination in how things work and an interest in science (Newton 1984; Ott 1978). In contrast girls are more likely to choose engineering relatively late and to see their choice as related to an interest in and talent for mathematics (Johnson 1975; Newton 1984; Ott 1978).

Although early commitment and dedication to a field is usually highly regarded by both admissions tutors and potential employers, the male's early commitment to engineering may represent immaturity and an attempt to avoid social contact. Male engineering students frequently report being uninterested in people, having few close relationships in childhood, and experiencing difficulty in social relationships. They appear to choose their career earlier than their male peers and be less likely to admit ever having had any doubts about their career choice. This psychological rigidity is accompanied by a highly conservative world-view, with associated political attitudes and values (Hacker 1981; Rubin 1969).

In comparison with male engineers, female engineers hold relatively liberal attitudes and values, although most of their views are still classified as 'conservative' when compared with female groups in other occupations (Cotgrove and Weinreich-Haste 1982). Perhaps the largest area of difference between female engineers and males in the field is in how they regard gender and the division of labour between the sexes. Although female engineers do not see themselves as 'feminists' and do not have more radical views than women entering traditionally feminine occupations, their attitudes towards women's roles are significantly more pro-feminist than those held by male engineers (Bryant 1984; Newton 1985).

187

Writing on the differences between female and male engineers, Robin (1969) observed that the 'problem' for women in engineering was one of incompatibility between females and males. He described male engineers as introverted, unsophisticated, narrow in interests, and relatively ininterested in cultural activities. He saw female engineers as having much broader interests. Similar observations have been made by other researchers (Brown 1975; Ott 1978). Davis (1975) noted that one of the major reasons why women students left engineering was because of the narrowness of the technical curriculum and lack of opportunity to explore wider interests. She asked female engineering students to describe their male classmates and found that the men were characterized as being dull and immature, as well as unfriendly. The gulf between female and male engineers has been described eloquently by Brown, a woman engineer who has written about her own career:

'Engineering is probably the toughest profession for a woman to make her mark in. The reason for this is that engineering has generally attracted to its ranks men who are extremely conservative . . . they are proving even slower than lawyers or doctors to accept women as their peers or superiors.'

(Brown 1975: 5)

A recent psychological theory, known as gender schema theory (Bem 1985) offers an explanation for the considerable psychological differences observed between female and male engineers. Coupled with recent empirical data, it suggests that male engineers are more likely than female engineers to see their career choice as representing an important aspect of their gender identity. To understand this line of argument it is necessary to summarize some changes in how 'femininity' and 'masculinity' are conceptualized and to introduce the concept of androgyny.

Femininity, masculinity, and androgyny

Until recently most people, including psychologists, have seen 'femininity' and 'masculinity' as polar opposites. Being 'feminine' has implied not being 'masculine' and vice versa. It has been popularly assumed that females should have only 'feminine' qualities and males only 'masculine' ones. However, these stereotyped notions remained largely untested and unverified. They seemed so obvious as to be unchallengeable.

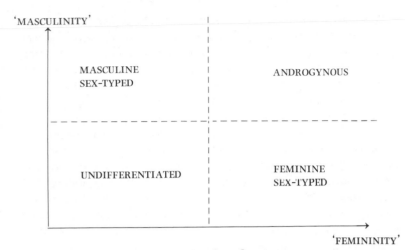

Figure 9.1 Four-fold androgyny classification

During the 1970s a number of psychologists challenged traditional notions of femininity and masculinity (Bem 1974; Constantinople 1973; Spence, Helmreich, and Stapp 1975). Working largely on the basis of empirical evidence, they suggested that rather than 'femininity' and 'masculinity' representing opposite ends of a continuum, they were independent and unrelated to each other. Out of this work came the revival of the notion of androgyny – the idea that people can simultaneously have both feminine and masculine characteristics. To understand how people saw gender in relation to their own personality, it was argued, it is necessary to ask people about the relative balance of their feminine and masculine characteristics.

As a concomitant of this line of research, psychologists have developed tests to measure psychological androgyny (Bem 1974; Spence and Helmreich 1978). Typically such tests yield both a 'femininity' score and a 'masculinity' score. Respondents are categorized according to the balance of the two scores, so that there are four possible outcomes (see *Figure 9.1*). Two outcomes represent 'sex-typing' – a significant difference in the proportion of 'feminine' and 'masculine' characteristics (feminine sex-typing or masculine sex-typing). The other two suggest a relative balance between 'feminine' and 'masculine' characteristics (those who are relatively high on both scales are classified as 'androgynous'; those who are relatively low on both scales are classified as 'undifferentiated').

Early research suggested that psychologically androgynous people were more psychologically flexible and had a wider repertoire of behaviours (Bem 1974). They were more likely than people who were traditionally sex-typed to be comfortable in engaging in behaviour which is usually seen as characteristic of the opposite sex (Bem and Lenney 1976). There was evidence suggesting that they had higher self-esteem and were less likely to suffer from depression (Williams 1978). These early studies brought about an explosion of research using androgyny measures. Some of these studies confirmed the early findings and suggested that psychological androgyny represented a new standard of mental health for both females and males – thus contradicting the conventional notion that women should have predominantly 'feminine' characteristics and men should have predominantly 'masculine' characteristics. Other studies questioned these conclusions and suggested that in a male-dominated society it was 'masculine' characteristics which conferred psychological health and stability for *both* sexes (Kelly and Worell 1977; Taylor and Hall 1982).

One of the leading proponents of research on androgyny has been the American psychologist, Sandra Bem (1981, 1983, 1985) who has suggested that gender schema theory provides an explanation of how people learn about gender. Bem argues that people differ in the extent to which they organize and process information according to gender. As part of this process, they also differ in the extent to which they see their various personal characteristics as relating to gender. Gender schema theory suggests that people who are sex-typed (those who are classified either as traditionally sex-typed or as cross-sex-typed) are more likely than people who are not sex-typed (those who are classified as androgynous or undifferentiated) to use gender as a basis for categorizing information. [3] Traditionally sex-typed people are also more likely than non-sex-typed or cross-sex-typed people to feel uncomfortable in engaging in behaviour which is usually considered gender-inappropriate. They tend to see such behaviour as detracting from their sense of 'femininity' or 'masculinity'. Bem suggests that traditionally sex-typed people actively avoid gender-inappropriate behaviour, observing that 'sex-typed individuals are motivated to restrict their behaviour in accordance with cultural definitions of gender appropriateness' (Bem 1985: 207).

My own research has been concerned with how schoolgirls choose engineering as a career. In the research female engineering trainees were compared with two main groups: male engineering trainees and young women entering traditionally 'feminine' occupations. It was hypothesized that there would be differences between the groups in how they thought about gender and how they defined their own 'femininity' and 'masculinity'.

The choice of engineering as a career

The primary subjects in this research were a group of young women who were being trained as technicians in engineering under a special scholarship scheme run by the Engineering Industry Training Board (Engineering Industry Training Board 1983; Newton 1981). They were trained in two types of engineering in two regions of England, London and the Midlands. The women in London were trained in electronics and electrical engineering, whereas those in the Midlands were trained in light mechanical engineering. These young women training to be engineers were compared with two groups – their female schoolfriends, and male trainee engineers being trained on the same sites. The female schoolfriends had either left school at sixteen to enter traditionally 'feminine' jobs or had stayed on at school to do A-levels. In London the female engineering trainees and their female schoolfriends were compared with two additional groups, young women undertaking a course in business studies which included training in secretarial skills, and young women following a nursery nursing course.

During their first few weeks of training all those participating in the research completed the Bem Sex Role Inventory, a measure of psychological androgyny. Based on the balance of their scores on the 'femininity' and 'masculinity' scales of this test, respondents in each group were classified in one of the four categories referred to above: feminine sex-typed, masculine sex-typed, androgynous, or undifferentiated.[4] The results of this analysis are shown in *Table 9.1*.

When female engineering trainees were compared with their female friends and with male engineering trainees, they were significantly more likely to be classified as androgynous (high on 'femininity'; high on 'masculinity') than either their friends or male engineers. Conversely, they were significantly less likely to be feminine sex-typed than their friends, whereas male engineers were more likely to be masculine sex-typed than either female group. The proportions of female engineers and their female friends who were classified as masculine sex-typed (27 per cent and 25 per cent) were

191

Table 9.1   *Four-fold androgyny classification for male engineers,
female engineers, and female friends*[1]

	Androgynous[2]		Masculine[3] sex-typed		Feminine[4] sex-typed		Undifferentiated	
	N	%	N	%	N	%	N	%
Male engineers (N=31)	5	16	22	71	1	3	3	10
Female engineers (N=37)	16	43	10	27	6	16	5	14
Female friends (N=57)	12	21	14	25	28	49	3	5

Notes
1 All significance levels reported are for a two-tailed test.
2 Female engineers are significantly more likely to be classified as androgynous than male engineers (Chi squared =4.61, 1 df, p > .04), and than their female friends (Chi squared =4.28, 1 df, p < .04).
3 Male engineers are significantly more likely to be classified as masculine sex-typed than female engineers (Chi squared =11.37, 1 df, p > .001), and than their female friends (Chi squared =16.02, 1 df, > .0001).
4 Female engineers are significantly less likely to be feminine sex-typed than their female friends (Chi squared =9.15, 1 df, > .003).

virtually the same. Perhaps the most dramatic finding was that 71 per cent of male engineers were classified as masculine sex-typed, thus suggesting the importance of stereotypically 'masculine' characteristics to their own self-conceptions.

Table 9.2 shows the results for the London female respondents – engineering trainees, their schoolfriends, and students on business studies and nursery nursing courses.

In the London female groups there was further substantiation of these findings. Female engineers were significantly more likely to be androgynous than any other group. They were also significantly less likely to be feminine sex-typed than any other group. Whilst female engineers were slightly more likely to be classified as masculine sex-typed than women in the other groups, these differences were not statistically significant.

Why is the prospective female engineer so likely to be classified as androgynous – having both 'feminine' and 'masculine' characteristics? Why is she so unlikely to be classified as feminine sex-typed?

Who becomes an engineer?

Table 9.2 *Four-fold androgyny classification for female engineers, female friends, and female students of business studies and nursery nursing*[1]

	Androgynous[2]		Masculine sex-typed		Feminine[3] sex-typed		Undifferentiated	
	N	%	N	%	N	%	N	%
Female engineers (N=17)	9	53	3	18	3	18	2	12
Female friends (N=14)	5	36	1	7	7	50	1	7
Female business studies students (N=13)	2	15	0	0	9	69	2	15
Female nursery nursing students (N=12)	2	17	1	8	8	67	1	8

Notes
1 All significance levels reported are for a two-tailed test.
2 Female engineers are significantly more likely to be classified as androgynous than women in business studies (Fishers exact = .03) and women in nursery nursing (Fisher exact = .05).
3 Female engineers are significantly less likely to be classified as feminine sex-typed than female friends (Fishers exact = .05), than women in business studies (Chi squared = 6.16, 1 df, p < .02), and than women in nursery nursing (Fishers exact = .01).

Two interrelated sets of factors shed some light on these findings. The first group of factors is linked with the image of engineering and the procedure for selecting female trainees. It suggests that women entering engineering and the people who select them find it necessary to balance the masculine image of the field by emphasizing the feminine qualities of female engineers. The second group of factors is concerned with the antecedents of androgyny. It suggests that the precursors of androgyny can be seen in early childhood experience and in the independence these young women felt from their families in making their career choices.

Looking at the first set of factors, it is not surprising that a woman choosing engineering is likely to perceive herself as having 'masculine' qualities. However, the cultural values placed on 'femininity' make it unlikely that the prospective female engineer will wish to see herself as 'unfeminine' and, indeed, the decision to study engineering may encourage her to emphasize her 'feminine' as well as her 'masculine' qualities. Informal conversations with male engineers and training officers who were involved in selecting the women in this sample suggested that the selectors did not want girls whom they felt were 'too masculine'. They preferred girls whom they saw as 'fairly tough' and 'able to cope', but who at the same time also retained 'feminine' qualities. Therefore women who choose engineering as a career (and are allowed into it) are more likely to see themselves as having both 'feminine' *and* 'masculine' characteristics. Past research on androgyny measures (Kelly and Worell 1977) suggests that such women are more likely to be high on both 'femininity' and 'masculinity' scales than to be low on both scales and thus be classified as 'undifferentiated'.

Examination of the 'femininity' and 'masculinity' scores obtained by the various groups in this research suggests the importance of occupational stereotyping. Female engineers differed from other female groups in that they tended to see themselves as having more 'masculine' characteristics, whereas young women entering nursery nursing were distinguished from other women in the research by their high levels of 'femininity'. However, female engineers did not differ from their friends in perceived levels of femininity. As expected, male engineers conformed to the popular stereotype of being masculine sex-typed, although it would have been useful to have had males in other occupations for purposes of comparison.[5]

The need to consider 'femininity' and 'masculinity' as independent dimensions is seen clearly in the present sample, where (as in Bem's research discussed earlier) the scores have a low negative correlation $(r = -.16)$. Writers who have conceptualized 'femininity' and 'masculinity' as polar opposites have frequently portrayed the future female scientist or technologist as being less 'feminine' and more 'masculine' than her friends or schoolmates studying arts subjects (Smithers and Collings 1981; Harding 1981). Although these researchers appear to have been describing the relatively high degree of 'masculine' traits possessed by these young women, their measures precluded their assessing the levels of 'feminine' traits also possessed by them.

Who becomes an engineer?

Turning now to a discussion of the antecedents of androgyny, in exploring early childhood and family factors there were several indications that the female engineers being studied were relatively independent and determined to follow their own interests. These factors would appear to be related to their subsequent self-definitions as androgynous. When female engineers were asked to recollect early childhood experiences, they were somewhat more likely than their friends to have played with both girls and boys in their childhood and less likely than the other groups to have had only girls as playmates. They were significantly more likely to have played with unconventional ('boy's') toys in their childhood than all other groups (Newton 1984). This link between childhood activities and achievement in non-traditional fields has also been reported by Standley and Soule (1974) and by Connor and Serbin (1977). However, there was little evidence that female engineers in this study came from unconventional families.

Unlike the findings of previous research on women in non-traditional work roles (Hennig and Jardim 1976), there was no tendency for female engineers in the present study to be first or only children. In this study both female engineers and their friends were most likely to be second or third children. There was no difference in the numbers of brothers and sisters they had, or in other important aspects of their families. Mothers in both groups were usually in paid employment, and there was no difference in their occupations or their pattern of working. The only noteworthy family background factor found was that female engineers were more likely than their friends or the male engineers to have fathers who were in professional jobs – the Registrar General's Class I, with 19 per cent of the sample having fathers who fell into this group. This confirms the results of several other studies in suggesting that professional families are most likely to support a daughter's non-traditional career choice (Standley and Soule 1974; Wolpe 1971).

There were relatively few other differences between the families of female engineers and those of their friends. Female engineers were quite likely to be the daughters of engineers, but this was also true of their friends and the control group of male engineers. Forty per cent of the female engineers had fathers in engineering, but the figure was almost as high amongst their friends, with 34 per cent reporting that their fathers were engineers. The explanation of this finding may lie in how girls perceive their father's influence on their career choice and, when in the process of career choice, how the father's attitudes are expressed or perceived to be expressed. (As noted below, the parallel process for boys appears to operate quite differently.)

Previous data on this sample of female engineers suggest that fathers were unlikely to suggest engineering as a possible career choice for their daughters (Newton 1981); however, they were usually highly supportive and encouraging to their daughters after the initial decision had been made (Newton and Brocklesby 1982). This interpretation is in line with Wolpe's (1971) study of graduate engineers. She found that although 59 per cent of her sample had fathers or brothers in engineering, they rarely saw their family as influential in their career decision. It appears that fathers may serve as important exemplars of engineers and that they are often described as being positive about their daughters' interest in engineering (Weinreich-Haste and Newton 1983); however, they are not seen as directly influencing career choice. Their influence is perceived indirectly and their role in providing a model of an engineer is often not recognized. This pattern contrasts sharply with the parental influences reported by the male engineers and the female groups in traditional roles (female friends, women in business studies courses, and women in nursery nursing courses). Both male engineers and females in these traditional groups saw their parents and family friends as directly and highly influential in their career choice, whereas female engineers saw teachers and the media as being most important in their choice of engineering. Female engineers were also more likely than respondents in any other group to say that no one had influenced them in their career choice (Newton 1981; Newton and Brocklesby 1982).

As previous studies of entrants to engineering suggest, girls were more likely to make their career choice relatively late in their school careers, whereas boys were more inclined to make an early choice of engineering. These findings reinforce the notion that girls and boys choose engineering out of different psychological needs and interests.

Policy implications

The success of the Engineering Industry Training Board's 'Insight' programme and related programmes at technician level has demonstrated that women can be interested in engineering, and that such programmes offer a useful introduction to engineering and related careers. Access and conversion courses can provide women with the academic and practical experience necessary to enter a variety of training and educational programmes in science and engineering. However, a more basic problem remains – male engineers and managers must be convinced that increasing the proportion of women in the field is a positive and necessary step. Unfortunately this seems unlikely to occur quickly. As has been suggested, the typical male engineer is conservative in attitudes and values and is reluctant to accept change. He has a highly traditional view of women's roles and is unlikely to favour special programmes which will treat female candidates differently from male candidates (Davidson 1984). He sees engineering as a highly 'masculine' world and may regard the introduction of women as a personal threat (Bryant 1984).

Although current government policy regards increasing the numbers of science and engineering graduates as a national priority, both polytechnics and universities are having great difficulty in attracting suitably qualified students of either sex (*Times Higher Educational Supplement* 1985). Rather than trying to change student preferences by exhortation, a more effective policy might involve changing training and education in engineering to make it more appealing to both sexes. In their review of engineering education, Beuret and Webb (1983) have argued for a broadening of engineering education, so that engineers are prepared for more active roles in decision-making in industry. Echoing similar concerns, McKay (1983) calls for 'humanizing' the technological aspects of engineering. He goes so far as to suggest that entry requirements for engineering courses might be relaxed to allow students with qualifications in arts and humanities to enter.

At first glance these suggestions appear heretical, particularly in the face of the widely acknowledged problem of the low status of engineers in the United Kingdom (Committee of Enquiry into the Engineering Profession 1980; Herriot and Ecob 1980). The notion of changing entry requirements for degree courses appears to contradict the major recommendations of the Finniston Report on the Engineering Profession which suggests making engineering education both longer and more rigorous. Although it can be argued that relaxing entry requirements would lower academic standards, this outcome is neither necessary nor inevitable. Attracting a wider variety of students and broadening the curriculum in engineering might actually increase the proportion of highly intelligent and talented people in engineering and provide industry with people who have a wider experience and perspective. Such changes would be likely to benefit women, both by making engineering accessible without the usual complement of maths and science examinations and by making it a more appealing career. However, these changes remain a long-term goal and represent only one aspect of the basic question of how to increase the numbers of women in engineering. Until women form a significant proportion of the workforce employed as technician and graduate engineers, special programmes for women will continue to be necessary. These forms of positive action are needed both to interest women in engineering as a career and to provide them with the support necessary to withstand the pressures they currently face when working in the industry. Because both women and men working in engineering believe that childcare is a woman's responsibility and because most female engineers want to have children (Bryant 1984; Newton and Brocklesby 1982), childcare is a necessary feature of programmes designed to retain women in engineering. Although a number of employers claim to regard the needs of individual women sympathetically, the lack of comprehensive policies for maternity leave and childcare places a heavy burden on women having or intending to have children.

The stress experienced by female engineers appears to be a serious problem and can be traced at least in part to the extra 'performance pressures' they feel as 'token women' (Kanter 1977). In a recent study investigating the position of women at British Petroleum, Davidson (1984) found that of all employees interviewed, both male and female, women engineers reported being under the most stress. Their feelings of stress were linked directly to prejudice and discrimination and they were more likely than their male colleagues to be considering leaving the company. Contrary to the popular stereotypes of women employees, their reasons for leaving were not related to family intentions, but rather to dissatisfaction with the job and pressures at work.

Although there is ample evidence that women are capable of being engineers, both the institutions training and educating them and the industries employing them remain unconvinced of their value. This situation is not unique to engineering, although the proportion of women entering the field remains much lower than in most other professions. As the industry is changing in response to new technology and some fields of engineering are expanding, there is an opportunity to reconsider traditional patterns of work and to revise employment practices which have been designed to fit the usual patterns of men's careers. A few companies, such as British Petroleum, are showing interest in developing policies which will help to retain women. They are recognizing that such policies are not an expensive 'extra' for women but a sensible investment in valuable, trained employees (Davidson 1984).

Notes

1 This film is distributed by C.F.L. Vision, Chalfont Grove, Gerrards Cross, Bucks SL9 8TN.

2 GIST was an action research project funded by the Equal Opportunities Commission, the Social Science Research Council, the Department of Industry, and Shell UK. The project was designed to explore why girls underachieve in physical science and technical subjects at school and to examine the effectiveness of various interventions. Further information is available in the final report on the project (Kelly, Whyte, and Smail 1984).

The EITB began a series of 'Insight' programmes in 1979. These were residential programmes lasting from three days to one week, designed to encourage high-calibre girls (currently studying mathematics and physics) to consider engineering as a career and to opt for a relevant degree course at university or polytechnic. Further information about 'Insight' is available in EITB Occasional Paper 10, 'Insight: A Review of the Insight Programme to Encourage More Girls to Become Professional Engineers'. Information about 'Insight' and other EITB programmes to encourage women to become engineers is available from the EITB, 54 Clarendon Road, Watford WD1 1LB.

3 'Traditionally sex-typed' refers to females who are 'feminine' sex-typed and males who are 'masculine' sex-typed. 'Cross-sex-typed' refers to females who are 'masculine' sex-typed and males who are 'feminine' sex-typed.

4 Subjects in the research were classified as 'masculine' or 'feminine' sex-typed if their scores on the 'masculinity' and 'femininity' scale of the Bem Sex Role Inventory were significantly different (t < 2.025); see Bem (1974). Group medians were used to determine whether subjects' scores were 'high' or 'low' for assignment to the androgynous and undifferentiated groups.

5 For a full consideration of these 'femininity' and 'masculinity' scores, see Newton (1985).

References

Bachtold, L.M. and Werner, E. (1973) Personality Characteristics of Creative Women. *Perceptual and Motor Skills* 36: 311–19.

Bem, S.L. (1974) The Measurement of Psychological Androgyny. *Journal of Consulting and Clinical Psychology* 42: 155–62.

— (1981) Gender Schema Theory: A Cognitive Assessment of Sex Typing. *Psychological Review* 88: 354–64.

—(1983) Gender Schema Theory and Its Implications for Child Development: Raising Gender Aschematic Children in a Gender Schematic Society. *Signs* 8: 598–616.

—(1985) Androgyny and Gender Schema Theory: A Conceptual Integration. *Nebraska Symposium on Motivation* 32: 179–226.

Bem, S.L. and Lenney, E. (1976) Sex Typing and the Avoidance of Cross-sex Behaviour. *Journal of Personality and Social Psychology* 33: 48–54.

Beuret, G. and Webb, A. (1983) *Goals of Engineering Education.* Leicester: Leicester Polytechnic.

Breakwell, G.M. and Weinberger, B. (1983) *The Right Woman for the Job: Recruiting Women Engineering Technician Trainees.* Report to the training division of the Manpower Services Commission.

Brown, J.M. (1975) A Woman in the World of Engineering. *IEEE Transactions on Education* E–18 (1): 3–10.

Bryant, L. (1984) *Women in Engineering: Images and Identifications.* Paper presented to British Sociological Association Conference, University of Bradford.

Committee of Enquiry into the Engineering Profession (1980) *Engineering Our Future.* The Finniston Report (Cmnd. 7794). London: HMSO.

Connor, J.M. and Serbin, L.A. (1977) Behaviourally Based Masculine and Feminine Activity Preference Scales for Preschoolers: Correlates with Other Classroom Behaviour and Cognitive Tests. *Child Development* 48: 1411–416.

Constantinople, A. (1973) Masculinity–Femininity: An Exception to a Famous Dictum? *Psychological Bulletin* 80: 389–407.

Cotgrove, S.F. and Weinreich-Haste, H. (1982) *Career Choice with Special Reference to Engineering.* Final report to the Social Science Research Council.

Davidson, M. (1984) *Career Development and Women Engineers: An Equal Opportunities Audit in BP (UK).* Paper presented at Women into Science and Engineering Education and Training Conference, London, October.

Davis, S.O. (1975) A Researcher's Eye View: Women Students, Technical Majors, and Retention. *IEEE Transactions on Education* E–18 (1): 25–9.

Engineering Industry Training Board (1983) *The Technician in Engineering (Part 4): Employment, Education and Training of Women Technicians.* Research Report No. 9. Watford: EITB.

— (1984) *Women in Engineering.* Occasional Paper No. 11. Watford: EITB.

Hacker, S.L. (1981) The Culture of Engineering: Women, Workplace and Machine. *Women's Studies International Quarterly* 4: 341–53.

Harding, J. (1981) Sex Differences in Science Examinations. In A. Kelly (ed.) *The Missing Half: Girls and Science Education.* Manchester: Manchester University Press, pp. 192–204.

Hennig, M. and Jardim, A. (1976) *The Managerial Woman.* New York: Pocket Books.

Herriot, P. and Ecob, R. (1980) *Engineers and Their Functions in Manufacturing Industry.* Paper presented at international workshop on social psychology and social policy, University of Kent, April.

Johnson, D.C. (1975) The Chronology and Support of Educational Choices. In M.D. Ott and N.A. Reese (eds) *Women in Engineering . . . Beyond Recruitment.* Ithaca, NY: Cornell University Press.

Kanter, R.M. (1977) Some Effects of Proportions on Group Life: Skewed Sex Ratios and Responses to Token Women. *American Journal of Sociology* 82: 965–90.

Kelly, A., Whyte, J., and Smail, B. (1984) *Girls into Science and Technology*. Final report to the Joint Panel on Women and Underachievement of the Equal Opportunities Commission and Social Science Research Council.

Kelly, J.A. and Worell, J. (1977) New Formulations of Sex Roles and Androgyny: A Critical Review. *Journal of Consulting and Clinical Psychology* 45: 1101–115.

Kundsin, R.B. (ed.) (1973) Successful Women in the Sciences: An Analysis of Determinants. *Annals, New York Academy of Sciences*, 208.

McKay, A. (1983) News Release. Institution of Mechanical Engineers, 18 November.

Newton, P. (1981) Who Says Girls Can't Be Engineers? In A. Kelly (ed.) *The Missing Half: Girls and Science Education*. Manchester: Manchester University Press, pp. 139–49.

— (1984) *Female Engineers: How Different Are They?* Paper presented to Conference on 'Girl Friendly' Schooling. Manchester Polytechnic, September.

— (1985) *Female Engineers: Femininity Re-defined?* Paper presented to the British Association for the Advancement of Science, University of Strathclyde, August.

Newton, P. and Brocklesby, J. (1982) *Getting on in Engineering: Becoming a Woman Technician*. Final report to the Engineering Industry Training Board and to the Equal Opportunities Commission/Social Science Research Council Panel on Women and Underachievement.

Ott, M.D. (1978) Differences between Men and Women Engineering Students. *Journal of College Student Personnel* 19: 552–57.

Ott, M.D. and Reese, N.A. (eds) (1975) *Women in Engineering . . . Beyond Recruitment*. Ithaca, NY: Cornell University Press.

Roberts, V. (1964) The Choice of Career: A Study of the Attitudes of Grammar School Girls in Seventeen Schools towards Science-based Careers. In N. Seear, V. Roberts and J. Brock (eds) *A Career for Women in Industry?* London: Oliver and Boyd, pp. 9–58.

Robin, S.S. (1969) The Female in Engineering. In R. Perrucci and J.E. Gerstl (eds) *The Engineer and the Social System*. New York: Wiley, pp. 203–18.

Rossi, A.S. (1965) Barriers to Career Choice of Engineering, Medicine or Science among American Women. In J.A. Matfeld and C. Van Aken (eds) *Women and the Scientific Professions*. Cambridge, MA: MIT Press, pp. 51–127.

Rothwell, S. (1982) Women's Career Development: An Overview of the Issues for Individuals and Organisations. In C.L. Cooper (ed.) *Practical Approaches to Women's Career Development*. Sheffield: Manpower Services Commission, pp. 14–23.

Smithers, A. and Collings, J. (1981) Girls Studying Science in the Sixth Form. In A. Kelly (ed.) *The Missing Half: Girls and Science Education*. Manchester: Manchester University Press, pp. 164–79.

Spence, J.T. and Helmreich, R.L. (1978) *Masculinity and Femininity*. Austin: University of Texas Press.

Spence, J.T., Helmreich, R.L., and Stapp, J. (1975) Ratings of Self and Peers on Sex-role Attributes and Their Relation to Self-esteem and Conceptions of Masculinity and Femininity. *Journal of Personality and Social Psychology* 32: 29–39.

Standley, R. and Soule, B. (1974) Women in Male-dominated Professions: Contrasts in Their Personal and Vocational Histories. *Journal of Vocational Behaviour* 4: 245–58.

Taylor, M.C. and Hall, J.A. (1982) Psychological Androgyny: Theories, Methods and Conclusions: A Review. *Psychological Bulletin* 92: 347–66.

Times Higher Educational Supplement (1985) 25 October.

Weinreich-Haste, H. and Newton, P. (1983) A Profile of the Intending Woman Engineer. EOC Research Bulletin No. 7, Summer.

Williams, J.A. (1978) Psychological Androgyny and Mental Health. In O. Hartnett, G. Boden, and M. Fuller (eds) *Sex-Role Stereotyping*. London: Tavistock, pp. 200–19.

Wolpe, A.M. (1971) Factors Affecting the Choice of Engineering as a Profession among Women. Unpublished MA dissertation. University of Bradford.

© *1987 Peggy Newton*

10

Class and Gender among Professional Women in India

Joanna Liddle and Rama Joshi

Introduction

An increasing number of studies of middle-class women and women in professional occupations has appeared over the last decade, both in the West and in India. Few of these studies, however, have examined the impact on such women of their position in the class structure, or attempted to analyse how the divisions of gender are related to the hierarchy of class, preferring instead to focus exclusively on the discriminatory effects of gender. Research which examines the interrelation of gender and class has looked primarily at working-class women. A notable exception is the work of Catherine Hall (1981), who studied the relationship between gender divisions and the development of the middle class in an English town in the late eighteenth and early nineteenth centuries. In the Indian context, Blumberg and Dwaraki (1980) considered class, but did not relate it in any analytical way to the hierarchy of gender, whilst Rama Mehta (1970) looked at attitudes to caste but did not go beyond attitudes to consider structures.

It is important to study middle-class and professional women from the perspective of class and gender for two reasons. One is to fill the gap in the description of and theorizing about this group from such a perspective. Attempts so far to understand the contradictions experienced by professional women between their gender position and their occupational status have foundered on the failure to make the link between gender and class. As we show below, the contradictions arise precisely from the dual effect of class privilege and gender discrimination. The second reason is the importance of this group's position in the class/gender structure for clarifying the connections between the two systems of hierarchy. In particular, middle-class women who are employed in professional jobs stand at an important intersection of the class structure and the gender structure, since they are employed at the top of the occupational hierarchy where many of the material benefits of class are located for middle-class men. But whereas professional and middle-class men reap the benefits of both gender and class privilege and working-class women suffer the disadvantages of both class and gender oppression, professional women experience the advantages of class and the penalties of gender. By looking at this group of women, it is possible to disentangle some of the connections between class and gender and to examine the nature of these connections.

Paradoxically, the lead in this approach has been taken not by socialist feminist writers, who have concentrated almost exclusively on working-class women, but by radical feminists seeking to demonstrate both that gender operates independently of class and that gender generally takes priority over class divisions. In the debate on women's subordination, the socialist feminists' emphasis on class and their refusal to see the gender hierarchy as independent of the class structure have been criticized for reducing every female oppression to the class system, thereby ignoring the impact of male supremacy and exonerating men from responsibility in the subjugation of women (Delphy 1980). The radical feminist analysis, however, which suggests that all women share a common class position, has been criticized for neglecting class differences in women's oppression and the ways in which gender and class relate (Barrett and McIntosh 1979). To demonstrate the independence of gender and class hierarchies, Diana Leonard (1982: 173) has shown some of the particular ways in which middle-class women, whether professionally employed themselves or the wives of middle-class men, still suffer sexual oppression from men, arguing that gender subordination therefore cuts across and outweighs class privilege.[1]

Diana Leonard's argument is important because it points to the specific position of middle-class women in the class and gender hierarchies as a means of distinguishing some of the connections between gender and class. But the examples from India show (perhaps more clearly because of the continuing relevance of 'semi-feudal' structures) that the particular ways in which gender subordination develops in the middle class is not distinct from, but has its roots in, the forms of gender subordination in the traditional caste structure, the divisions of gender and class developing together in a dialectical way.[2]

This chapter aims to describe some of the class/gender contradictions that professional women experience in India and to examine the argument about the pattern of priority and independent development of gender and class. To do this we explore two aspects of class and gender, in the areas of education and employment, that are specific to professional women in India, using empirical evidence from 120 women working in Delhi.[3] The evidence suggests that the privilege of class outweighs the subordination of gender to the extent that the women have access to higher education and are able to secure employment in the professions, helping to break down the sexual division of labour in one section of the class hierarchy. But the subordination of gender outweighs the privilege of class inasmuch as female education is used to improve women's commodity value on the marriage market, and the restrictions on their physical mobility outside the home hamper their work performance, helping to perpetuate women's position as male sexual property and reinforcing their domestic dependence. We argue that the contradictions of professional women's experiences cannot be explained without reference to both gender divisions and class divisions. Finally, we show how an examination of professional women in India can inform the debate on the nature of the relationship between class and gender.

The middle class in India

The formation of social classes arose mainly from the British colonization of the country and the integration of the Indian economy into world capitalism (Desai 1959). The traditional mercantile capital of India was destroyed by the British during the eighteenth and the first half of the nineteenth centuries. The new Indian bourgeoisie began to develop in the second half of the nineteenth century from the merchant bankers and moneylenders who had begun to accumulate small amounts of capital (Chandra 1974: 398–99). This new capitalist class developed independently of British capitalism. The professional groups and government servants, however, did not grow out of an expanding bourgeois economy, as happened in the West, but instead were developed directly by the British to administer the country under

British supervision. For this, English-educated administrators were needed, as well as lawyers, accountants, teachers, and other professionals (Sen 1982: 80–6).

In 1835, English was made the official language of India and the medium of higher education. The intention behind the establishment of English education was, as revealed in the famous quote of Macaulay's: 'to form a class who may be interpreters between us and the millions we govern: a class of persons, Indian in blood and colour, but English in taste, in opinions, in morals and in intellect' (quoted in Misra 1961: 154). The selection of this group was explicitly elitist:

> 'It was absolutely necessary to make a selection, and they therefore selected the upper and middle classes as the first object of their attention, because by educating them first, they would soonest be able to extend the same "advantages" to the rest of the people.'
>
> (Trevelyan, quoted in Misra 1961: 151–52)

Although unstated, this selection was also gendered. The women of the middle class were not allowed to serve as government officials, nor was any provision made for their education (Mathur 1973: 20–30). The British created the professional class out of the existing public officials who had served the Mughals (the previous rulers), out of the moneylenders, and out of the literary class of educated brahmins (the highest caste in the Hindu social hierarchy) – what Trevelyan termed 'the rich, the learned, the men of business' (quoted in Misra 1961: 151). These groups were predominantly from the rural power elite. The industrialists developed largely from the middle strata, but this group constituted a minority in the middle class compared with the professionals (Misra 1961: 307, 338–40). The middle class thus emerged primarily out of those groups which had been powerful in the rural areas (Sen 1982: 80–1). The rural power structure was originally based on the Hindu caste system, successively subordinated to the Mughals after the Muslim invasions and to the British after the arrival of the Europeans.

In the twentieth century, the middle class found their ambitions thwarted by the paucity of government jobs, which failed to expand as fast as the number of educated men who desired them, and by British domination of senior posts in government and the professions (Nehru 1939: 434–39). The Indian bourgeoisie was inhibited in its accumulation of capital by British domination of the market and control over private investment and public finance (Chandra 1974: 394–97). The middle class therefore supported and eventually took over the leadership of the freedom movement and, after independence, it was the middle class who took over the machinery of state. Thanks to the inhibition of the Indian economy by British colonialism before independence (and by Western economic imperialism since independence), the middle class has been unable to expand sufficiently to replace the rural power structure based on caste with an urban structure based on class (Chandra 1974: 413). The economic, political, and ideological structures of caste and class therefore coexist in a state of mutual transition.

The formation of the middle class from the upper castes and the persistence of caste influence on contemporary Indian society has had a dual effect on middle-class women. In the first place, the continued relevance of high-caste structures and ideals has meant the retention of certain traditional caste strictures on women of the middle class. Although the earliest Hindu writings, the Vedas, prescribed education for both sexes and show that women worked as scholars, poets, teachers, and in business, agriculture, and crafts, the later law books advocated the exclusion of women and the lower castes from studying the scriptures and the withdrawal of high-caste women from their previous employment (Altekar 1962: 10–24). At this time, too, the law books laid down women's total dependence on men, as in the famous statement from the Code of Manu: 'A woman should never be independent. Her father has authority over her in childhood, her husband in youth, and her son in old age' (Manusmriti, Dharmashastra IX, 3).

Women's position declined further in succeeding centuries when child marriage became compulsory for women of the higher strata, widows were forbidden from remarrying, and sati (widow burning) was introduced (Thapar 1966: 151–52). These harsh controls over women were reinforced with the Muslim invasions beginning around AD 1000 when purdah and the seclusion of women became common among the upper echelons of both Hindus and Muslims (Mies 1980: 60). Purdah is a variable set of specific behavioural constraints, involving the removal of women from the public gaze of men and restricting women's physical mobility, particularly outside the home (Papanek 1973: 289). Seclusion is a more general approach to how women should behave in a patriarchal society, ranging from strictest purdah, through various forms of sex segregation, to the idea that 'a woman's place is in the home'. It enforces the dual control of men over women's sexual and economic autonomy by confining women to the home as exclusive sexual property and by preventing women from contributing to the economic income of the family or gaining economic independence. Women's economic contribution becomes restricted to the domestic sphere and the physical restrictions are overlaid with the ideology of domesticity, which not only proposes that the domestic sphere is natural for women, but also links domesticity with moral respectability. These material controls are linked with the 'pativrata' ideal, the 'husband-worshipper', which embodies the woman's obedience and subordination to the husband and his family in marriage. As Mehta has written:

'Just as Pativrata was the moral code, the Purdah system was part of the feminine code of modesty. High caste women in some parts of India were segregated from men and their social life was confined to the home or to the company of other women. Even in parts of India where Purdah was not practised, wellborn women were still discouraged from being with men or treating them as equals, with the exception of parts of South India.'

(Mehta 1970: 19)

These forms of gender subordination were very far from being independent of the social hierarchy. On the contrary, the sexual and economic control of women in the higher castes and the upwardly mobile lower castes, through seclusion or purdah, was intimately connected with control over the accumulation and maintenance of both movable property, inherited by daughters in the form of dowry, and non-movable property in the form of land inherited through the male line (Liddle and Joshi 1986: 57–62).[4] In the transition to a class society, the tradition of seclusion and the ideology of domesticity prevalent among the upper castes were retained for women of the middle class, although in significantly different forms, as we will show. Kamla Bhasin has called this the middle-class woman's predicament:

'In spite of the quantitative changes in the education of women and an increase in their job opportunities, the plight of women has remained more or less unchanged. . . . Education creates in them analytical faculties, ambitions and desires, but the social laws which still govern their marriage, family life and social behaviour force on them unquestioned fidelity, obedience and subservience.'

(Bhasin 1972: 35)

Professional women in India

At the same time, however, the development of the middle class has opened up opportunities for economic independence through education and professional employment to women of this class, who had previously been subject to dependence and seclusion. As Rama Joshi has written elsewhere:

> 'We are, today, witnessing a transitional period in the status of women in India. This is especially true of the middle class women who have been more obsessed with the traditional past while at the same time aspiring for modern values.'

(Joshi 1972: 50)

This tension between the traditions of caste and the new values of class finds expression in the specific ways in which education and employment have developed for professional women of today.

Class, gender, and education

We have argued that the development of the professional class was the direct result of the British requirement for local administrators. By the time of Britain's colonization of the country, female dependency, early marriage, seclusion, and the undesirability of female education were entrenched among the higher strata. When the British introduced English education for future government servants in 1835, their exclusion of women went unremarked (Mathur 1973: 20-1, 29). The British first acknowledged the importance of female education in 1854, but little was achieved until the Indian social reform organizations later in the century began to campaign for women's education (Thapar 1963: 482–84). The first two women graduated from Calcutta University in 1883 (Mathur 1973: 38) and in 1885 the Countess of Dufferin founded the National Association for Supplying Medical Aid by Women to Women, to include the training of women doctors (Lazarus 1929: 57). But as the reformer Mary Carpenter pointed out as early as 1866, the major barrier to female education at every level and in every field was the lack of women teachers – a point rejected by the government on grounds of cost (Mathur 1973: 30, 36).

In the early twentieth century, women's organizations such as the Women's Social Conference and the All-India Women's Conference took up the cause of female education as well as the lack of medical care for women, and linked them with purdah and child marriage (Forbes 1982: 527–29). The importance of women teachers for female students and women doctors for female patients both stemmed from the same cause: the segregation of the sexes and the strict control over female sexuality among the upper strata of society. An Indian women doctor wrote in 1929 about 'her suffering sisters and their children . . . who would suffer silently even to death rather than be examined by men' (Lazarus 1929: 51).

The only way that secluded women of the upper castes could receive education or health care was by training women doctors and teachers, which began to break down sex segregation and undermine the sexual and economic control of women by men. Those women who took professional training not only came out of seclusion but also became economically independent. Such opportunities were taken up initially by women from reformist families, but later women from more orthodox families began to see possibilities for change. This process was still occurring among the women we interviewed – women like Reeta Rao, a lecturer aged forty-nine who came from a strict Bengali brahmin background: 'I wanted education desperately. . . . My father thought education for girls was ridiculous, but my mother said, "Let her go till we find the right man." I fought my father to let me have an education.'

Soon educated men of the middle class began to be dissatisfied with uneducated wives, which is how Rekha Rohtagi's father developed such liberal attitudes to women's education. Rekha was fifty, a high-caste Hindu originally from Pakistan who was also a lecturer:

'My father was very liberal. From the beginning he inculcated the attitude that daughters should have equal education. He was unusual. Partly it was because he was educated, partly because he couldn't find companionship with his wife, who was a very fine woman but uneducated. I always felt the incompatability between my mother and father. I felt that women should have economic independence as well as equivalent intellect.'

So the education of middle-class men led to demands for female education both from men who wanted educated wives and from middle-class women themselves who were 'desperate for education' and wanted to provide professional services to their secluded sisters.

Once women began to campaign for female education, facilities slowly increased. In 1881 0.2 per cent of women were literate and by 1946 the figure had risen to 6 per cent (Department of Social Welfare 1974: 238). After independence opportunities were further expanded and female literacy stood at 19 per cent in 1971 (Department of Social

Welfare 1974: 265). In spite of this expansion, the data show that women who have received higher education are still an extremely select and privileged group even within the middle class. Their position can be used as an indicator of professional women's class privilege in comparison with the rest of the population.

WOMEN'S CLASS PRIVILEGE: ACCESS TO HIGHER EDUCATION

We have noted above that in 1971 19 per cent of women were literate in all India (42 per cent of all women in the urban areas); only 0.2 per cent and 1 per cent respectively were graduates (Department of Social Welfare 1978: 120–22). For most people in India, however, a college education is barred for both financial and cultural reasons. Although state schools are free up to class VIII, higher education is fee-paying. Equally important regarding the access to higher education of the children of the poor is the fact that although state schools teach in the local languages, higher education, since its inception by the British, has used English as the teaching medium. English-medium schooling is not provided in the state system and has to be bought in the private sector. A further barrier to the poor is that school attendance is not enforceable, because the level of poverty in India demands children's labour in domestic, agricultural, and waged work (Department of Social Welfare 1978: 181–82; Mathur 1973: 81–2, 112). In this connection, Wasi's study of education concluded that 'about 65 % of the wastage that occurs in India today is due to poverty' (1971: 23–4).

The women we interviewed were very highly qualified, more than two-thirds having a postgraduate degree, and more than a third having three or more degrees. A significant proportion (14 per cent) had studied abroad. Most came from financially well-off homes. A quarter of their mothers and four-fifths of their fathers were graduates (compared with 1 per cent of urban females and 4 per cent of urban males in the total population). Many of the women were positively encouraged by their families and most of them experienced no difficulties of any kind in acquiring an education. Even among the women interviewed, however, a small proportion of families found themselves in financial difficulties over their daughters' education. Shikha Munshi, a brahmin lecturer of forty-three, had worked as a secretary in order to finance further study:

'I left school in 1948 at the age of fourteen because my parents couldn't afford any more education for me. I started working at

211

eighteen, studied in the evenings, and got my BA at twenty-two. Then a friend said, "Don't give up, do an MA," so I continued on my own and did an MA in political science as an external degree.'

Shikha went on to take a PhD and only finished her education at the age of thirty-six. Other women took loans and won scholarships to solve the money problem. Meeta Sanatani, a doctor aged thirty-five, said:

'My family was happy that I wanted to be a doctor, but when I passed the entrance exam, my father's income was low – he was a businessman – and he couldn't afford to pay for my study and felt bad about it. My relatives pestered him, especially my sister's husband, because they thought I was good enough. There was no money to pay the fees, but I got loans and a scholarship.'

The problems of cultural imperialism in the teaching medium, which inhibits the schooling of ordinary Indian children, affected education even at the highest levels. Puja Shukla, a thirty-seven-year-old brahmin lecturer from Assam, remarked:

'The Western influence is so powerful that Indian culture has nothing to do with my day-to-day life now. At work I have to communicate in English even though I'm teaching my own regional language. I would prefer not to speak English, but there is no practical alternative.'

Until the economy expands, a professional education will remain the privilege of the wealthier middle class. Apart from economic and cultural barriers, however, there is another factor which creates difficulties for women who want an education. This is the impact of gender.

WOMEN'S GENDER SUBORDINATION: EDUCATION FOR MARRIAGE

Female literacy is approximately half, and female graduation a quarter, of that of men. Only 0.2 per cent of all Indian women and 0.8 per cent of men are graduates, rising to 1.3 and 3.7 per cent in urban areas (Department of Social Welfare 1978: 120–22). Although the figures for graduate women compared with the general population show that graduate women are a highly privileged group, it is clear that women are much less likely than men to become graduates. The privileges which graduate women gain from their class position are undermined in some way by their position in the gender hierarchy.

Of the professional women interviewed, 38 per cent had experienced problems in acquiring an education and the majority found that the root of their difficulty lay in the divisions of gender. The major inhibitor of female education in the middle class lay in the primacy of women's domestic role. Neelam Bhatia was thirty-three, a brahmin from Lucknow who worked as a lecturer. The older members of the joint family had opposed her education: 'My grandparents were very much against education for girls. They thought it would be a waste because I'd just get married.' Rekha Rohtagi's family encountered similar attitudes, although they were a liberal high-caste family: 'Our neighbours used to say, "Why educate daughters? They don't have to go in for jobs." My father used to protest against that kind of attitude.' But the 'protection' of female sexuality remained important for the middle class. Nirmala Verma, aged forty-six, a professor of medicine from a high-caste family, reported:

'My elder sister also wanted to be a doctor, but there was no women's medical college in Lahore and my father wouldn't allow us to go to the co-ed college. My father was of the view that education wasn't essential for girls.'

The problem with the establishment of education for women of the middle class was that it threatened to disrupt the economic and sexual control previously accorded to men under the caste system, by allowing women access to professional employment. Middle-class men attempted to contain this threat to male supremacy by imposing limits on women's education, retaining the advantages of marrying an educated wife without losing the benefits of women's domestic services. Women were allowed education but not employment, and female education came to be valued, not for itself or as a means of economic security, but as a commodity on the marriage market. This development was already being reported in the *Quinquennial Review of Education in India, 1917–22*:

'The demand for women's education, among higher caste Hindus and Muslims was on the increase from year to year. People did not educate their daughters to get them employment but to marry them on better and easier terms. But as soon as a suitable bridegroom was available, the girl was at once placed in the seclusion of the purdah.'

(quoted in Mathur 1973: 62)

In A Man's World

A study in 1972 suggested three main reasons for women obtaining professional education: as something worthwhile to do until a marriage was arranged; to increase her marriage potential; and, for poorer middle-class parents, to avoid excessive dowry demands (Dhingra 1972). All three reasons saw women's education as instrumental for marriage rather than for self-development, employment, or economic independence. Many of the women interviewed confirmed that these views were widespread and held by women as well as men. Rekha Rohtagi said:

> 'I always had different ideas from people at college. I was politically motivated and in women's organizations – I wasn't interested in clothes or a rich marriage. . . . Many girls at college were getting qualifications for marriage.'

Rupali Sinha, a brahmin lecturer of thirty-nine from Bengal, similarly remarked:

> 'Girls get a degree but they don't go on to a job because of the family set-up. They're happy to get married. They get married into high-status families because of the degree, but they aren't respected.'

Mumtaz Ahmad, a lecturer of forty-two from Lucknow, encountered the same attitude from her orthodox Muslim family:

> 'I was a very serious student, a very literary figure at college. My parents just expected me to marry. They wanted to educate their children but only for show. They were angry when I wanted to work.'

Reeta Rao, the woman who fought her father to let her have an education, discovered that her husband added *her* achievement to *his* status: 'My husband expected me to be a good housewife and help his career. Since he was well-educated, he wouldn't marry a non-graduate – but it was for his own image, not mine.'

Neither Mumtaz's nor Reeta's family wanted the women to use their education in the way men do – for professional employment – because this would lead to women's economic independence and possibly to sexual independence (such as finding their own marriage partner), thus undermining the subordination of women to men in the gender hierarchy and breaking down the sexual division of labour between domestic and paid work. Nor was too high a level of education desirable, since this could undermine the subordination of

214

women to men in the family. When Moyna Ghosh got her PhD, her aunts wrote to Moyna's mother not with congratulations, but 'saying how worried they were: how would I get a husband?'. To contain the threat to male supremacy posed by the new opportunities for women of the middle class, women's education is kept subordinate to the education of middle-class men and its value transformed into a commodity for marriage.

So the education which the social reform organizations and the women's organizations fought to attain on an equal basis with men has become another marketable asset along with attractiveness, domestic skills, and dowry, increasing women's value on the marriage market and helping to reinforce middle-class women's position in the family as domestic dependents subordinate to men in the hierarchy of gender. The use of female education for the maintenance of women's subordination in marriage, rather than for social and economic independence, contains within it its own contradictions, as Vimla Gupta, a middle-caste manager of fifty-three, observed from her own experience:

> 'When women are educated but given no outlet for their talents, this has a bad effect on them and the family. You can't give glimpses of the future, then shut off the possibilities. Women must be able to use their education, with all the problems.'

As a result of this contradiction, although many women still receive an education only in order to achieve a better class of marriage, there are also women who use their education to reject domesticity, take up employment, and attain economic independence, as will now be shown.

Class, gender, and employment

Much of the discussion on the slow development of women's education is also relevant to employment, for the two went hand in hand in terms of women's exclusion among the Hindu and Muslim upper strata. But whereas the effect on female education of the strict controls over women was to exclude them from learning, the effect on women's work was differentiated by their position in the social hierarchy. Lower-caste women continued to work in agriculture, manufacture, and crafts, while upper-caste women were confined in the home, performing exclusively domestic work and forbidden from undertaking any form of work in the public sphere (Srinivas 1977: 224–26). British views on women's work coincided with the upper-caste view, for in their selection of upper and middle-class men for administrative positions, they too excluded women (Choksi 1929: 63). Women were not allowed to compete for civil services jobs under British rule, even after they had begun to acquire the necessary education. Only after independence were the legal barriers to women's employment removed.

The progress of women's employment in the professions was considerably slower than that of female education. Not all the women who received education entered or remained in employment, either because of the pressure of domestic work or because of the continued opposition to women's employment from orthodox families (Lazarus 1929: 53). But the struggle for female education, the existence of middle-class professional jobs, and the demand for medical services for secluded high-caste women led inevitably to women working in professional occupations. This last factor was crucial to the change in attitudes over female employment. Medicine and education became acceptable professions for women precisely because they could be undertaken whilst maintaining sex segregation (though not, of course, seclusion) and minimizing contact with men.

The campaigns of the social reform movement and the women's organizations focused much more specifically on women's education than on their right to paid work although, of course, the employment of women as teachers and doctors was implied. But, for example, the exclusion of women from government posts does not appear to have figured largely in their campaigns. Instead, the women's organizations concentrated their efforts on influencing the leadership of the Indian National Congress, who took over the positions of power after independence. In 1928 Congress published a report on Indian self-government which, thanks to the activities of the women's movement, included the principle of sexual equality and universal adult franchise. In 1931 Congress adopted the report and its proposed principles for a new constitution, pledging support for sexual equality before the law and no discrimination in employment or offices (Everett 1981: 133).

At independence, Indian women achieved a constitutional guarantee of sex equality, the right to education and to adequate means of livelihood. They acquired political rights including the right to vote, to contest elections, and to enter the administrative services (Mehta

1982: 104). The Factories Act 1948, the Plantation Labour Act 1951, and the Mines Act 1952 legislated for equal pay for equal work, maternity benefits, crèches, and nursing time, and specified a maximum load and maximum hours for women in workplaces where fifty or more women are employed. It is illegal to employ women on night work, on underground or dangerous work, to restrict the recruitment of women, or to terminate employment on the grounds of pregnancy (Mankekar 1975: 19).

These reforms benefited middle-class women the most, for the majority of poor, illiterate women were unaware of their legal rights and had no resources to fight for them through the courts (Mehta 1982: 125–26). Even for middle-class women the improvements were limited, but there is no doubt that economic opportunities for professional women increased after independence. Not only were public services expanded at this time, with women's needs particularly in view (Mathur 1973), but legal and customary bars to women's employment were removed, notably in government service. Before 1947, no women were employed as government officers. In 1960 the ratio of women to men passing the Indian Administrative Service and Indian Foreign Service examinations was 1:82. In 1972 it was 1:8 (Department of Social Welfare 1974: 210). Nevertheless, the actual number of women entering these select professions is tiny and those who do so are an even more privileged group than educated women as a whole.

WOMEN'S CLASS PRIVILEGE: ACCESS TO PROFESSIONAL EMPLOYMENT

It is not possible to estimate the number of employed women with any accuracy because the definition of 'work' has been changed in the censuses of 1951, 1961, and 1971, the latest definition particularly underestimating the extent of women's work (Gulati 1975: 1692–693). In 1971, women were estimated to be 17 per cent of the workforce (Department of Social Welfare 1978: 212) – although the figure was 30 per cent in 1961 (Nath 1968: 1205) – and 17 per cent of professional workers (Department of Social Welfare 1974: 206). The definitional problems of the census are more likely to underestimate women's total work participation rate than that of full-time professional workers, although it neglects women in part-time professional employment. A study of Chandigarh city showed that the largest proportion of employed women was among the wives of men in the lowest occupational class, the proportion dropping sharply towards the middle levels, then rising slightly towards the higher levels (D'Souza 1980: 129). D'Souza's figures fail to account for unmarried women in employment, but they do show that middle-class wives work predominantly in the home.

In terms of their socio-economic position, the education, occupation, and income of our respondents' parents indicate that these women come from a very select group of families. A high proportion of their fathers and mothers were graduates, most of the fathers' occupations were in the top two occupational categories, and the fathers' incomes were significantly higher than the average salaries of qualified male employees. This pattern suggests a formidable array of privileged circumstances, allowing our women access to the professions.

Having gained access to the professions the women interviewed benefited from a further array of privileges which come with membership of an elite. Two of these are material – the economic benefits of financial independence and the social benefits of increased autonomy in their own lives. Two others are psychological – an increase in esteem and respect from other people and a concomitant rise in self-identity and self-confidence.

The mean per capita income of the families of the women interviewed was 938 rupees per month, compared with only 29 rupees per month in all India (Das and Chatterji 1972). Almost all the women referred to economic independence as one of the major benefits of professional employment, and 64 per cent said that they worked in paid employment for that specific reason, regardless of other financial resources. Economic independence not only brings material privileges in the class hierarchy, but also gives women independence from men in the gender hierarchy. The importance of this factor can be seen by the startling difference in the marriage rates of the professional women interviewed, compared with Indian women as a whole – 36 per cent were single, compared with 19 per cent in the 20–24 age group and only 5 per cent in the 25–29 age group of women as a whole (Bose 1975: 155–56).

The psychological benefits of being a professional woman stem from the material benefits. Her income and autonomy mean that family, friends, and community accord her recognition as an individual (rather than by defining her merely in terms of her husband), which increases her confidence and identity. Bhavna

Kharbanda, thirty-two, a government servant from a high-caste, north Indian family, said:

'I have my own status, I can do things the way I want. I'm at par with men in all fields. I'd like all women to have jobs; it makes them more independent-thinking. They can be what they are, not what their husbands are. They have their own status and circle of friends. Women who don't have jobs have no friends of their own. They lose their own, take their husband's and lose their individuality. The feeling still has to develop that women should have an independent life, thought, interests.'

The privileged home and family circumstances which allowed the women respondents access to the select group of professional workers and the privileges they gained when they obtained such occupations, all stem from their position in the class hierarchy. When their position in the gender hierarchy is considered, however, many of the privileges gained through class are eroded by the divisions of gender.

WOMEN'S GENDER SUBORDINATION: MOBILITY RESTRICTIONS ON EMPLOYMENT

The 1971 census showed that among qualified employees, women received lower pay than men (Department of Social Welfare 1978: 269). The segregation of women into relatively few occupations is shown by the fact that 80 per cent of women employees are found in only twelve occupations (Directorate-General of Employment and Training 1973: 26–7).[5] In the professions, women are much more likely to be found in medicine and tertiary level teaching (21 and 18 per cent) than in high-level government and management jobs (9 and 2 per cent women) (Department of Social Welfare 1978: 278, 284, 290–91; Directorate-General of Employment and Training 1971: 19, 21; 1973: 29–30). An examination of the academic qualifications of professional men and women has shown that 'women are, by and large, better equipped than men in most of the [professional] occupations' (Directorate-General of Employment and Training 1971: 23), suggesting not that women are better qualified than men in general, but that women employed in the professions have to be more highly qualified than men to be selected for the same jobs.

Among the women interviewed, the doctors, lecturers, and government servants all received equal pay with men, but 12 per cent of the managers received lower pay than their male equivalents. Job segregation within each profession occurred, with few women teaching science, maths, or engineering, most women doctors in gynaecology, obstetrics, and paediatrics, and women predominantly in 'desk jobs' rather than 'field jobs' in government and management. Sixty-three per cent of the women believed there was sexual discrimination in employment and in selection, assessment, and promotion. Reva Sahborwal's was only one story among many. She was a young export executive for a small private company, from a high-caste, north Indian family:

> 'There's discrimination in every job. . . . DCM [a private firm in Delhi] refuse all women. I had applied to them, and they said I had a job – I should call to collect the letter in a few days. But the director refused to sign the letter offering me the job, because I was a woman. Promotion is *not* equal. When they take you on, you are on a scale, and you have to be exceptional to get higher. In the export business, men can move around India and abroad and prove themselves, whereas women are office-bound and can't do so. We must sit at a desk and turn out "wonders" before we're ac-knowledged as much as a boy who is out proving himself.'

The reluctance to allow middle-class women to take paid employment outside the home and the desire to restrict their movements if they do take employment, stem from ideology about women in traditional high-caste society. During the formation of the social classes, female seclusion and the ideology of domesticity in the upper castes continued to influence the middle class. We have argued that those structures and ideas affect the way education for middle-class girls is seen and used, transforming female education into a commodity value for marriage. They also affect views of female employment in the middle class. The concern to maintain control over women's sexuality, despite their emergence from seclusion, is expressed in attempts to contain female employment within professions which could operate in parallel with, but segregated from, men. It is also expressed in attempts to restrict women's freedom of movement in the workplace, on the streets, on public transport – in fact anywhere that women might come into contact with unknown men.

In the extreme case, this means that educated women are not allowed to have jobs at all. Paramjit Caroli, a lecturer of twenty-eight from a Delhi Sikh family, commented:

'The conflict of values makes it more difficult for women to have jobs – the Indian definition of a good wife and mother. Some traditional well-off families wouldn't like you to work at all. It's a prestige symbol for the wife not to work.'

The 'conflict of values' between domestic seclusion in orthodox caste society and professional employment in the middle class means that women who have fought to acquire an education and a professional job find their new-found freedom limited by a restriction on their physical mobility. Women cannot travel alone easily, go out at night, stay away from home, go on tour, take fieldwork trips, or work on-site. This restriction does not apply to *men* of the middle class, but it is enforced on middle-class women by the family, by employers, and by unknown men who may be encountered on such trips who use intimidatory behaviour known in India as 'Eve-teasing'. Renu Deb, a young high-caste manager from Delhi, said: 'The lack of mobility is a disadvantage. My parents need to know I'll be safe. If I had to go off and they didn't know where, they wouldn't like it, whereas if it were a son they'd say "It's his job."' Similarly, Anita Shukla, a thirty-year-old brahmin civil servant from Benares, remarked:

'Some superiors have an overprotective attitude towards women. For instance, if you're the magistrate, the district magistrate will tell you not to go out at night. Colleagues do it too, sometimes, but they're less protective because there's an element of competition.'

The restriction on women's mobility is not merely an inconvenience – it also hampers their job performance. Ragini Nanda, a lecturer of forty-one from a high caste, north Indian family, commented: 'When I want to take students on fieldwork, the committee says I cannot go alone. I must go with someone who can look after the party properly.' Gita Ralham, a civil servant of thirty-eight, also from a high-caste, north Indian family said, similarly:

'I wanted to do something active, with authority, so I wanted to work in the districts, not desk work. The districts are a round-the-clock headache but I love it. In Uttar Pradesh (my state) they tend to keep women in secretarial jobs, when I particularly wanted a field job for job satisfaction and career prospects. Without certain experience, your promotion is hindered; for instance, you can't get to be joint secretary if you haven't done the districts.'

The restriction on their mobility also posed problems for women managers, as Uma Sudha, a manager of forty-nine from Rajasthan, remarked:

'Sometimes men have an advantage when things have to be done out of normal hours, working at night and so on. I don't want anyone to be able to score over me, so I make sure I'm equally mobile. If you're not mobile they take advantage. There's a latent idea in men's minds of the things women shouldn't do. You're always aware of it.'

In the Indian women's liberation magazine *Manushi*, Charu Sehgal has described her struggle to be treated as a responsible adult in the male-dominated profession of accountancy. She was one of a group of trainees who were asked to stay late one day to finish an audit. When the partner of the firm realized that she included herself in his request, he told her to go home because it wasn't 'safe' for women to travel home later than 5.00 p.m. Charu Sehgal commented: 'Surely, at the age of twenty-two, I should have the right to decide at what hour the city becomes unsafe.' On a different occasion, she and another woman volunteered to go on an audit but were refused permission by their superiors because their male colleagues would not agree to take 'responsibility' for them. As she went on to point out: 'It is pathetic to think that these same men are going to refuse admission to new women applicants because "girls can't stay late and can't go on outstation audits"' (Sehgal 1985: 21–2).

The tradition of seclusion and the ideology of domesticity for middle-class women have developed in such a way as to encompass prohibitions on women's professional activities which are quite incompatible with their occupational status. Whilst restrictions on women's mobility clearly stem from ideas about seclusion and domesticity, the domestic ideology is now too narrow a concept to explain the extension of restrictions into the occupational arena. Such restrictions, and the ideas that go with them, mean that women in professional jobs find themselves in quite a different position from that of professional men. Apart from direct discrimination in selection, assessment, and promotion, which are common to women all over the world, professional women in India are subject to a specific form of constraint on their physical movements which makes it difficult to stay late at the office, go out at night, or travel away from home on business. This constraint, although dressed up as 'protectiveness' and concern about 'safety', is actually concerned with preventing sexual autonomy, and serves as a continual reminder to women who have achieved a measure of economic and social independence that they are still men's sexual property and that those who stray out of the domestic sphere are 'deserving' of male harassment. Significantly, it also serves to reduce women's work performance, discouraging them from taking up employment or entering male areas of work and thus confirming men's belief that women are less competent in and committed to their professions.

Conclusion

The barriers to women entering the professions in India are formidable. They are such that those women who do get professional jobs are an extremely privileged elite. The privileges they gain from being members of this elite help to liberate them from many of the constraints with which less fortunate women are still burdened. They can develop their talents and interests through education. They receive the material and social benefits of economic independence and a fulfilling occupation. They are given greater respect by family, friends, and community, and they acquire an identity aside from their relation to men. However, simply because they are *women*, they do not share all the privileges of their class. The freedoms which they gain are limited by the structure of male domination even at the top of the occupational hierarchy. Male control over female education is retained by requiring that a woman's education should not exceed that of her husband, and by using a girl's education to increase her value as a commodity on the marriage market. Male control over female employment is maintained not only through direct discrimination and occupational segregation, but also by imposing restrictions on women's physical movements which severely hamper their professional activities. In the transformation of women's education into a commodity for marriage, fathers obtain family connections with a higher class of family for less dowry. In the extension of physical restrictions to women's professional activities, men receive a greater proportion of jobs and encounter less competition from women of the same class.

Among the women interviewed, the privileges of class outweighed the subordination of gender to the extent that middle-class women were able to afford higher education and to enter the professions.

These privileges of class help professional women to break free of their domesticity and dependence on men and to begin to undermine the sexual division of labour in the employment structure. In these ways, the privileges of class outweigh the subordination of gender, helping to break down the gender divisions in one section of the class hierarchy. These privileges are limited, however, by the ways in which the subordination of gender outweigh the advantages of class. For middle-class women, gender oppression is paramount inasmuch as higher education is used primarily to improve their marriage chances and the restriction on their movement hampers their employment opportunities, reinforcing their domestic dependence within marriage and helping to perpetuate women's position as male sexual property. In these ways, the subordination of gender outweighs the privileges of class, helping to contain women's economic and sexual independence and perpetuating the dominance of men in the hierarchy of gender. The economic and sexual control of high-caste women, expressed particularly in seclusion under the caste system, is revealed in different forms of control over middle-class women under the class structure. The specific forms of control which have developed to contain women of the professional class can be seen to have their roots in the particular class, cultural, and gender history of professional women.

The ways in which the systems of gender and class have developed together for professional women suggest that the two systems do not operate independently, but neither does there appear to be any fixed pattern of priority between the two hierarchies in their impact on women. Each outweighs the other in different and specific ways depending on particular patterns of historical development. In education, the existing traditions of marriage are accommodated to incorporate a completely new activity arising out of women's class position, such that education becomes a new criterion for a good marriage. In employment, an existing form of constraint on women's mobility is extended to a completely new form of activity stemming from their class position, such that women's professional movements are restricted. Two quite different processes can be seen to be operating here, suggesting not that one structure has greater impact on women than the other, but that the two develop together in a dialectical way. To understand the subordination of women in any particular sector of society, therefore, it is vital to examine both systems of hierarchy and the ways in which they relate, rather than attempting to reduce women's oppression to *either* the class system *or* the gender system alone, or attempting to say which system has priority as a general rule.

The implications for women's liberation of a study of professional women from a class/gender perspective are twofold. First, although professional employment brings women significant benefits and helps to reduce their domesticity and dependence on men, the limits on their freedom of action are such that employment, even at the top of the occupational hierarchy, cannot be said to constitute liberation. Second, despite the ways in which women's achievements in the middle class have been transformed to maintain their sexual and economic subordination to men, such developments help the cause of women's liberation by heightening the contradiction for middle-class women between the proffering of new opportunities for independence on the one hand and the imposition of new constraints on the other.

Notes

1 Diana Leonard emphasizes that this implies, not 'that gender is not differently constituted in different classes, but rather that *structurally* patriarchal power is common throughout society' (Leonard 1982: 173).
2 We refer to traditional caste structures as 'semi-feudal' because they do not follow the same forms as Western feudal systems – see Bailey and Llobera (1981).
3 The empirical data are based on questionnaires and interviews obtained in 1977 from 120 women working in Delhi in four professions: medicine, university teaching, the Indian Administrative Service, and management. Medicine and education are regarded by the middle class as suitable occupations for women. Women have only been allowed to compete for government jobs since independence in 1947, and access to management posts in public and private sector industry is relatively recent. Within the middle class, such women are placed socially and economically below women in elite jobs such as judges and ambassadors, but above the majority of middle-class women employees in white-collar and lower professional work such as clerks, secretaries, nurses, and school-teachers. The women in the sample were all educated to degree level and were employed in posts where higher education was a requirement. They were aged between 22 and 59, and included single, married, separated, divorced, and widowed women. They represented all the major religions of India and some of the minor ones. They comprised a cosmopolitan selection of people, having been born in nearly every state in India as well as those regions which are now Pakistan and Bangladesh.
4 Constraints of space mean that we cannot discuss the connection between gender divisions and the development of caste in any detail.
5 This pattern is exactly the same as in the United Kingdom.

In A Man's World

References

Altekar, A.S. (1962) *The Position of Women in Hindu Civilisation*. Delhi: Motilal Banarsidas.

Bailey, A.M. and Llobera, J.R. (1981) *The Asiatic Mode of Production*. London: Routledge and Kegan Paul.

Barrett, M. and McIntosh, M. (1979) Christine Delphy: Towards a Materialist Feminism? *Feminist Review* 1: 95–106.

Bhasin, K. (ed.) (1972) *The Position of Women in India*. Srinigar: Arvind Deshpande, pp. 35–49.

Blumberg, R.L. and Dwaraki, L. (1980) *India's Educated Women*. Delhi: Hindustan Publishing Corporation.

Bose, A. (1975) A Demographic Profile of Indian Women. In D. Jain (ed.) *Indian Women*. New Delhi: Government of India, pp. 127–84.

Chandra, B. (1974) The Indian Capitalist Class and British Imperialism. In R.S. Sharma (ed.) *Indian Society: Historical Probings*. New Delhi: People's Publishing House, pp. 390–413.

Choksi, M. (1929) Impressions of Women's Colleges. In E. Gedge and M. Choksi (eds) *Women in Modern India*. Bombay: Taraporewala, pp. 63–77.

Das, A.B. and Chatterji, M.N. (1972) *The Indian Economy: Its Growth and Problems*. Calcutta: publisher not known.

Delphy, C. (1980) A Materialist Feminism is Possible. *Feminist Review* 4: 79–105.

Department of Social Welfare (1974) *Towards Equality: Report of the Committee on the Status of Women in India*. New Delhi: Government of India.

— (1978) *Women in India: A Statistical Profile*. New Delhi: Government of India.

Desai, A.R. (1959) *The Social Background of Indian Nationalism*. Bombay: Popular Book Depot.

Dhingra, O.P. (1972) *The Career Woman and Her Problems*. New Delhi: Shri Ram Centre for Industrial Relations and Human Resources.

Directorate-General of Employment and Training (1971) *Occupational-Educational Pattern in India (Public Sector)*. New Delhi: Government of India.

— (1973) *Occupational Pattern in India (Private Sector)*. New Delhi: Government of India.

D'Souza, V.S. (1980) Family Status and Female Work Participation. In A. de Souza (ed.) *Women in Contemporary India and South Asia*. New Delhi: Manohar, pp. 125–39.

Everett, J.M. (1981) *Women and Social Change in India*. New Delhi: Heritage.

Forbes, G. (1982) Caged Tigers: 'First Wave' Feminists in India. *Women's Studies International Forum* 5: 525–36.

Gulati, L. (1975) Occupational Distribution of Working Women. *Economic and Political Weekly*, 25 October.

Hall, C. (1981) Gender Divisions and Class Formation in the Birmingham Middle Class, 1780–1850. In R. Samuel (ed.) *People's History and Socialist Theory*. London: Routledge and Kegan Paul, pp. 164–75.

Joshi, R. (1972) Contemporary Change in the Socio-Economic Role of Women in India – Its Impact on Family Life. In K. Bhasin (ed.) *The Position of Women in India*. Srinigar: Arvind Deshpande, pp. 50–9.

Lazarus, H. (1929) Sphere of Indian Women in Medical Work. In E. Gedge and M. Choksi (eds) *Women in Modern India*. Bombay: Taraporewala, pp. 51–62.

Leonard, D. (1982) Male Feminists and Divided Women. In S. Friedman and E. Sarah (eds) *On the Problem of Men*. London: Women's Press, pp. 157–73.

Liddle, J. and Joshi, R. (1986) *Daughters of Independence: Gender, Caste and Class in India*. London: Zed.

Mankekar, K. (1975) *Women in India*. New Delhi: Government of India.

Mathur, Y.B. (1973) *Women's Education in India (1813–1966)*. Delhi: University of Delhi.

Mehta, R. (1970) *The Western Educated Hindu Woman*. Bombay: Asia Publishing House.

Mehta, S. (1982) *Revolution and the Status of Women in India*. New Delhi: Metropolitan.

Mies, M. (1980) *Indian Women and Patriarchy*. Delhi: Concept.

Misra, B.B. (1961) *The Indian Middle Classes*. London: Oxford University Press.

Nath, K. (1968) Women in the Working Force in India. *Economic and Political Weekly*, 3 August.

Nehru, J. (1939) *Glimpses of World History*. London: Lindsay Drummond.

Papanek, H. (1973) Purdah: Separate Worlds and Symbolic Shelter. *Comparative Studies in Society and History* 15: 289–325.

Sehgal, C. (1985) Handicapped – by Gender or by Men's Attitudes? *Manushi* 29: 21–2.

Sen, A. (1982) *The State, Industrialization and Class Formations in India*. London: Routledge and Kegan Paul.

Srinivas, M.N. (1977) The Changing Position of Indian Women. *Man* 12: 221–38.

Thapar, R. (1963) The History of Female Emancipation in Southern Asia. In B. Ward (ed.) *Women in the New Asia*. Paris: UNESCO, pp. 473–99.

— (1966) *A History of India*, vol. 1. Harmondsworth: Penguin.

Wasi, M. (1971) Perspective: The Educational System and the Educated Woman of India. In YWCA (ed.) *The Educated Woman in Indian Society Today*. Bombay: Tata-McGraw Hill, pp. 17–44.

© *1987 Joanna Liddle and Rama Joshi*

Name Index

Name index

Chiplin, B. 84
Choksi, M. 216
Cockburn, C. 105
Collings, J. 194
Collinson, D. 105
Connor, J.M. 195
Constantinople, A. 189
Cooper, C.L. 58
Coote, A. 97, 107
Coser, L.A. 155
Coser, R. 55
Cotgrove, S.F. 184, 187
Coyle, A. 91
Crichton, D. 38
Crompton, R. 88
Crowther Hunt, Lord 12
Culler, J. 57
Curran, L. 89, 92

Das, A.B. 218
Dasey, R. 34
Davidson, M. 58, 184, 186, 197, 198–99
Davidson, N. 61
Davies, C. 2, 4, 83, 84, 85, 91, 103; on National Health Service 61–86
Davies, J. 55–6, 57
Davies, S.O. 184, 188
Day, P. 108
de Beauvoir, S. 107
Deb, R. 221
Delphy, C. 204
Desai, A.R. 205
Dhingra, O.P. 214
Dinerman, B. 131
Dixon, M. 62, 66
Downs, P. 56
Drummond, P. 61
D'Souza, V.S. 218

Dufferin, Countess of 209
Dwaraki, L. 203

Ecob, R. 197
Edwards, P.K. 98–9
Elliott, P. 139, 141
Elston, M.A. 108, 138–39
Epstein, C.F. 55–6, 57, 113, 139, 178–80
Everett, J.M. 216

Farrell, C. 84
Ferry, G. 89, 93
Finch, J. 70, 134
Fogarty, M. 23, 24–5, 55, 131
Forbes, G. 209
Fry, J. 136

Garmaniko, E. 103
Ghosh, M. 215
Gill, T. 87
Goffman, E. 176
Gowler, D. 51, 52, 57
Gray, J. 139, 141
Greig, N. 84
Griffiths, D. 58, 90
Groves, D. 70
Guest, D. 44, 46, 50–1, 52, 54, 57
Gulati, L. 217
Gupta, V. 215

Hacker, S.L. 187
Hakim, C. 57
Hall, C. 203
Hall, J.A. 190
Handy, C. 46, 52
Harding, J. 194
Hargreaves, G. 38
Hartmann, H. 91

229

Name index

Mies, M. 207
Misra, B.B. 206
Moore, J. 93
Mueller, A. 13, 23
Munshi, S. 211–12
Murphy, Y. and R.F. 57

Nath, K. 217
Nehru, J. 206
Newby, H. 129
Newton, P. 8–9, 89, 184, 186, 187, 191, 195, 196, 198, 199; on engineers 182–202
Nicholson, N. 57
Niven, M.M. 34–42 *passim*
Novarra, V. 56, 57, 87

Ott, M.D. 184, 187, 188

Papanek, H. 207
Pattullo, P. 97, 131, 140
Peters, T.J. 52
Phillips, A. 91
Phizacklea, A. 97
Podmore, D. 6, 155; on lawyers 113–33
Prandy, K. 88
Prather, J. 131
Prentice, G. 56
Purcell, J. 44

Quandango, J. 113

Ralham, G. 221
Ramazanoglu, A. 176
Rao, R. 210, 214
Raymond, J.G. 168
Reese, N.A. 184
Reid, S. 88
Rendel, M. 33

Rhodes, P. 140
Roberts, B.C. 100
Roberts, H. 141
Roberts, V. 185, 186
Robin, S.S. 113, 187–88
Roff, H.E. 43
Rohtagi, R. 210, 213, 214
Rose, R. 15, 29, 30
Rosser, J. 2, 4, 91, 96, 103; on NHS 61–86
Rossi, A.S. 185–86
Rothwell, S. 184
Rowntree, S. 38, 39
Roy, D. 180

Sabhorwal, R. 220
Sachs, A. 131
Salaman, G. 50, 51
Sanatami, M. 212
Saraga, E. 90
Scullion, H. 98–9
Sedley, A. 105
Seear, N. 131
Sehgal, C. 222
Sen, A. 8, 206
Serbin, L.A. 195
Shaw, C. 62, 66
Shore, E. 31
Shukla, A. 221
Shukla, P. 212
Siltanen, J. 98, 109
Silver, P.H.S. 139
Sinha, R. 214
Sisson, K. 44
Sloane, Prof. 84
Smail, B. 89, 199
Small, J. 140
Smith, M. 58
Smith, P. 62, 66
Smith, R. 34, 139

Subject Index

233